in search of DRACULA

Ein wunderliche vnd erschröckenliche hystori von einem großen wüttrich genant Dracole wayda Der do so gar vnkristenliche martter hat an gelegt die menschē. als mit spissen. auch dy leüt zu tod geslyffen ꝛc

Gedruckt zu bamberg im Lxxxxi. iare.

Fifteenth-century woodcut portrait of Dracula from a pamphlet that was published in Bamberg in 1491; a copy of it was purchased by the British Museum and perhaps was consulted by Bram Stoker. The Old German caption reads: "A wondrous and frightening story about a great bloodthirsty berserker called Dracula the voevod who inflicted such un-Christian tortures such as with stakes and also dragged men to death along the ground."

in search of

DRACULA

a true history of Dracula and vampire legends

Raymond T. McNally
and Radu Florescu

New York Graphic Society • Greenwich, Connecticut

Dedicated to the memory of Bram Stoker
on the seventy-fifth anniversary of
his masterpiece—*Dracula*.

Copyright © 1972 by Raymond T. McNally and
     Radu Florescu
First published 1972 by the New York Graphic
     Society Ltd.
140 Greenwich Avenue, Greenwich, Conn.
Third Printing, 1972
All rights reserved.
No portion of the contents of this book may be repro-
duced or used in any form or by any means without
written permission of the publishers.
Manufactured in the U.S.A.
International Standard Book Number 0-8212-0485-8
Library of Congress Catalog Card Number 72-80419

CONTENTS

LIST OF ILLUSTRATIONS

ACKNOWLEDGMENTS

This book would not have been possible without the collaboration of Professor Constantin Giurescu, the distinguished historian from the University of Bucharest, George Florescu, Romania's most knowledgeable genealogist, and Matei Cazacu, a brilliant young assistant from the Nicolae Iorga Institute in Bucharest.

Special gratitude is owed to the Dracula team we assembled on both shores of the Atlantic, a team whose members are far too numerous to be named individually. Among our Romanian colleagues and friends whose help we particularly appreciate are H.E. Cornel Bogdan, Romania's dynamic Ambassador to the United States; Professor Stefan Stefanescu, director of the Nicolae Iorga Institute in Bucharest; Professor Ion Pop, director of the Folklore Institute, who provided the assistance of his team of experts; and Lidia Simion, who was in charge of foreign scholars at the University of Bucharest and who became our crucial anchor-woman.

For their editorial assistance, thanks go to Donald D. Ackland and to Pat Lambdin Moore.

Finally, we gratefully acknowledge the genius of Bram Stoker, who created the fictional Dracula; the expertise of Bela Lugosi in portraying the vampire count in films; and America's love affair with the imagined Dracula, which partly inspired our efforts to document the real one.

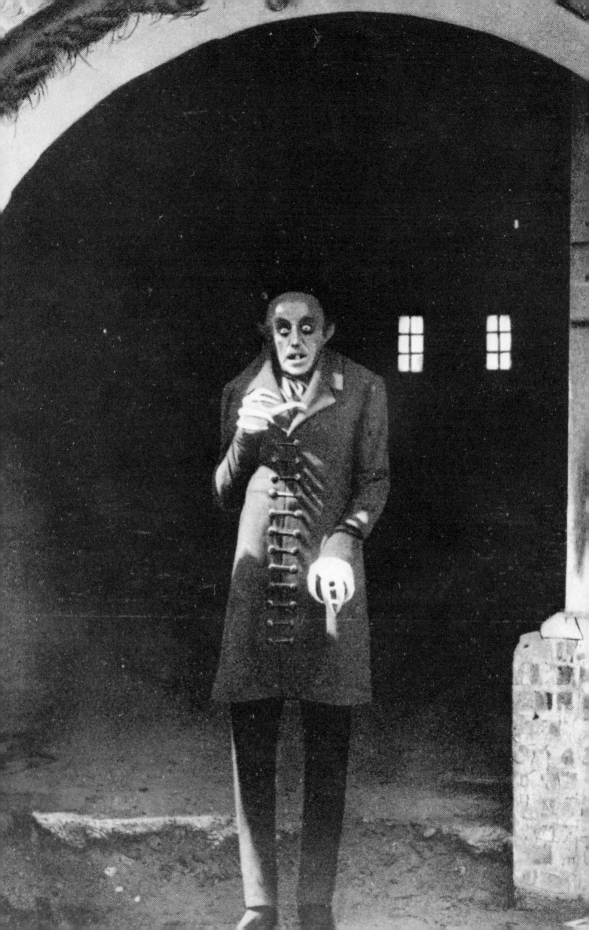

CHAPTER 1

Introducing the Dracula of Fiction, History and Folklore

"Welcome to my house! Enter freely and of your own will!" He made no motion of stepping to meet me, but stood like a statue, as though his gesture of welcome had fixed him into stone. The instant, however, that I had stepped over the threshold, he moved impulsively forward, and holding out his hand grasped mine with a strength which made me wince, an effect which was not lessened by the fact that it seemed as cold as ice—more like the hand of a dead than a living man.*

So the vampire Dracula first appears in Bram Stoker's novel. Published in 1897, *Dracula* is as popular now as when it was written. Millions not only have read it but have seen it at the cinema. Among the filmed versions are *Nosferatu,* made with Max Schreck in 1922, *Dracula* with Bela Lugosi in 1931, and *Horror of Dracula* with Christopher Lee in 1958. By now there are more than a hundred Dracula films and still others are in the making.

As for the book before you, it has been written by two authors. One of us—but let Raymond McNally speak for himself: "More than 15 years ago, as a fan of Dracula horror films I began to wonder

9

Count Orlock (Dracula) portrayed by Max Schreck in the greatest Dracula film ever made: *Nosferatu,* 1922, directed by Felix Murnau.

whether there might be some historical basis for their vampire hero. I re-read Stoker's *Dracula,* and noted that not only this novel but almost all of the Dracula films are set in Transylvania. At first, like many Americans, I assumed that this was some mythical place—in the same imaginary region, perhaps, as Ruritania. I found out, however, that Transylvania is real—a province that belonged to Hungary for almost a thousand years and that now is part of modern Romania. In Stoker's novel there were some fairly detailed descriptions of the towns of Cluj and Bistrita,* and the Borgo Pass in the Carpathian mountains. These, too, proved real. If all that geographical data is genuine, I reasoned, why not Dracula himself? Most people, I suspect, have never asked this question, being generally thrown off by the vampire story line. Obviously, since vampires do not exist, Dracula—so goes popular wisdom—must have been the product of a wild and wonderful imagination.

"Eventually I read an authentic late 15th-century Slavic manuscript, in an archive in Leningrad, which described the deeds of a Wallachian ruler named Dracula. And after researching the little that was available about the historical Dracula in various other languages, I consulted with my Boston colleague, Professor Radu Florescu, who was in Romania at the time. With his encouragement and enthusiasm, I took up the study of the Romanian language and traveled directly to the very homeland of Dracula to see what more I could discover about this mysterious man and legend. There, underlying the local traditions, so I found, was an authentic human being fully as horrifying as the vampire of fiction and film—a 15th-century prince who had been the subject of many horror stories even during his own lifetime; a ruler whose cruelties were committed on such a massive scale that his evil reputation reached beyond the grave to the firesides where generations of grandmothers warned little children: 'Be good or Dracula will get you.'

"Unlike myself, an Austro-Irish American who knew the fictional Dracula through late-night movies, my colleague Radu Florescu is a native Romanian who

10

For the sake of simplicity, all Romanian spellings have been presented without accents or diacritical marks.

Mr. Bram Stoker as portrayed in 1885, twelve years before the publication of his novel *Dracula*.

knew of an historical Dracula through the researches of earlier Romanian scholars. But his ties with this history go deeper than that. As a boy he spent many hours on the banks of the river Arges, which bounded his family's country estate deep in the Wallachian plain. At the time he was ignorant that several miles to the north, and many centuries earlier, a brutal drama involving a large group of boyars had bloodied the banks of this same river. That knowledge came to light when Florescu and myself discovered along the banks of the Arges the authentic site—and cruel beginnings—of Castle Dracula.

''In addition, George Florescu, Radu's uncle and Romania's leading genealogist,

11

has discovered that the Florescus trace back to a boyar family of Dracula's time, and one prominent in 15th-century Wallachian history.''

During the late 1960's, together with George Florescu and the Romanian historians Constantin Giurescu and Matei Cazacu, we formed a team to research the actual sites of the real Dracula's exploits and to probe the folklore concerning not only this fearsome real-life prince but also the vampire. Legends are still very much alive among the Romanian peasants in the mountainous regions of Transylvania and Wallachia, and they were the key to some of the startling discoveries that were made.

It was autumn of 1969 when we tracked down Castle Dracula—a castle in ruins and one known to the peasants as the castle of Vlad Tepes, or Vlad ''the Impaler''—a ruler notorious for mass impalements of his enemies. Vlad Tepes was in fact called Dracula in the 15th century, but this is not known by the peasants of the castle region today. As for Stoker's mythical vampire, Dracula, he is completely unknown to these peasants.

Using dozens of ancient chronicles and maps of European provenance, documents contemporary with Dracula, and 19th- and 20th-century philological and historical works, and drawing on folklore and peasant traditions, we have pieced together a dual history: an account not only of the real 15th-century Dracula, or Vlad Tepes, who came from Transylvania and ruled in Wallachia, but also of the vampire who existed in the legends of these same regions. In addition, we have studied how Bram Stoker, in the late 19th century, united these two traditions to create the most horrifying and famous vampire in all fiction: Count Dracula.

What was known of this dual history before these researches? In 1896, a Romanian Slavicist, Ioan Bogdan, noted that there existed various 15th-century German pamphlets which described the Wallachian Prince Vlad Tepes as ''Dracole,'' and the Romanian historian Karadja published the texts, but neither made the connection between this reference and Stoker, nor did Bogdan, as a philologist, concern himself with the folklore. A few pertinent discoveries were later made by others. For instance, in 1922, Constantin Giurescu, then a young scholar, discovered the foundation stone of the Church of Tirgsor, which indicated Vlad Tepes as its founder and patron. And in the 1930's, Dinu Rosetti with George Florescu opened the grave of Vlad Tepes at Snagov, but this was only part of a general excavation at the site, not a deliberate exploration of Vlad's grave. It was not until the 1960's that part of the story began to be unraveled by Grigore Nandris. He studied the philological relationship of the names Dracole and Vlad Tepes and noted that for some reason Bram Stoker had associated these names in his vampire story. The German Slavicist Striedter compared Slavic manuscripts and German pamphlets about Dracula; the Soviet Slavicist Lurie analyzed Slavic documents. But it was Nandris's philological studies which prepared the ground for the present study. Harry Ludlam's *The Biography of "Dracula": Bram Stoker* (1962) was also invaluable. Ludlam, without knowing the story of the historical Vlad Tepes or the folklore traditions, described Stoker's meeting in London in the 1890's with Arminius Vambery, a scholar at the University of Budapest. Stoker learned of "Dracula" from this Hungarian friend who evidently knew—but never himself wrote about—parts of the Vlad Tepes or Dracula story and also the peasant beliefs in vampires.

What follows is a complex story, for it involves a 15th-century prince known in his time as both "Vlad Tepes" and "Dracole"; the fictional Dracula created by Bram Stoker in 1897; and the beliefs of the Romanian peasants in Transylvania and Wallachia both today and in the 15th century. This complex story brings up many questions. Was the real Dracula a vampire? Did the peasants of his time consider him a vampire? What connection is there between the real prince and the vampire-count created by Stoker? What do the Romanian peasants believe today about Vlad Tepes and vampires? And have we been dealing simply with "history" or are there mysteries here beyond the reach of historical research?

13

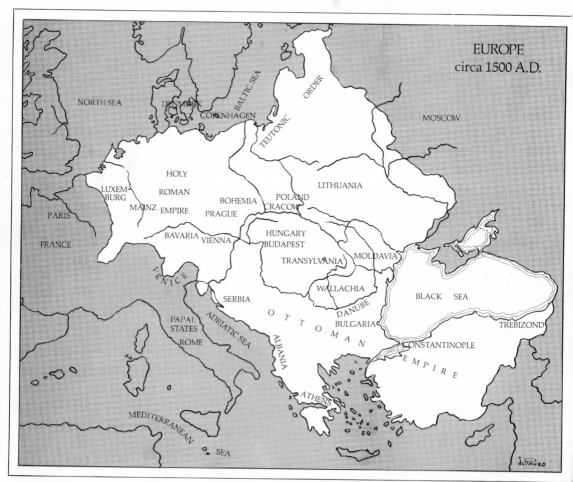

EUROPE
circa 1500 A.D.

During the 15th century all phases of European life were undergoing transformation. Religious reformers were challenging the authority of the papacy. The invention of movable type, rediscovery of classical education, and development of the arts were raising the level of intellectual life. Feudal localities were becoming associated into states or other units of increased political power. Voyages into unknown seas were expanding man's knowledge of his world. And with the fall of Constantinople to the Ottoman Turks in 1453 came the end of the Eastern Christian Empire, of which the great city had been the center for more than a thousand years. As the Turks pressed outward, dominating the whole of Asia Minor and the Balkan peninsula, throughout Europe fear grew that the entire continent would come under the control of Islam.

CHRONOLOGIES

PRINCES OF WALLACHIA	KINGS OF HUNGARY

PRINCES OF WALLACHIA

Basarab I 1310-52
Nicolae Alexandru 1352-64
Vladislav I 1364-77
Radu I 1377-83
Dan I 1383-86
Mircea (the Old; the Great) 1386-1418
Mihail 1418-20
Dan II 1420-31
Alexandru Aldea 1431-36
Vlad Dracul (the Devil) 1436-42
Basarab II 1442-43
Vlad Dracul 1443-47
Vladislav II 1447-48
Vlad the Impaler (Dracula)
  October-November 1448
Vladislav II November 1448-56
Vlad the Impaler (Dracula) 1456-62
Radu the Handsome 1462-73
Basarab Laiota (the Old) 1473-74
Radu the Handsome 1475
Basarab Laiota (the Old)
  1475-November 1475
Vlad the Impaler (Dracula)
  November-December 1476

KINGS OF HUNGARY

Sigismund of Luxemburg 1387-1437
  (Holy Roman Emperor, 1411-33;
  King of Bohemia, 1420)
Albert II 1438-39
Interregnum 1444-46
Governor: Ioan de Hunedoara (John Hunyadi)
  1446-53
Ladislaus V (the Posthumous) 1440-57
  (King of Bohemia, 1453)
Mathias Corvinus 1458-90
  (crowned 1464; King of Bohemia, 1469)
Pretender: Frederick III 1440-93
  (Holy Roman Emperor; crowned King of
  Hungary, 1459)

SULTANS OF THE OTTOMAN EMPIRE

Murad II 1421-51
  (for brief period gave power to his
  son Mohammed II)
Mohammed II 1444-46; 1451-81

EMPEROR OF THE EASTERN ROMAN EMPIRE

Constantine XI Palaeologus 1448-53
(last of the emperors of the Eastern Roman
Empire; killed by Turks when they captured
Constantinople)

EVENTS

1422	Unsuccessful siege of Constantinople by the Turks.
1427	Turkish domination in Serbia.
1431	Birth of Dracula. His father, Vlad II, invested with the Order of the Dragon, an organization dedicated to fighting the Turks.
1440	Unsuccessful siege of Belgrade by the Turks.
1442-43	Victories of John Hunyadi over the Turks in Transylvania and Wallachia.
1443	Dracula and his brother Radu the Handsome are hostages in the Ottoman Empire.
1443-44	The "long campaign" of Hunyadi in the Ottoman Empire.
1444	The Crusade of Varna. Dracula and his brother in danger of death.
1445	The campaign of the Burgundian fleet on the Danube.
1446	Sultan Murad II invades Greece. Mistra becomes a vassal state of the Turks.
1447	Death of Dracula's father, Dracul, and of Dracula's brother Mircea.
1448	Turkish victory over Hunyadi at Kosovo. First reign of Dracula in Wallachia. Turkish domination in the Balkans, excepting Albania.
1453	Fall of Constantinople to the Turks. Death of Constantine XI, last of the emperors of the Eastern Christian Empire.
1456	Unsuccessful siege of Belgrade by the Turks. Death of John Hunyadi. Moldavia pays tribute to the Turks. Dracula begins his second and major reign in Wallachia.
1457	Dracula's cousin Steven (the Great) becomes Prince of Moldavia. Victories of Scanderbeg over the Turks in Albania.
1458	The Turks conquer Athens. Mathias Corvinus becomes King of Hungary.
1460	The Turks conquer Mistra and Thebes.
1461	Fall of Trebizond to the Turks.
1462	Turkish campaign against Wallachia. Dracula taken prisoner by King Mathias.
1463-65	The Turks invade Bosnia and Hertzegovina.
1468	Death of Scanderbeg.
1474	Dracula granted freedom by King Mathias.
1475	The Tartar Khan of Crimea becomes a vassal of the Turks. Hungarian campaign in Bosnia. Dracula given a military command by King Mathias.
1476	Dracula's third reign in Wallachia begins in November; ends in December when he is killed during the course of a battle near Bucharest.

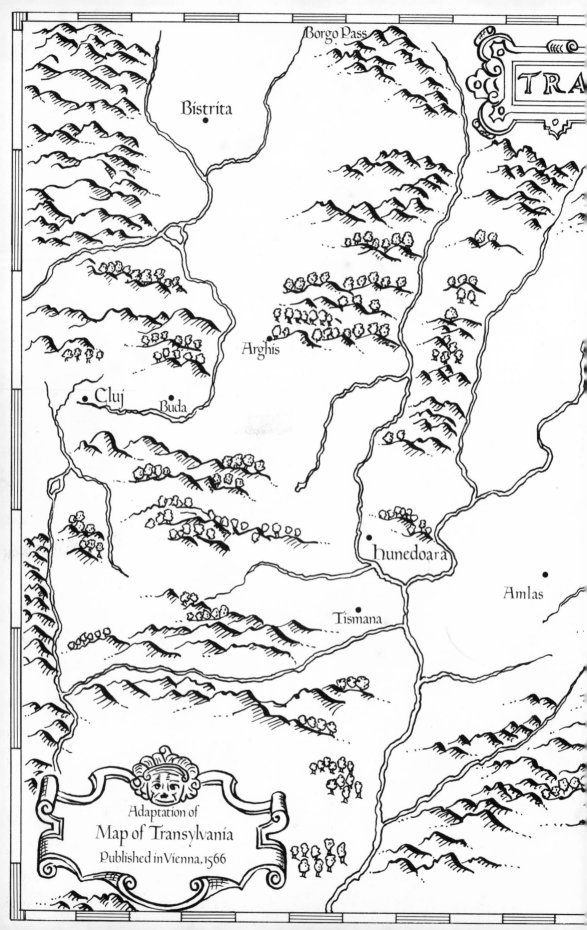

Map of Transylvania

Borgo Pass

Bistrita

TRA

Arghis

Cluj · Buda

Hunedoara

Amlas

Tismana

Adaptation of
Map of Transylvania
Published in Vienna, 1566

CHAPTER

Bram Stoker and the Search for Dracula

High up in the Transylvanian mountains we came to a halt. There, atop a black volcanic rock formation, bordering the river Arges and framed by a massive Alpine snow-capped landscape, lay the twisted battlements of Castle Dracula, its remains barely distinguishable from the rock of the mountain itself. This was hardly the grandiose, macabre mausoleum described by Bram Stoker in his famous novel, *Dracula*. Yet, no matter how modest nor how tortured by time, it was an *historic* edifice, one challenging the historian to solve its mystery, to push back an unconquered frontier.

For our party of five, composed of two Americans and three Romanians, this was the end of a long trail. Our search for Castle Dracula had begun in a light vein—over a glass of plum brandy at the University in Bucharest. It continued as an expedition marred by every possible frustration and by mysterious accidents.

This search began, as did so many other Dracula hunts, because of the extraordinary hold the Dracula vampire

19

Castle Dracula in ruins. The original caption for this photograph, taken in 1930, identified Dracula's mountain retreat as "the fortress of Poenari in the district of the Arges." The authors later identified the ruins as those of Castle Dracula. The castle is now being restored by the Romanian government.

mystique still exercises upon the popular imagination of western Europe and the United States. Unperturbed by the vampire myth, however, a handful of skeptics have always claimed that there was a *factual basis* for the Dracula story and that the setting indeed lay in Transylvania.

Bram Stoker, at the very beginning of his story, tells of his own painstaking efforts both to consult well-known orientalists such as Arminius Vambery, professor at the University of Budapest and a frequent visitor to England, and to study the available literature concerning the frontier lands between the Christians and Turks. Even Stoker's mention of his difficulties in consulting maps of the area available at the British Museum Library in London are intended to stress the historicity of the plot; he tells us they were not too reliable, but they proved to be far more accurate than he thought.

In Stoker's novel, the town of Bistrita, for instance, is accurately described and located, as are such small villages as Fundu and Veresti (which, by the way, you will not find marked on any modern tourist map). The famed Borgo Pass leading from Transylvania to Moldavia, the northernmost province of Romania, really exists, and is beautifully described to the point of detail in Stoker's novel. The historic context, the century-old struggle between Romanians and Turks that was sparked in the 15th century, is authentic. The ethnic minorities of Transylvania—the Saxons, Romanians, Szekelys, and Hungarians—are known and are distinguished from each other by Stoker.

Dracula was in fact an authentic 15th-century Wallachian prince who was often described in the contemporary German, Byzantine, Slavonic, and Turkish documents and popular horror stories as an awesome, cruel, and possibly demented, ruler. He was known mostly for the amount of blood he indiscriminately spilled, not only the blood of the infidel Turks—which, by the standards of the time, would make him a hero—but that of Germans, Romanians, Hungarians, and other Christians. His

The Borgo Pass.

ingenious mind devised all kinds of tortures, both physical and mental, and his favorite way of imposing death has caused Romanian historians to label him "the impaler."

In a rogues' gallery Dracula would assuredly compete for first prize with Cesare Borgia, Catherine de Medicis, or Jack the Ripper, owing not only to the quantity of his victims, but to the refinements of his cruelty. To his contemporaries, the story of his misdeeds was widely publicized—in certain instances by some of the intended victims, mostly Germans—from Budapest to Strasbourg. The Dracula story, in fact, was a "best-seller" throughout Europe 400 years before Stoker wrote his account. Many of the German-originated, 15th-century versions of the Dracula story have been found in the dusty archives of dozens of monasteries and libraries.

The names of Dracula and his father Dracul are of such importance to this story that they require a precise explanation. To begin with, both father and son had the given name "Vlad." The names "Dracul" and "Dracula" (Dracule in some manuscripts) are really nicknames. What's more, both of these nicknames had two meanings. "Dracul" meant "devil," as it still does in Romanian today; in addition it meant "dragon." In 1431, the Holy Roman Emperor Sigismund invested Vlad the father with the Order of the Dragon, a semi-monastic, semi-military organization dedicated to fighting the Turkish infidels. "Dracul" in the sense of "dragon" stems from this. It also seems probable that when the simple, superstitious peasants saw Vlad the father bearing the standard with the dragon symbol they interpreted it as a sign that he was now in league with the devil.

As for the son, we now know that he had two nicknames: he was called Vlad Tepes (pronounced tsep-pesh), which signifies Vlad the Impaler, and he was called Dracula, a diminutive meaning "son of the dragon" or "son of the devil." A final point in this discussion of nomenclature: the interchangeability of the words "devil" and "vampire" in many languages may be one reason for the association of Dracula with vampirism.

GENEALOGY

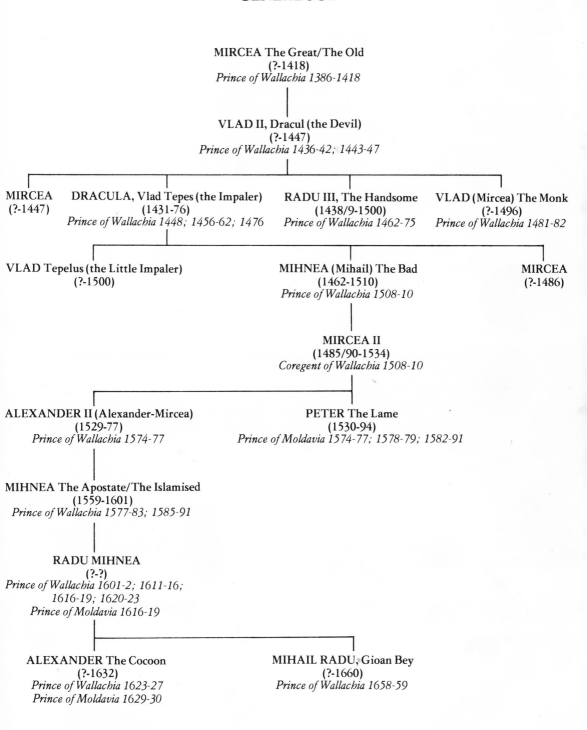

MIRCEA The Great/The Old
(?-1418)
Prince of Wallachia 1386-1418

VLAD II, Dracul (the Devil)
(?-1447)
Prince of Wallachia 1436-42; 1443-47

MIRCEA
(?-1447)

DRACULA, Vlad Tepes (the Impaler)
(1431-76)
Prince of Wallachia 1448; 1456-62; 1476

RADU III, The Handsome
(1438/9-1500)
Prince of Wallachia 1462-75

VLAD (Mircea) The Monk
(?-1496)
Prince of Wallachia 1481-82

VLAD Tepelus (the Little Impaler)
(?-1500)

MIHNEA (Mihail) The Bad
(1462-1510)
Prince of Wallachia 1508-10

MIRCEA
(?-1486)

MIRCEA II
(1485/90-1534)
Coregent of Wallachia 1508-10

ALEXANDER II (Alexander-Mircea)
(1529-77)
Prince of Wallachia 1574-77

PETER The Lame
(1530-94)
Prince of Moldavia 1574-77; 1578-79; 1582-91

MIHNEA The Apostate/The Islamised
(1559-1601)
Prince of Wallachia 1577-83; 1585-91

RADU MIHNEA
(?-?)
Prince of Wallachia 1601-2; 1611-16;
1616-19; 1620-23
Prince of Moldavia 1616-19

ALEXANDER The Cocoon
(?-1632)
Prince of Wallachia 1623-27
Prince of Moldavia 1629-30

MIHAIL RADU, Gioan Bey
(?-1660)
Prince of Wallachia 1658-59

The end of the direct male descendants of Dracula

Other male Draculas, too, were known by epithets expressing deviations of character. Dracul's eldest son was Vlad the Little Impaler; his second son was Mihnea the Bad; and another descendant was Mihnea II, the Apostate. In an age of violence all the Draculas lived violently and with few exceptions died violently.

In his lifetime Dracula had fame and notoriety throughout much of Europe, and rarely has such recognition of a public figure become so lost to posterity. Indeed, when Stoker wrote about Dracula in the late 19th century, few of his readers knew he was writing about an historical character. One obstacle to understanding arose from the fact that the Dracula stories circulated in diverse languages (German, Hungarian, Romanian, Slavic, Greek, Turkish) and in different worlds having little relation with each other. A chief difficulty, however, was the confusion caused by the name itself. Was it Dracula ''the son of the devil,'' Dracula ''son of the man invested with the Order of the Dragon,'' or simply Dracula ''the impaler''? Small wonder that the Byzantine scholar reading the chronicles referring to Dracula's deeds of heroism against the Turks, the German reading of the atrocities of the ''Devil'' against his fellow Saxons, and the Romanian studying the ''Impaler's'' achievements, failed to attribute these actions to one and the same man. It is only of very recent date that Romanian historians themselves have pieced together some of the fragments of this formidable Dracula story.

If Stoker's Dracula story was essentially correct in points of history, if Dracula existed, why not a Castle Dracula? Since the geographic setting of Transylvania was so minutely described by Stoker, what could be more logical than to begin the hunt in northeastern Transylvania, where the author set his plot on an isolated mountain peak, a few miles east of Bistrita on the road leading to the Borgo Pass.

Over the years, many persons had set out to find Castle Dracula in this general direction. They had traveled the way of Stoker's hero, Jonathan Harker, from Cluj to Bistrita and from Bistrita to the Borgo Pass. They found the countless superstitious

24

Romanian peasant who lives near Castle Dracula and who recounted tales about Vlad the Impaler (Dracula). Photo taken by Dr. McNally in the autumn of 1969 while with an expedition seeking Dracula folklore in the castle area.

peasants; were struck by the majestic beauty of this abandoned Carpathian frontier region separating Transylvania proper from Bukovina to the northeast and Moldavia to the east. But none had found the castle. Half-a-dozen expeditions, undertaken with the same purpose in mind, all ended on the same dismal note—not a trace of *any* castle.

Undeterred by past failures, the authors of the present volume decided to undertake the venture and set forth on the Stoker trail, if for no other reason than to satisfy their curiosity.

From the standpoint of sheer scenery, it is easy to excuse Bram Stoker for setting the story in the wrong part of Transylvania, thus leading the Dracula hunter some 100 miles or more astray. The anchor town of Bistrita, the actual departure point for any Dracula excursion, is a quaint medieval city, more German than Romanian in its characteristics, with a mixed population of Romanians, Hungarians, and those mysterious Szekelys, whom Stoker erroneously took to be possible ancestors of Dracula. The Szekelys themselves claim just as formidable a pedigree of horror, tracing themselves to Attila's Huns. From the crumbling walls of the old city, the most unsophisticated traveler can judge that at one time Bistrita must have been an impressive frontier point; from its oversized marketplace surrounded by the colorful baroque German-styled homes of the well-to-do, he may safely conclude that the town was an important trading center with goods plying northward from Transylvania to Poland and Bohemia and eastward to Moldavia.

Beyond Bistrita, the road finally climbs to the Borgo Pass, along the Dorne depression, passing through several rustic mountain villages where life has not changed much in a thousand years. The peasants still wear their traditional garb—the fur cap, or *caciula*, the embroidered shirt with motifs that vary from village to village, the sheeplined vest, or *cojoc* (lately sold as *après*-ski apparel in the elegant resorts of Europe), the roughly stitched pigskin shoes, or *opinci*. These farm people are not without an artistic side. The women embroider; the men mold clay products with a

Voronets Monastery in Moldavia. Religious scenes painted on the exterior walls are a distinctive feature of the 15-century churches built in this region.

technique kept secret, although the quality of the local clay certainly contributes to its success. The peasant house, almost entirely of wood, delights one with the imaginative carvings of its *pridvor*, a kind of porch surrounding the house, and the decorative patterns of the main gate, giving the only access to the courtyard. Local folklore is rich: the *Doinas*, the *Strigature* or lyrical poetry, the *Basme* or fairy tales, the ballads, and the *legende* or popular epics, all combine natural and supernatural elements. In the Doinas there are frequent references to the wolves, which, traveling in packs at night in the midst of winter, do their worst to man and beast alike. In the Basme, the bat is often mentioned, and in Romania this creature is an element of bad luck. In the legends of old, the vampire is a supernatural being of demonic origin, fighting Fat-Frumos, the fairy prince who embodies moral power, and is typified as a dragon monster-serpent, the motif used on the ancient standard of the Dacians.

Also interesting for our purposes are the historical ballads which speak of the ancient battleground between Romanians, Tartars, Turks, and Poles. These ballads commemorate countless heroes and villains, though in the Borgo region no Dracula is remembered by the old generation, perhaps the last one preserving by word of mouth a fascinating, distorted history, one quite as remarkable as what the sagas of the Vikings record.

Of late, the more wily peasants, impressed by the number of foreign tourists seeking Dracula's castle, have decided to play along with the search; and they do it well for the price of a few cigarettes and packs of chewing gum. Unwilling to disappoint the Dracula hunter, one imaginative peasant from the village of Prundul-Birgaului made numerous allusions to a "castle" that was *mai la munte*, a favorite expression of Romanian vagueness which means "a little farther up the mountain" (of course, when you reach one peak, as every Alpinist knows, there is always another behind). However, as the historians have often found in regard to folklore, where there is smoke, there is fire. It so happened that the folklore references spurred by gain, implying the existence of a castle near the Borgo Pass, were quite correct. Only it was *not* Castle Dracula—though Dracula visited it during his lifetime, since he often traveled along the solitary highway winding through the Borgo Pass.

This historic route was initially traveled by Romania's feudal leaders at the close of the 14th century, when they set forth from their haven in the Transylvanian plateau to found the Principality of Moldavia. It goes through majestic country—Stoker's Mittle-Land "green and brown where grass and rock mingle in an endless perspective of jagged rock and pointed crags."

Beyond the lower mountains, surrounding the Dorne depression and rising to 3000 feet, lie the higher peaks, often snow-capped even during the summer; these are the Rodna Mountains of Bukovina, a favorite Alpinist playground which demands the skill and sometimes the equipment of the expert for tricky ascents of upwards of 7500 feet. On the Moldavian side of the border, one reaches the watering spa of Vatra Dornei. Today this town is an important tourist center, not only because of the health-restoring springs, but because it gives approach to a dozen famed monasteries, located in Bukovina and Moldavia proper, and representing extraordinary jewels of 15th-century Romanian artistry. The biblical scenes on the exterior walls of the monasteries, dating back to Dracula's time, are painted in shades of deep blue and purple, and they have survived virtually unscathed through some 500 rigorous winters in this region.

Castle Bistrita, located near the Borgo Pass, may have served as the model for the castle in Stoker's novel. It was John Hunyadi who actually completed Castle Bistrita around 1449, five years before the fall of Constantinople. The Voevod or Warlord of Transylvania, Papal Prince and foremost Balkan crusader, Governor of Severin, hereditary Duke of Timisoara and of Bistrita, and in charge of the Hungarian kingdom, John Hunyadi was, in fact, in control of the political destinies of what was left of the east and central European lands in their last and desperate struggle with the

29

Turks. He died in 1456 while defending Belgrade, the last great Christian bastion on the Danube, the year that Dracula was enthroned as prince. Hunyadi was the father of Mathias Corvinus, the Hungarian king who kept Dracula imprisoned in his citadel on the Danube for some twelve years, from 1462 to 1474. Relations between the Hunyadis and the Draculas, however, were initially friendly, though never intimate for reasons which will be explained later in this book.

During the years 1451 to 1456, Dracula may have lived at Castle Bistrita. We know that he stayed in nearby Suceava with his cousin, the future Prince Steven of Moldavia, from 1449 to 1451.

Not a trace of Bistrita Castle remains today—only legends. It is probable that Stoker heard of these legends connecting Dracula to this region. The Saxon population of Bistrita, who disliked the Romanians and the Hungarians, doubtless heard of Dracula's atrocities against their brethren farther south in the towns of Brasov and Sibiu, where most of the horrors were committed and recorded, and it is quite plausible that some Saxon refugee from southern Transylvania may even have written a description of them in Bistrita itself. However, if there is a Bistrita document about Dracula, it is not known today. In any event, Bistrita Castle was attacked, ransacked, and totally destroyed by the German population of the city at the close of the 15th century, an apparent gesture of defiance against the Hungarian kings, who, as we know, were allies of Dracula. The full story of the precise circumstances which led to the German attack may never be known.

From the few descriptions we have of the former castle, it seems to have been a smaller version of Hunyadi's formidable castle of Hunedoara, located 100 miles to the southwest; a most impressive structure tracing back to 1260 and today completely and beautifully restored. This is the castle of the Hunyadis where Dracula was greeted as an ally and friend in 1452, but as a foe in 1462. It corresponds closely to the ''Castle Dracula'' in Stoker's novel. With its imposing donjon, smaller towers, massive walls,

Hunedoara, castle of John Hunyadi.

battlements, and drawbridge, it seems custom-made for the Dracula and vampire setting. In the impressive Hall of Knights, with its lovely marble columns, once hung all the portraits of the ''greats'' of Dracula's time, including the great John Hunyadi himself and Dracula. A hostile hand, possibly that of a revengeful German, destroyed all these portraits. Fortunately, three paintings of Dracula, plus a number of woodcut portraits, have survived the furies of the past.

In his novel, Bram Stoker describes Dracula as ''a tall old man, clean-shaven save for a long white mustache and clad in black from head to foot without a single speck of color around him anywhere.'' The author depicts Dracula's mustache as heavy, his teeth as sharp and white, and his skin as sallow and pallid. In the portrait of Dracula that survives in the collection at Castle Ambras, the real Dracula is as startling and arresting in appearance as the figure created in words by Stoker, or the character Nosferatu created some years later by Max Schreck in Murnau's 1922 classic horror film.

◄ Portrait of Dracula; at Castle Ambras, near Innsbruck, Austria. The artist is unknown, but undoubtedly this striking oil was painted in the late 15th or the early 16th century and accurately portrays Prince Dracula. The painting is part of the original collection of Ferdinand II, who owned Castle Ambras in the 16th century.

33

Wooden cane carved with head of Dracula. Origin unknown. A Florescu family heirloom, the cane is now owned by Dr. McNally.

CHAPTER

3

The Historical Dracula: 1430/31-62

Tyrant from Transylvania

In a broad sense, Bram Stoker was quite correct in setting his Dracula story in romantic Transylvania, even though he located his fictional castle 140 miles away from the site of the authentic one. Dracula was born in Transylvania, in the old German fortified town of Schassburg (in Romanian, Sighisoara). One of the most enchanting Saxon burghs, and certainly the most medieval, Schassburg is located about 65 miles south of Bistrita. The date of Dracula's birth, as close as we can ascertain, is 1430 or 1431. The house in which he was born is identified by a small plaque dedicated to his father Dracul. This marks the threshold of a typical German burgher's house, attached to a row of similar ones of 15th- and 16th-century vintage. Distinguished from each other only by their bright colors, they line a narrow cobbled lane leading up to the site of the old fortress which commands the city.

Dracula spent his youth in this peculiarly Germanic atmosphere, making frequent trips to the Germanies. As an infant, he may have been taken in

35

Dracula's birthplace in Sighisoara, Transylvania. The plaque on the house states that "Vlad Dracul," Dracula's father, lived there in 1431.

February 1431 to Nuremberg, site of the Court of the Holy Roman Emperor Sigismund of the Luxemburg line, when his father was invested with the insignia of the Order of the Dragon. On that same occasion, in the presence of a few dissident boyars from his native principality, Dracul was also made prince of the southern Romanian principality of Wallachia as well as duke of the Transylvanian districts of Almas and Fagaras. The formal oath that was taken in Nuremberg affected the future of all the Draculas. The Order of the Dragon, in the eyes of those charitably inclined, baptized the whole family as heirs and successors to the man initially so honored. The Draculas were thus, by their Dragon standard, dedicated to fight the Turks. This formal investiture also bound the Draculas to the hazardous task of seeking the insecure Wallachian throne, ruled at the time by Prince Alexandru Aldea, Dracul's half brother. This was to mark the beginning of a lengthy feud between rival members of the ruling family, one featuring numerous crimes, of which the 15th century bears many instances, particularly in Eastern Europe.

When the recently invested "Dragon" was finally able to make good his title of prince by expelling Alexandru Aldea from Wallachia in the winter of 1436-37, the seat of Wallachian power continued close to the Transylvanian border, where Dracul essentially drew his support. Historically, Transylvania had always been linked to both the Moldavian and the Wallachian principalities. After the Roman legions evacuated the more recently conquered province of Dacia in 271 A.D. the bulk of the Romanized population withdrew to the mountains, seeking escape from the turmoils of Eastern invasion in the Transylvanian plateau. In this way, the Daco-Romans survived untouched by the Gothic, Avar, Hunnish, Gepidae, Slav, Hungarian, and Bulgarian avalanches, which would surely have destroyed their Latin language and customs had they continually resided in the plain. Only after the torrent of invasions had receded did these Romanians descend into the plain, but cautiously, maintaining tentatively their mountain hideout. By and large, each generation of Romanians from the 13th century onward advanced a little farther into the plain. Eventually they reached the Danube and the Black Sea to the south, the Pruth and the Dniester to the northeast— in other words, to the limits of modern Romania, and also in part to the former limits of ancient Dacia. In the case of Wallachia, nothing is more typical of its tendency to turn to Transylvania for security, and nothing better demonstrates the reticence in abandoning the mountains as a haven of shelter, than the choice of the early capitals of the principality. The first, early 14th-century capital, Campulung, borders the Transylvanian Alps.

Dracula's capital, Targoviste, lies somewhat lower down in the plain, but still provides easy access to the mountains. The choice of this site already marks a period of increased self-confidence in the country's history. Bucharest, Romania's present capital, was fortified by Dracula in 1459, as a defensive bastion against the Turks. It was known as the citadel of the Dambovita river. Lying much closer to the Danube, it reflected the country's power in the continued conquest of the eastern lands, not-withstanding the pressures of the Turks. Dracula's youngest brother and successor, Radu the Handsome, chose to reside more often in Bucharest for precisely opposite reasons; he wished to be closer to his Turkish masters. Rumor had it that Radu, owing to his lengthy sojourn in the Turkish capital, also wanted to be close to Con-stantinople, as he was not insensible to the pleasures of the sultan's harem. Idle gossip accused him, largely because of his good looks, of being one of Sultan Mohammed's long-haired boys, thus one required to be constantly at his master's disposal. In any case, Radu's reign marked the reversal of the heroic stage in Wallachia's history and the beginning of conditional surrender to the sultan. Conditional, since the relationship of Wallachia to Constantinople continued to be regulated by treaty, with the local princes as vassals to the sultan.

When secure on his throne, Dracul, a wily politician, sensed that the tenuous balance of power was rapidly shifting to the advantage of the ambitious Turkish Sultan

Murad II. By now the Turks had destroyed both Serbs and Bulgars and the sultan was contemplating a final blow against the Greeks. Thus, Dracul began the first of his numerous deceptions, treacherously signing an alliance with the Turks against his former patron, the Holy Roman Emperor. In 1438, in admittedly difficult circumstances, Dracul and his two sons Mircea and Dracula accompanied Sultan Murad II on one of his frequent incursions of Transylvania, murdering, looting, and burning on the way, as was the Turkish practice. This was the first of many occasions when the Draculas, who in a sense labeled themselves ''Transylvanians,'' returned to their homeland as enemies rather than as friends. But the Transylvanian cities and towns, though cruelly raided and pillaged, evidently still believed that they could get a better deal from a fellow citizen than from the Turks. This provides the explanation for the eagerness of the mayor and burghers of the town of Sebes to surrender specifically to the Draculas, on condition that their lives be spared and that they not be carried into Turkish slavery. Dracul, sworn to protect the Christians, was at least on this occasion able to save Sebes from complete destruction.

Many such incidents made the Turks suspect the true allegiance of the Romanian prince. Accordingly, Sultan Murad beguiled Dracul into a personal confrontation in the summer of 1444. Insensitive to the snare, Dracul crossed the Danube with his second son, Dracula, and his youngest one, Radu, only to be ''bound in iron chains'' and brought into the presence of the sultan, who accused him of disloyalty. In order to save his neck and regain his throne, after a brief imprisonment Dracul swore renewed fidelity to Murad, and as proof of his loyalty, he left Dracula and Radu as hostages. The two boys were sent to Egrigoz in Asia Minor, and placed under house arrest. Dracula remained a Turkish captive until 1448, Radu stayed much longer, and because of his weaker nature submitted more easily to the refined indoctrination techniques of his jailors. To all intents and purposes, perhaps because of his effeminate looks, he became a minion of the sultan and eventually the official Turkish candidate to the Wallachian throne, and in due course he succeeded his brother.

Dracula's reaction to these dangerous years, dangerous because his very life was at stake should his father's policy change, was quite the reverse. In fact, these years of Turkish imprisonment already form a clue to his shifty nature and perverse personality. They taught Dracula, among other things, the Turkish language, which he mastered like a native; acquainted him with the pleasures of the harem (for the terms of confinement were not too strict); and completed his training in Byzantine cynicism, which the Turks had merely inherited from the Greeks.

Dracula from that time onward held human nature in low esteem. Life was cheap—after all, his own was constantly threatened—and morality was nonessential in matters of state. He needed no Machiavelli to instruct him in the amorality of politics.

He also developed during those years, as related by his Turkish captors, a reputation for trickery, cunning, insubordination, and brutality, and inspired fright in his own guards, in contrast to his brother's sheepish subserviency. Two other traits were entrenched in Dracula's psyche because of the plot into which father and sons had been ensnared. One was suspicion; never again would he trust himself to the Turks or for that matter to any man, whether friend or foe. The other was revengefulness; Dracula would not forget, nor forgive, those whether high or low who crossed him; indeed, this became a family trait. The sultan's representative who had arranged the trap which led to Dracul's imprisonment was captured by Dracula in the course of his campaign against the Turks in 1462, and summarily executed after the cruelest tortures—this despite Dracula's promise of safe conduct.

In December 1447, Dracul the father died a victim of his own plotting—murdered by the henchmen of John Hunyadi, who had become angered by the Dragon's flirtations with the Turks. Dracul's pro-Turkish policies are easily accountable, if on no other basis than to save his sons from inevitable reprisals and possible death. The assassination of Dracul took place in the marshes of Balteni, on the site of an ancient monastery that still exists. The father's murder was compounded by the brutal killing of Dracula's elder brother, Mircea, who had fought valiantly on the side of the Hunyadi crusade. There were more legitimate, personal reasons for the Hunyadi-inspired, double assassination, and they deserve a brief explanation here.

At the time of his imprisonment at Adrianople, Dracul had sworn that he would never bear arms against the Turks, a flagrant violation of his previous oath as a member of the Order of the Dragon. Once safely restored to his position as prince, and in spite of the fact that his two sons were hostages of the Turks, Dracul hesitantly resumed his oath to the Holy Roman Emperor, and joined the anti-Turkish struggle. He was, in fact, absolved of his Turkish oath by the Papacy. This implied that he could participate in the Balkan crusades, at that time organized by John Hunyadi against Sultan Murad. Dracul's hesitancy can be readily understood; the risks he took were nothing less than the decapitation of his sons Dracula and Radu. Indeed, it is little short of a miracle that the Turks did not behead these two captives.

The elder brother, Mircea, not Dracul, took the lead more actively in what is described as the long campaign of 1443. From the Wallachian point of view, this campaign proved an outstanding success. It led to the capture of the citadel of Giurgiu, built at great cost to Wallachia by Dracula's grandfather, Prince Mircea. However, the Varna campaign of 1444, though organized on a far more ambitious scale and reaching the Black Sea, was a disaster. The young, inexperienced King of Poland, Vladislav, fell to his death along with the papal legate Cesarini, and Hunyadi himself, it is said, was able to flee and survive only because the Wallachians knew the terrain well enough to lead him to safety. In the inevitable recriminations which followed, both Dracul and his son Mircea held Hunyadi personally responsible for the magnitude of the Christian debacle. "The Sultan goes hunting with a greater retinue," reproached the Wallachian prince, "than the 20,000 Christian crusaders," who had relied upon the support of a shoddy Burgundian and Genoese fleet to prevent the

Turkish landing from Asia Minor. A council of war held somewhere in the Dobrogea judged Hunyadi responsible for the Christians' defeat, and, largely upon the entreaties of Mircea, sentenced him to death. But Hunyadi's past services and his widespread reputation as the ''white knight'' of the Christian forces saved his life, and Dracul ensured him safe passage to his Transylvanian homeland.

From that moment on Hunyadi bore the Draculas, and particularly Mircea, Dracula's brother, a deep hatred. This vindictiveness was to be satisfied by Dracul's and Mircea's assassination. After 1446, Hunyadi once again placed the Wallachian crown in the more reliable hands of a Danesti claimant. (The rival Danesti family traced back to Prince Dan, one of Dracula's great-uncles.)

What is far more difficult to account for is Dracula's attitude upon his escape from Turkish captivity in 1448. We know that the Turks—undoubtedly impressed by Dracula's ferocity and bravery, and obviously opposed to the Danesti princes since they were thoroughly identified with the Hungarian court—tried to place Dracula on the Wallachian throne as early as 1448, an attempt which succeeded for two months. Dracula, then about 20 years old and fearful of his father's Transylvanian assassins, and equally fearful about returning to his former captors, fled to Moldavia, the northernmost Romanian principality, at that time in the hands of Prince Bogdan, whose son, Prince Steven, was Dracula's cousin. During these years of Moldavian exile, Dracula and Steven developed a close and lasting friendship, each promising the other that whoever might succeed to the throne of his principality first would help the other to power swiftly—by force of arms if necessary. The Moldavian princely residence was then at Suceava, an ancient city and today the point of departure for visits to a number of famous monasteries in one or more of which both Dracula and Steven undoubtedly continued their scholarly Byzantine education under the supervision of erudite monks and abbots.

Dracula stayed in Moldavia until 1451, when Steven's father, Bogdan, was brutally assassinated by a rival faction. Perhaps because of a lack of alternatives, Dracula then reappeared in Transylvania, where he threw himself upon the mercies of John Hunyadi, who had instigated his father's and brother's assassination. He was undoubtedly taking a chance, though by that time owing to Turkish pressure the reigning Danesti prince of Wallachia, Vladislav II, had adopted a pro-Turkish policy, thus estranging him from his Hungarian patrons. It was essentially history repeating itself at the expense of the Danesti.

It was in Hunyadi's interests once again to have a pliable tool, a prince in reserve, just in case the Danesti prince might turn to the Turks completely. Thus, mutual self-interest, rather than any degree of confidence, bound Dracula and John Hunyadi together from 1451 until 1456, when Hunyadi died at Belgrade. During this time, John Hunyadi was Dracula's last tutor, political mentor, and, what is more important, military educator. Dracula could have had no finer instruction in anti-Turkish strategy. Like a chivalrous vassal he personally took part in many of Hunyadi's campaigns. He was invested, as his father Dracul had been, with the duchies of Fagaras and Almas. In addition, he rapidly became the official claimant to the Wallachian throne. It was for this reason that he did not accompany his suzerain in the Belgrade campaign of 1456, when the great Christian warrior was finally felled by the plague. Dracula at the time had finally been granted permission to cross the Transylvanian mountains and oust the unfaithful Danesti from the Wallachian throne.

During the years 1451-56 Dracula once again resided in Transylvania. Abandoning the family home at Sighisoara, he took up residence in Sibiu, mainly to be closer to the Wallachian border. In Sibiu, Dracula heard news which had the effect of a bombshell in the Christian world: Constantinople had fallen to the Turks, and the Emperor Constantine Palaeologus, at whose court Dracula may have been a page in the 1430's, had died. Dracula at least could take comfort in the fact that Sibiu was considered the most impregnable city in Transylvania. This may have influenced his decision to stay there. Yet in one of those inconsistent, illogical acts that make a riddle of his personality, barely four years after he had left the city of Sibiu, Dracula mercilessly raided this haven of refuge and its vicinity with a Wallachian contingent of 20,000 men and killed, maimed, impaled, and tortured some 10,000 of his former fellow citizens and neighbors. Pillaging and looting took place on a more ferocious scale than had been the case with the Turks in 1438. As we shall see, the spiteful Germans of Sibiu were to have some retributive satisfaction in Dracula's lifetime.

Hard-pressed by the Turks in 1462, Dracula threw himself upon the mercies of John Hunyadi's son, Mathias, appealing for at least a safe asylum. Mathias, King of Hungary, had previously given some indication of offering military aid, but when Dracula found him at Castle Fagaras (today restored), the king instead of granting sanctuary had Dracula incarcerated on the spot, then sent in chains to Budapest and later to the fortress of Visegrad, 30 miles up the Danube. Here Dracula spent the next 12 years of his life.

What is the explanation of this strange and unexpected reaction on the part of Mathias? Apparently the Germans of Sibiu, hearing of Dracula's predicament, had forged three letters in his name which revealed him as meekly submitting to the Turks, and then had allowed them to be intercepted by servants of the Hungarian king. The original letters were published in the correspondence of Pope Pius II. One can safely presume they were forgeries, since no prince about to demand asylum from a friendly monarch would be so demented that simultaneously he would write to the enemy and promise him military aid against this friend. Such coincidence is incredible even in view of Dracula's notorious perfidy. Surely, the forgery was simply a device of the Saxons of Sibiu for avenging Dracula's depredation of their town two years earlier. Not only was Dracula imprisoned, but his character was defamed by political pamphleteering.

The palace of Mathias was located on a mountain dominating the famous bend of the

Danube. Just a few hundred yards below stood the Tower of Solomon, where maximum-security prisoners of the realm were detained. Very early in his long period of incarceration Dracula somehow caught the eye of Mathias' sister. Either because of the intervention of this young lady, whose name has been carefully omitted from the Hunyadi family registers owing to her association with Dracula, or for some unknown cause, the terms of Dracula's imprisonment became progressively more lenient. Moreover, there were all sorts of secret passages under the mountain, one or more of which probably led from donjon and cell to the private quarters of the princess.

Dracula's first wife had died, or, more probably, had committed suicide by throwing herself from the high tower of Dracula's castle shortly before the arrival of the Turks in 1462. He was thus free to marry again. His new marriage to Mathias' sister, plus renunciation of his Orthodox faith, ultimately led to his liberation and his return to the Wallachian throne.

When released from prison in 1474, Dracula was given a house by Mathias in the ancient town of Pest, across the Danube from Buda, but he lived there for only a few months. A local legend circulating at the time spoke of the brutal death of a Hungarian captain who had surreptitiously entered the house and been decapitated by Dracula himself. The event might well have passed unnoticed but for the motive of the killing, so typical of Dracula's egomania in any and all circumstances. He did not kill the man because the house had been subjected to theft, but because his deranged vanity had been insulted. "Is this the way," he asked, "in which one enters the house of a prince, without a formal introduction?" The thief, interesting to say, was allowed to go free.

After leaving Pest, Dracula spent close to two years at Sibiu with his wife. He had seemingly reconciled himself to the German burghers, who could do little against him anyhow because of his marriage connections with the Hungarian crown. In the heart of Sibiu to this day lies the ancient Gothic cathedral with its impressive 200-foot steeple, the construction of which was begun before Dracula's time. Within this church is buried Dracula's only legitimate son, known to history, not surprisingly for a Dracula, as ''Mihnea the Bad.'' Mihnea had fewer opportunities to exploit his evil instincts, simply because he reigned more briefly than his father—from April 1508 to October 1509. He died as did all the Draculas, assassinated by one of his numerous political adversaries, and in the very city where, like his father, he had sought refuge after a turbulent rule. One of Mihnea's male descendants committed the supreme offense, of which Dracula himself had been suspected in 1462; he converted himself to Islam, and thus some of his offspring bore Moslem names.

Another Transylvanian town which is linked with Dracula's name is Brasov (in German, Kronstadt). Brasov seemingly holds the distinction of having witnessed on its surrounding hills more stakes with Dracula victims rotting in the sun or chewed and mangled by the Carpathian vultures than any other place in the same principality. Although statistics are very difficult to establish, particularly for that time, some 30,000 persons were probably killed in Amlas on the morning of St. Bartholomew's Day, August 24, 1460—more than were butchered by Catherine de Medicis on the same saint's-day in Paris more than a century later. Dracula was meticulously accurate when counting Turkish heads, but notoriously vague when the impaled victims were either Saxons or Romanians. Somehow Dracula's St. Bartholomew's massacre has escaped the eye of the historian (though not that of contemporary publicists), while that of Catherine has made her the object of enduring reprobation.

Dracula's crimes, the refinements of his cruelty, deserve a chapter unto themselves. Impalement, hardly a new method of torture, was his favorite method of imposing death. A strong horse was usually harnessed to each leg of the victim, while the stake was carefully introduced so as not to kill instantly. At times Dracula issued special instructions to his torturers not to have the pales too sharp—rather, rounded-off—lest gaping wounds kill his victims on the spot. Such quick death would have interfered with the pleasure he sought in watching their agonies over a period of time, as the stakes were propped in the ground. This torture was often a matter of several hours, sometimes a matter of days. There were various forms of impalement depending upon age, rank, or sex. This is the reason why, in Romanian history, Dracula is known to this day as Vlad Tepes—Vlad the Impaler—even though his contemporaries knew him as Dracula.

There were also various geometric patterns in which the impaled were displayed. Usually the victims were arranged in concentric circles, and in the outskirts of cities where they could be viewed by all. There were high spears and low spears, according to rank. There was impalement from above—feet upwards; and impalement from below—head upwards; or through the heart or naval. There were nails in people's heads, maiming of limbs, blinding, strangulation, burning, the cutting of noses and ears, and of sexual organs in the case of women, scalping and skinning, exposure to the elements or to the wild animals, and boiling alive.

Dracula's morbid inventiveness may well have inspired the Marquis de Sade, who was no doubt familiar with his crimes. In regard to the cruel techniques practiced in our so-called enlightened 20th century, Dracula set another shining precedent. He generally demanded confessions prior to punishment, sometimes as a way of escaping partial or even total violence. And often he scaled the severity of the punishment to the instinctively self-preservative wit of his potential victim. There were instances when a man doomed to destruction was able to save his life with some happy or flattering phrase.

The historical ballads tell us that Dracula victims were principally seen in the larger Transylvanian towns such as Sibiu or Brasov, in smaller villages such as Sercaia and Mica, and outside hostile fortresses such as Fagaras. Most of Dracula's Transylvanian atrocities occurred between 1459 and 1461. The decomposed bodies of impaled prisoners frightened the Turks who encountered them at Giurgiu on the Danube. Even the stout-hearted conqueror of Constantinople, Mohammed II, was sickened when he saw the remains of 20,000 prisoners, taken several months before, rotting outside Dracula's Wallachian capital of Targoviste. They included many Turks, perhaps more Germans, some Bulgarians, Hungarians, and Romanians, particularly of the upper class—all those who in some manner had crossed the demented tyrant.

The scene of Dracula's most publicized act of atrocity, which began early in the morning, April 2, 1459, is a small knoll within the city of Brasov. In Dracula's time a small chapel dedicated to St. Jacob dominated the hill until the tyrant prince had it destroyed by fire. (One of the best-known, medieval, local German woodcuts depicts Dracula and his boyars dining and feasting in an open area below this church, while attendants are busily cutting off heads and limbs of the unfortunate.) The story relates that by the end of that April day thousands of Saxon burghers were neatly arranged on stakes around the party. Another incident tells that one of Dracula's more sensitive boyars had the audacity to hold his nose, presumably owing to the stench of the carnage. Dracula, with a twisted sense of humor all his own, immediately ordered one of his officers to impale the man on a stake, but one even higher than those reserved for the rest, so that the boyar might not be perturbed in his agony by the stench of the corpses and blood all around.

In reviewing such horrors, one must remember that there are two sides to Dracula's personality. One is that of the demented psychopath, the torturer and inquisitor who turns to piety to liberate his conscience. The other reveals the disciple of Machiavelli, the premature nationalist, the amazingly modern statesman, who can always justify his actions in accordance with *raison d'état*. The citizens of Brasov and Sibiu after all were ''foreigners'' who attempted to perpetuate their monopoly of trade in the Romanian principalities. They were intriguers as well. The Saxons, conscious of Dracula's authoritarianism, were busy, as was their wont since earlier times, subverting his regime and granting asylum to would-be contenders from the Danesti clan.

47

It is far too easy to explain Dracula's personality, as some have done, on the basis of insanity alone. There was certainly a method along with his madness.

Although Dracula ruled the principality of Wallachia on three separate occasions and died near the city of Bucharest, which he fortified, both his family homestead—the magnet of authority during his actual rule—and his many massacres take us back to Transylvania. Moreover, the site of Dracula's castle, though technically in Wallachia, skirts the Transylvanian mountains, and the secret passage below the castle leads straight to the snow-capped peaks of the Fagaras mountains. To this extent the tradition borne out in Stoker's story is quite correct. Dracula is inexorably and historically connected with romantic Transylvania.

Prince of Wallachia

But no matter how closely Dracula was bound to Transylvania, his associations with Wallachia are a major part of his story. Dracula's ancestors stemmed from Wallachia, the southernmost of the three Romanian provinces. It was here that he ruled three separate times: briefly in 1448; from 1456 to 1462; and for two months in 1476. It was here, too, that Dracula's capital was located: therein lay the center of his political power, the scene of many of his horrors, and the official headquarters of the Orthodox Church. He also built all of his monasteries in this province, and fought many campaigns against the Turks on its southern frontier along the Danube.

On the northern frontier of Wallachia, facing Transylvania, Dracula erected his infamous castle. On a tributary of the Danube, the Dambovita, he built yet another fortress, which in 1659 became the city of Bucharest, the capital of modern Romania. Close to Bucharest, Dracula was killed, and at the island monastery, Snagov, 20 miles north of the city, he was buried. From Wallachia come our internal sources concerning Dracula, and in essence they tend to confirm the German, Russian, Hungarian, and Byzantine narratives.

At the Military Museum in Bucharest is an assortment of mementos from Dracula's time, and in the park outside is a reconstructed version of the tyrant's notorious castle. The document with the first mention of Bucharest is located at the Academy of the Romanian Socialist Republic. However, the only existing life-size Dracula portrait is located in Castle Ambras near Innsbruck. Ferdinand II, Archduke of the Tyrol, who owned Castle Ambras during the 16th century, had a perverse hobby of documenting the villains and deformed personalities of history. He sent emissaries all over Europe to collect portraits of such persons, and reserved a special room in the castle for displaying them. It made no difference whether the subjects were well-known or comparatively obscure. What did matter was that they be actual human beings, not imagined ones. If such persons could be found alive, the archduke tried to settle them, at least temporarily, at his court, where paintings could be made of them on the spot. A few giants, a notorious dwarf, and the wolfman from the Canary Islands stayed on at the Castle Ambras for some years. Dracula was already dead at the time when this degenerate Hapsburg began his hobby, but the prince's reputation as a mass murderer was already largely established in the Germanic world because of the tales of the Saxons of Transylvania concerning the impalements. We do not know how or where Ferdinand's portrait of Dracula was painted or who the original artist was. It is possible that one of Dracula's descendants took the portrait with him when fleeing Wallachia some time in the 16th century and that following his death it fell into the hands of the Jesuits, who, knowing of Ferdinand's unusual interests, gave it to the archduke.

The fascinating and rather frightening gallery of rogues and monsters at Castle Ambras has hardly been disturbed since the days of its founding. The Dracula portrait hangs between that of the wolfman Gonsalvus from the Canary Islands and those of his two wolf children, who are completely covered with hair. A little to the left of Dracula is the portrait of Gregor Baxi, a Hungarian courtier who in the course of a duel had one eye pierced by a pale. The other eye degenerated into a bloodied and deformed shape. Baxi managed to survive this condition for one year, long enough for the portrait to be completed with the actual pale protruding from both sides of the head—which made medical history. It is strangely appropriate that this impaled victim should be located close to Dracula, whose eyes are depicted slightly turned to the left and seem to gaze in satisfaction at this macabre scene. A visit to Castle Ambras, particularly to the ''Frankenstein Gallery'' as the modern-day guides insist on calling it, is a startling experience, even for the most stout-hearted.

At Castle Anif, near Salzburg, yet another Dracula portrait once existed. It was discovered at the close of the last century in rather unusual circumstances. A member of the Florescu family, Demeter, a jurist by profession, was traveling through Salzburg in 1885, and by chance was invited to dinner by Count Arco-Stepperg, the owner of Castle Anif. After dinner the count showed his guest the well-known collection of oriental paintings in the large gallery of the castle. To his great surprise, Demeter saw among them a portrait of Dracula, which he immediately recognized, having seen the other portrait at Ambras Castle only a few days before. The owner was not able to explain to him how this painting had come into the hands of his family. In 1968, the authors of this book went back to Anif. They showed the present owner, Count Moye de Son, the notes made by Demeter Florescu concerning his visit in 1885. Unfortunately, the Dracula portrait was no longer in the castle. The Arco-Stepperg family had died out and inheritances had dissipated the collection.

Two other Dracula portraits exist. One, at the Vienna Art Gallery, is a miniature oil painting, probably a copy of the Ambras portrait. The other was discovered accidentally during the summer of 1970 by W. Peters, a German-born scholar of

The Wolfman from Munich; in the collection at Castle Ambras. This portrait, one of the Wolfman's daughter, and another of his son form an extraordinary family series—one that Wilhelm V, Duke of Bavaria, felt would make a welcome gift to his uncle Ferdinand II, who collected paintings of grotesque figures. This same family was depicted by the painter Georg Hoefnagel in his sketchbook in 1582. The Wolfman was one Petrus Gonsalvus from the Canary Islands, who had gone to Paris, refined his rough manners, and, as a gift from God, had found a pretty woman; after their marriage he complained that their children had inherited his hairy skin. This physical anomaly, by no means unique, was already being studied by the physician and professor Felix Plater in Basel at the time when the Wolfman and his family were passing through that city.

Romanian history. Entitled "St. Andrew's Martyrdom," it shows Dracula—a symbol of evil in the eyes of the 15th-century Austrian painter—as a simple spectator enjoying the scene. Crucifixion, after all, was just a variation of Dracula's favorite torture, impalement.

Several portraits of the prince survive in the primitive woodcuts on some of the German Dracula pamphlets. Whether these are true portraits is an open question since the German artists did their very best to deform Dracula's features. It is a twist of history and fate that the Dracula portraits exist in the Germanic world, and are totally absent in Romania—underlining the fact that in his day Dracula was better known in Western and Central Europe than in his native land. Owing to the popularity of Bram Stoker's novel outside Eastern Europe, this is still somewhat true today.

In Wallachia, Dracula is, of course, commemorated in popular ballads and peasant folktales, particularly in mountain villages surrounding Castle Dracula itself, the region where he is best remembered. Despite the perversions of time and trans-literation, or the distortions of the vivid imagination of the peasants themselves, it remains true that popular epic should play an important role in constructing the past. Dracula was not defined as all villain in Romanian folklore, in contrast to the German, Russian, and Turkish traditions which have an obvious *parti pris*. The German-Transylvanians bore him a grudge because he massacred them; the Russians because he abandoned the Orthodox faith; the Turks because he fought them. Romanian folklore—which is, of course, the product of peasant imagery, not that of the boyar chroniclers who labeled him "the Impaler"—has somehow attempted to explain away Dracula's cruel idiosyncrasies. Thus, it records him, in true "Robin Hood style," as cruel to the rich and a powerful friend of the poor. There is a little of the haiduc (the robber baron of the Balkans) in Dracula folklore. This peasant view of Dracula's deeds was probably a whitewash, an exaggeration; nevertheless it persisted. Moreover, Dracula *was* a brave warrior. The peasants were proud of his military ac-

St. Andrew's Martyrdom. Dracula appears at the far left of this crucifixion scene. The exact reason for his inclusion is not known. The late 15th-century Austrian painter who executed this oil apparently was familiar with portraits of Dracula and was able to create an excellent likeness of the prince.

Woodcut portrait of Dracula from Ioan Bogdan's 1896 publication *Vlad Tepes*, where its source is identified as a 15th—16th-century German pamphlet that was in Budapest.

53

complishments, no matter what methods he used to attain them. He *was* a national hero, defending Romania successfully against the rising Turkish tide. This one objective, ridding the country of the non-Christian, helped the peasant to excuse the impalement of the boyars, whose intrigues weakened the Wallachian state. It may also have helped them to forgive Dracula's attempts to eliminate those unfortunates, the poor and the crippled, who could not usefully serve the state. In Wallachian villages not far removed from Dracula's castle, there are peasants who claim to be descendants of the ancient warriors who fought for Dracula against the Turks, who defended him at the hour of need and guided him to safety across the mountains of Transylvania.

One thing is certain, the elderly peasants who still cultivate ''Dracula tales'' are a dying breed, and when the present generation is gone, the folkoric element may well die with them. The authors attempted to stimulate an interest in Dracula tales and ballads, and the first full-scale expedition to collect them was formed in the fall of 1969. As the search continues, it should include exploration of the abundant references to the supernatural, the vampire, and the wolf in Romanian folklore.

In a sense the whole of Wallachia (48,000 square miles) not just the castle region, is Dracula country from the mountains to the Danube, from the plain to the Black Sea. The main sites are Dracula's mountain castle, his capital of Targoviste, the ecclesiastical see at Curtea de Arges, the fortress of Bucharest, and his burial place at Snagov. Also of significance are Tirgsor (near Ploesti), the site of the most famous monastery Dracula built; Comana, erected close to the Danube in gratitude for a victory over the Turks; the tiny grotto of Getateni on the river Dambovita, where Dracula found haven and refuge in his escape from the Turks in 1462; and the proud and isolated abbey of Tismana, where Dracula was a frequent distinguished visitor and patron. Also included are part of Braila, the largest commercial center in the country; the fortress of Giurgiu on the Danube, the scene of Dracula's most successful campaign; Chilia farther up the mouth of the river, a strategic fortress that Dracula held precious enough not to yield even to his cousin Steven of Moldavia; the castle of Floci, a little beyond; and Enisala on the Black Sea, an older fortified bastion built by Dracula's grandfather, the remains of which can still be seen.

Apart from Dracula's famous castle on the Arges, there were minor fortifications erected by him, such as the fortress of Gherghita in the Carpathians. Dracula monasteries are still being discovered. At times one has the impression that the stones in each square foot of mosaic in a Dracula edifice wishes to tell the wayfarer its bloody story. There are no less than three villages scattered throughout the country which bear the name Vlad Tepes. It is safe to assume that they were named in his honor only when his crimes had somewhat faded from memory and his fame as a Christian warrior had helped wipe away his misdeeds.

Although Dracula's reputation had spread far and wide, much beyond Wallachia as we have noticed, the seat of his power was confined to a triangle just south of the Carpathians. At the apex, on the river Arges, a tributary of the Danube, was Castle Dracula, which will be discussed in the next chapter. The base lay between the ancient ecclesiastical seat of Curtea de Arges and Dracula's capital of Targoviste. Located between the two, but closer to the mountains, was Wallachia's first capital, oldest city in the land, Campulung. To the north are the two difficult mountain passes leading from Wallachia to Transylvania—one, by way of Turnu Rosu, reaches Sibiu, Dracula's Transylvanian residence; the other pass, closely guarded by the formidable German fortress of Bran, winds up the mountain to Brasov. This triangle just south of the Transylvanian border was the stage for the central scene of Dracula's six-year rule of Wallachia.

In Dracula's time the capital city of Targoviste was comparatively more significant than it is today, and certainly more imposing, spreading beyond the actual walls of the city. Like Versailles, Targoviste was not only the seat of power, but the nation's center of social and cultural life. Immediately surrounding the ostentatious palace, with its

Van deme quaden thyrāne
Dracole wyda·

Woodcut portrait of Dracula and text plate: these make up the first two pages of a late 15th-century German pamphlet that is in Budapest. Stoker's friend Arminius Vambery probably knew this pamphlet; moreover, Stoker may have seen a similar one that had recently been acquired by the British Museum, site of much of his research. The first three paragraphs of the text page shown here translate as follows:

Uan eyneme bosen tyranne
ghenomet Dracole wyda.

Na der bort vnses here ihesu cristi. M.cccc
lvj. yaer hefft desse Dracole wyda vele schreke
like wunderlike dink ghedan vnde bedreuen in
walechyen vnde ok in vngaren

Item de olde gubernator hefft den ol
den dracol wten laten Unde te dracole vnde sin
broer hebben aff ghetreten van creme loue. vn
hebben ghelauet vnde ghesworen den cristen lo
uen to beschermende

Item des suluen yares wart he ghesettet tho
eyneme heren in de Walachye Tohanth leth he
doden den Lasla wyda. de dar suluest heere ys
ghewest.

Item tohant dar na hefft he in zouenborgen
vn ok in wortelande mit namen beckenwrp laten vorbernen. Ock vrouwe vn ma iunk vn olt
Ethke hefft he mit syk gheuoret in de Walachye
an ysere kede. vn darsulues alle late werspeten.

Item he hefft alle iunge de in sin lant ghesant
weren vmme to lerende de sprake. de het hee al
le in eynen stauen besluten vn leth se vorberne.
der synt ghewest veerhundert

Item he heft eynen vrede ghemaket in sinen

Ex
Bibl.Com.
F. Széché-
nyi.

*About the evil tyrant called Dracula the voevod.
In the year 1456 after the birth of our Lord Jesus
Christ this Dracula the voevod did many
frightening wondrous things and threatened
[people] in Wallachia and also in Hungary.*

*Once the old governor had the old Dracul
killed; and Dracula and his brother, having
renounced their own faith, promised and swore
to uphold the Christian faith.*

*During these same years he was put on the
throne and became lord of Wallachia; he immediately had Ladislaus Waboda killed, who had
been ruler of that region.*

numerous components, its palatial gardens, and its princely church, were the Byzantine-styled houses of the boyars and their more diminutive chapels. On a smaller scale, within the comparative security of the walled courtyard, the upper class attempted to ape the etiquette of the Imperial court at Constantinople. Beyond and interspaced by gardens with stylish floral decorations, still a characteristic of modern Romanian cities to this day, were located the modest houses of the merchants, artisans, and other dependents of the princely and boyar courts. The three spiraled domes of the Orthodox churches and monasteries pierced the sky over the city. Targoviste, like Bucharest later on, was essentially a city of churches, some of which survive to this day, reflecting the intense zeal and piety of an earlier age. The monasteries, with their cloisters, chapels, and decorative courtyards, added to the colorfulness of the city. In fact, one Venetian traveler compared Targoviste to a "vast gaudy flower house." The inner sanctuary, containing most of the aristocratic homes, was surrounded by the defensive ramparts characteristic of the feudal age, though these were built on a far less impressive scale than the walls of the German-inspired fortresses in Transylvania. One almost gains the impression that each boyar household was itself a small fortified bastion, capable of defense not only against the foe without but against the far more crafty enemy within. Suspicion reigned in this Wallachian capital; anarchy was rampant; political assassination was frequent; and rapid succession of princes was the rule rather than the exception—all of which helps to account for some of Dracula's drastic measures against the boyars.

Shortly after ascending the throne in the spring of 1456, so runs one popular ballad, Dracula assembled several hundred of the great boyars of the land in the hall of the Targoviste palace, plus the five bishops, the abbots of the more important monasteries, foreign and native, and the Metropolitan. As Dracula surveyed the wily, tricky, and dishonest expressions of the boyars, he knew that among the guests were his father's and brother's assassins. Then he delivered a most untypical speech for a

Wallachian prince (who was more often than not the boyars' tool). "How many reigns," he asked, "have you, my loyal subjects, personally experienced in your lifetime?" There were chuckles and grimaces in the audience, then a tense moment of silence. "Seven, my Lord," was the reply of one man. "I," said another, "have survived thirty reigns." "Since your grandfather, my liege," retorted a third, "there have been no less than twenty princes—I have survived them all." Even the younger men admitted having witnessed seven. In this manner, almost a jocular one, each boyar stood his ground and tested the severity of the new ruler. The princely title and all that it implied had evidently been taken lightly. Dracula, his eyes flashing in a way that was to become characteristic, gave an order. Within minutes, his faithful attendants surrounded the hall. Some 500 boyars who had experienced more than a certain number of reigns (for Dracula knew that his father's assassins would be among them) were immediately impaled in the vicinity of the palace and left exposed until their corpses were chewed up by blackbirds. The lesson of this day did not escape the remaining boyars. Dracula was demanding either their total submission or exile to their respective estates. Woe to him who chose to disobey.

All that one can now see of Dracula's Targoviste are the remains of the princely palace, which was destroyed and rebuilt many times. Dracula's grandfather, the redoubtable Mircea, had placed the first foundation stone at the beginning of the 15th century. Nearby is the reconstructed 16th-century Chindeia watch tower, from the battlement of which the tourist can still survey the whole city if he has the heart to climb a steep and narrow winding staircase. Looking down on the courtyard below, one can clearly discern the remains of the palace's foundation, which indicate a structure of modest size. The cellar was probably used for the princely supply of wine. Here, too, would have been the prison or torture chamber where the unfortunate gypsy-slave or boyar opponent lucky enough to escape impalement was given the traditional bastinado. The notorious throne hall was evidently located on the ground floor. This

Dracula's palace at Targoviste. This was his main
palace. The city of Targoviste was his capital.

Tower at Targoviste; modern restoration.

61

was where Dracula, his father Dracul, and his grandfather Mircea, were invested princes of the land following a religious ceremony, and where they entertained the boyars, received audiences and petitions, and held official councils of state with the local Divan, which included every member of the upper aristocracy—the bishops, abbots, and the Metropolitan.

In this throne hall occurred a famous scene described in almost all the Dracula narrations: certain envoys of the sultan had come to greet the prince officially, and they refused to take off their turbans. Dracula, who was hyper-sensitive about any slight to his vanity, speedily ordered the turbans of the Turkish envoys to be nailed to their heads. The Turks agonized within a pool of blood at the very foot of the throne.

Many cruel scenes occurred in the throne room of Dracula's palace at Targoviste. Some of them included victims who escaped from the pale by slavish adulation, confessions, and self-incrimination. There was, for instance, the case of two monks from a neighboring Catholic monastery. According to the story, Dracula tactlessly showed them the rows and rows of impaled cadavers in the courtyard. One of the monks, rather than expressing moral reprobation (which Dracula expected and which would certainly have doomed the monk to impalement), meekly commented: ''You are appointed by God to punish the evil-doers.'' Dracula hardly expected enunciation of the doctrine of divine right, and consequently spared this particular monk. His colleague, however, who had the moral strength to disapprove of the ghastly scene, was impaled immediately.

Dracula took particular delight in ensnaring the unwary in a compromising statement. The following incident is typical; it occurred in September 1458, while Dracula was entertaining a Polish nobleman, Benedict de Boithor, who had come as the ambassador of an alleged ally, King Mathias Corvinus of Hungary. The usual trivial conversation was pursued in the dining hall of the palace at Targoviste. At the end of the repast, a golden spear was suddenly brought by some servants and set up directly in front of the envoy, who watched the operation cautiously, having heard of Dracula's reputation. "Tell me," said Dracula, addressing the Pole with some amusement, "why do you think that I have had this spear set up in the room?" "My lord," answered the Pole with verve, "it would seem that some great boyar of the land has offended you and you wish to honor him in some way." "Fairly spoken," said Dracula. "You are the representative of a great king. I have had this lance set up especially in your honor." Maintaining his *savoir faire,* the Pole replied: "My Lord, should I have been responsible for something worthy of death, do as you please, for you are the best judge and in that case you would not be responsible for my death, but I alone." Dracula burst into laughter. The answer had been both witty and flattering. "Had you not answered me in this fashion," said Dracula, "I would truly have impaled you on the spot." He then honored the man and showered him with gifts.

Of Dracula's married life, we know far too little during this period. His first wife, a boyar's daughter, probably died in 1462. From the native Romanian Dracula tales, it would appear that their marriage was not a happy one, for the prince was often seen wandering alone at night on the outskirts of the city, usually in disguise, seeking the company of the beautiful but humble woman who in time became his mistress. This relationship, among many others, indicated both Dracula's distrust of the boyars and his plebeian instincts. Needless to say, this particular idyl did not last; the woman was assassinated—for infidelity, according to peasant tales. Another mistress died in mysterious circumstances, with her sexual organs cut out.

Dracula was always concerned for the survival of the souls of his faithful followers, a reflection of the morbid religiosity inspired by the enormity of his crimes. He was careful to surround himself with priests, abbots, bishops, and confessors, whether Roman Catholic or Orthodox. He often spent long moments of meditation within the saintly confines of individual monasteries, such as Tismana in western Wallachia, where he was known as a generous donor. All the Draculas seemed intent upon belonging to a church, receiving the sacraments, being buried as Christians, and at least being identified with a religion. Even the famous Apostate Mihnea in due course became a devout Moslem. Like the average penitent of pre-Lutheran times, these men felt that good works, particularly the erection of monasteries along with rich endowments, would contribute to the eradication of their sins. Mircea, Dracul, Dracula, Radu, Vlad the Monk, and Mihnea, just to name six of the family, were collectively responsible for no less than 50 monastic foundations or endowments of which Dracula alone was responsible for five.Dracula's half brother, the notorious Vlad, was a monk before he became prince. Even the degenerate Radu, Dracula's brother, who was known as a Turcophile erected a monastery, Tanganul, and was probably buried there. Monastic interest was, of course, a perfect pretext for interfering in, and controlling the affairs of, both Catholic and Orthodox churches in Wallachia.

Dracula had a close relationship with the Franciscan monks in Targoviste and with the Cistercian monastery at Carta, and he frequently received monks from both orders at the palace. But the religious of various orders—including Benedictines and Capucins—sought refuge in German lands after they had incurred Dracula's wrath by refusing to toe the line. One of the monks, Jacob by name, from the monastery of "Gorion," may well have been the original author of the manuscript found at the Monastery of St. Gallen in Switzerland, the oldest document (1462) in the anti-Dracula publicity campaign, which made such a profound impact on the 15th-century Germanic world.

As late as the period of World War I, not a single ecclesiastical foundation was specifically attributed to Dracula. But in 1922, a brilliant young Romanian student, Constantin C. Giurescu, was passing casually through the village of Strejnicu, and stopped to converse with a local priest; by chance his eye noticed an inscription on a half-buried stone which lay in the backyard of the church. The stone had evidently been carved out from the main portico of some medieval church. Suspecting an interesting find and knowing both the Cyrillic script and ancient Church Slavonic, the young historian to his amazement, and that of the priest, deciphered the following inscription: "By the grace of God, I Vlad Voevod, Prince of Wallachia, son of the great Vlad Voevod, have built and completed this church on June 24 in the year 1461." The discovery was, to say the least, revolutionary. Giurescu took the translation of his inscription to Bucharest, where Professor Nicholas Iorga, the internationally known Romanian historian, confirmed the stone's authenticity.

Giurescu, who went on to become a professor at the University of Bucharest, can in many ways be considered the greatest living historian in Romania. In 1968, he came to America for a nationwide lecture tour. He was amazed and elated to find that American students had a strong interest in Dracula, even though much of that interest was due to Stoker's and Hollywood's vampire stories.

The foundation stone accidentally discovered by Giurescu in the courtyard of the village church of Strejnicu belonged to a church located only a few miles away at Tirgsor, where excavations have since revealed two more 15th-century churches. The erection of a Dracula church at Tirgsor had nothing to do with the importance of this town as a trading center. The date coincides clearly enough with the year of the murder of a rival Danesti claimant to the Wallachian throne. Dracula found this man, Vladistav Dan III, at Fagaras Castle in Transylvania, sheltered by his Saxon protectors. Incensed by the intrigue of this rival, Dracula ordered him to dig his own grave and to read his own funeral service, then decapitated him. It should be added that Tirgsor was also near the place where Dracula's father had been murdered in 1447. Thus there were at least two powerful motives that may have led Dracula to erect this particular monastery—a need to expiate his murder of Vladistav Dan and a desire to show filial piety.

Beyond the suburbs of Targoviste lies an extensive network of lakes. These were

Tirgsor. The ruins of a 15th-century monastery
built by Dracula. In 1930, Constantin Giurescu
discovered an inscription indicating Dracula as
the founder of this monastery.

used by Dracula mostly for fishing stocked trout, and for lakeside picnics and orgies. One outing, probably held in this area on Easter Day of 1459, was climaxed by the notorious mass murder of 500 boyars, a scene immortalized by the 15th-century Romanian painter Teodor Aman. The hilly region is similarly enshrined in popular memories. Here, in 1462, took place the famous impalement of the Turkish soldiers captured the previous winter when Dracula campaigned along the Danube.

Just outside Targoviste, high up in what is essentially an area of vineyards (the famed *podgorie*—hill region), lies an edifice far more handsome with its pure Byzantine profile than any existing church within the city itself. This is the Monastery of the Hill (Manastirea Dealului), known more traditionally as the Monastery of St. Nicholas of the Wines. Although it is reputedly one of the most beautiful ecclesiastical structures in Romania—second only to the Church of Arges, a few miles away—an atmosphere of gloom pervades it. At one time it served as a prison, later as a somewhat harsh military academy. Today it is a retreat for elderly priests and monks. Within the interior, virtually every stone which one steps on marks a tomb. No church in Romania speaks more eloquently about death.

The Monastery of the Hill was initially built and endowed by Dracula's cousin, Prince Radu the Great (1495-1508), one of the few members of the family not linked with bloodshed. Prince Radu (not to be confused with Radu the Handsome, Dracul's brother) gained renown as a patron of learning and a builder of churches; his reward was a majestic tomb at the foot of the mountain altar. Tradition suggests that the body of Dracula's father was brought by some pious monks to a frame church (which preceded the monastery) shortly after his assassination at Balteni. His tomb was unmarked because of the obvious dangers that threatened the monks at a time when a prince of the rival Danesti family was in power. Dracula's elder brother, Mircea, who valiantly fought the Turks during Hunyadi's crusades, is alleged to have been buried close to his father, near the altar. He had been captured by the pro-Hunyadi boyars at

Balteni, taken in chains to Targoviste, and executed shortly after his father's murder. When Dracula became prince in 1456 he ordered Mircea's coffin, located in the public burial ground in Targoviste, to be opened. Mircea's head was found twisted and turned to the ground, proving that he had been buried alive and had struggled desperately for breath. Dracula ordered him to be reburied with pomp (in the old wooden church on the monastery site) and proceeded with his revenge against the boyars.

Crusader against the Turks

In the winter of 1461, Dracula hurled a challenge to no less a person than the proud conqueror of Constantinople, Sultan Mohammed II. The subsequent Danubian and Wallachian campaigns which lasted from the winter of 1461 through the summer and fall of 1462 undoubtedly constitute the best-known and most discussed episode in his fascinating career. To say the least, Dracula's resourcefulness, his feats of valor, his tactics and strategy, brought him as much notoriety throughout Europe as his gruesome treatment of his subjects. Whereas his impalements were recorded in what is referred to as *"la petite histoire,"* and, thus, were more easily forgotten, his acts of heroism during the Christian crusades against the Turks, who had reached the climactic point of their penetration of Eastern Europe, were enshrined in the official records of the time.

With the death of the great Hunyadi in 1456, what was left of the Christian forces in this last age of Balkan crusading was in acute need of leadership. The bitter squabbles raging in the Christian camp ever since the disastrous episode at Varna, which had led to Dracula's father's assassination, continued unabated. This absence of Christian unity greatly helped the Turkish cause and had contributed to the capture of Constantinople in 1453, three years before Dracula's second accession to the Wallachian throne.

With the disappearance of the last vestiges of Serbian and Bulgarian independence and the fall of the Greek Empire, Wallachia was placed at the forefront of the anti-Turkish crusade by circumstances of geography alone. Supporting the Wallachian cause, Moldavia lay safely in the hands of Dracula's cousin Steven, who emerged as a hero in the post-Hunyadi Christian world. With the assassination of Prince Steven's father, Bogdan, in 1451, Steven had accompanied Dracula in his Transylvanian exile. There, while both were sojourning in the castle of the Hunyadis at Hunedoara, Dracula had made the formal compact with Steven: that whoever succeeded to the throne first would help the other gain the sister principality. In any event, each committed himself to come to the other's assistance in case of need. Exactly one year after his accession to the throne in 1457, Dracula, true to his promise, sent a Wallachian contingent which helped Steven reconquer the crown of his ancestors. In this way, Dracula helped launch the brilliant career of the greatest soldier, statesman, and man of culture that the Romanian Renaissance produced. For Steven the Great, as he is called, was both a soldier and a lover of the arts. The number of monasteries that still survive in the region of Suceava, Steven's capital, are eloquent testimony to the cultural and architectural brilliance of his age.

The threatened Catholic powers of Central Europe were all interested in the ''Reconquista,'' and circumstances after the fall of Constantinople seemed right for the renewal of a joint Balkan crusade. Following a period of anarchy at Buda after John Hunyadi's death, Dracula formally swore allegiance to the young King of Hungary, Ladislaus Posthumous. Since its geographic location made his realm susceptible to Turkish conquest, Ladislaus was definitely committed to fight the Moslems. Wallachian princes, protégés of the Hungarian court, were virtually pledged to enter the new crusade. The Poles were anxious to avenge the death of their boy-King Vladislav, who had perished at Varna in 1444. The Venetian Republic, as well as the Genoese, was interested as always in any endeavor that might suppress some potential threat to its commercial glory. Besides all this, the conquest of Constantinople was too calamitous a setback for the Christian world to remain unchallenged. Even the protagonists of Western chivalry—particularly the knights in Burgundy—despite how little genuine religious valor and zeal had survived the immoral fourth crusade, could not entirely dismiss their role as defenders of Christendom.

Both the German and the Russian narrators are silent concerning Dracula's Turkish campaigns: the Saxons' aim, after all, was to vilify Dracula, not to praise him; and the Russians were too remote from the Danube at the time to be really interested, and if their hearts were with the Christians, the Grand Duke of Moscow was always suspicious of Dracula's Catholic sympathies. We know the Russian ambassador at Buda was more interested in denouncing Dracula as an apostate than in praising him as a general. We are fortunate, however, in possessing numerous Romanian stories which glorify Dracula and other national heroes, especially as the age in which this folklore was put in literary form preceded the birth of national self-consciousness. In respect to historical events, Romanian folklore can be judged as a more impartial source than the foreign pamphlets which concentrated exclusively on horror tales.

Official Turkish records, including an eyewitness account by a Serbian Janizary, Byzantine chronicles, the report of a veteran in Dracula's army, official dispatches of Venetian and Genoese ambassadors and of papal legates, plus the narratives of travelers are among the major sources of information on Dracula's military affairs. By 1461, Dracula's power at home was sufficiently strong that he could undertake a more active role in the Reconquista. On the Turkish side, the sultan could ill afford to accept indignities unchallenged, but before engaging in warfare, he attempted diplomacy; or, to put it more accurately, to ensnare Dracula by guile rather than brute force. The

Turkish governor of Nicopolis, Hamza Pasha, and a crafty Greek interpreter, Toma Catavolinos, were initially sent to the Danubian port of Giurgiu to invite Dracula to discuss disputed territories, nonpayment of tribute, and other matters affecting Wallacho-Turkish relations. Dracula, knowing Turkish perfidy from his lengthy imprisonment in Asia Minor, immediately sensed a trap. These Turks were attempting to lay an ambush identical to that into which his father had fallen 18 years before and which had resulted in Dracula's own captivity as a hostage at Egrigoz. To gain time, the Wallachians pretended to fall in with the Turkish plan, and Dracula informed the Turkish envoys that he would indeed come to the assigned place. When he reached Giurgiu, however, events unfolded in a way quite different from that which the Turkish authors of the plot had intended. Under cover of the forests, which in those days extended virtually to the Danube, Dracula instructed a contingent of cavalry, far larger than the available Turkish force, to surround the appointed meeting place just outside the citadel of Giurgiu. Accompanying the two Turkish envoys, Dracula then forced them to ask that the city open its gates. The garrison was overwhelmed by the Wallachian horsemen. With the two envoys bound to each other, the whole enemy contingent was led in chains to Targoviste. There, in circumstances already alluded to, the Turks were neatly drawn upon pikes in a meadow on the city's outskirts, stripped of their clothes and impaled, some head up, others feet up. Two special pikes, larger than the rest, were designed for the great Catavolinos and Hamza Pasha of Nicopolis. Then they were left for all to see how Dracula dealt with those who attempted to deceive him. After six months, the summer sun and the blackbirds had done their work. This was the spectacle which greeted the Turkish Sultan Mehemet when he finally invested Targoviste in the summer of 1462—a scene so horrible that the sultan is said to have decided personally to quit the campaign.

Dracula knew that this act of atrocity was tantamount to an official declaration of war. In fact, he meant to press his advantage immediately, and in the winter of 1461 he launched his Danubian campaign, the plans for which had been carefully laid. The Wallachians, numbering somewhere between 10,000 and 20,000 men, consisted essentially of a rapid moving cavalry, free peasants, yeomen, and those dutiful boyars who happened not to have incurred Dracula's wrath. The officers were almost entirely new appointees, for Dracula had created a court and military nobility of his own. The terrain, however, was familiar and had already been the scene of skirmishes with the Turks.

The fortress of Giurgiu, built by his grandfather, and a place that Dracula considered to be his own legitimate inheritance, was burned to the ground. From here he made diplomatic preparations for the renewal of a Hunyadi-style crusading campaign against the Turks. He dispatched envoys to all the crowned heads of what remained of independent Eastern and Central Europe; appealed to the Papacy for armed help; and sent King Mathias of Hungary a lengthy dispatch (dated February 11, 1462, and still preserved in the archives of Munich) which reported the capture of Giurgiu. In that letter, Dracula was able to record some remarkable statistics, for there had been an actual counting of Turkish heads, noses, and ears—23,809 in all. Bags of these were sent to Mathias. Though calculated to enlist the Hungarian king in the crusade, the morbid tidings met with failure.

Dracula's famous offensive along the Danube, which was to lead him from Giurgiu to the Black Sea, began as an amphibious operation, since the winter of 1461 was exceptionally mild. Wallachian barges carried the infantry, while the cavalry advancing along the right bank protected their flank.

One purpose of the campaign was liberation: when Dracula invaded Bulgaria proper, countless peasants joined the Christian ranks, greeting the Wallachian leader as their deliverer from the Turkish yoke. Later, when Dracula was compelled to retreat, whole Bulgarian villages sought to obtain the right of asylum on Wallachian soil, fearing the inevitable Turkish reprisal. Dracula's principal aim, however, was to destroy Turkish power along the Danube. Thus his advance became bogged down in a number of siege operations directed against Turkish fortresses from Zimnicea to the Black Sea. Dracula's forces besieged and sacked towns on both banks of the river: Oltenita, Silistria, Calarasi, Rasova, Cerna-Voda, Hirsova, and Ostrov. Local peasant traditions pinpoint one of Dracula's temporary headquarters in a village on the right bank which still bears his name.

It was the Danubian campaign which established Dracula's reputation as a Christian crusader and warrior. Throughout Central and Western Europe, Te Deums were sung, and bells tolled from Genoa to Rhodes in gratitude for Dracula's endowing the Christian crusade with a new lease on life and taking over the leadership of the Great Hunyadi. Dracula's bold offensive also sent a new hope of liberation to the enslaved people of Bulgaria, Serbia, and Greece. At Constantinople itself there was an atmosphere of consternation, gloom, and fear, and some of the Turkish leaders, fearing *Kaziklu Bey*—the Impaler—apparently contemplated flight across the Bosphorus into Asia Minor.

The winter campaign ended on the Black Sea coast within sight of the powerful Turkish invasion force that had crossed the Bosphorus for a full-scale invasion of Wallachia. With his flank unprotected, Dracula was compelled to abandon the offensive. He burned all the Turkish fortresses he could not actually occupy. Beyond that he could not go; the momentum of the offensive had spent itself.

Mohammed the Conqueror decided to launch his invasion of Wallachia in the spring of 1462; Dracula had hardly given the sultan any alternative. To defy the sultan by spoiling a probable assassination plot was one thing; to ridicule him and instill hopes of liberation among his Christian subjects was quite another—one far more dangerous to his recently established empire. One Greek chronicler, Chalkokondyles, set the total number of the twin Turkish invasion forces as no less than 250,000 men, including a powerful Janizary (infantry) force, the Spahi Calvary, and a massive artillery.

The main contingent, led by the sultan himself, was carried across the Bosphorus by a vast flotilla of barges, assembled for this purpose in the Turkish capital. The other major force had been collected at Nicopolis in Bulgaria, and was to cross the Danube, recapture the fortress of Giurgiu, and then unite with the main force in a combined attack on the Wallachian capital of Targoviste. If these figures are even approximately accurate, this was the largest Turkish invasion force since the one which had captured Constantinople in 1453.

Dracula undoubtedly expected reinforcements at least from Mathias of Hungary, in order to correct the disparity of numbers; he had, according to the Slavic narrative, no more than 30,900 men, even allowing for a levy en masse. In the meantime, he practiced the classical tactic of the outnumbered, namely, the strategic retreat, combined with what is known today as the "scorched earth policy." After preliminary skirmishes along the marshes of the Danube, aimed essentially at delaying the juncture of the two great Turkish armies, Dracula abandoned the line of the Danube and began his withdrawal northward. As the Wallachian troops gave up their own native soil to the Turks, they reduced the country to barrenness, burning crops, poisoning wells, herding the cattle northward, and consuming all that they could not carry with them. The villages were emptied of people, the houses destroyed. The peasants usually accompanied the armies in their retreat. The boyars and their families, hearing of the impending attack, withdrew from their estates to the mountains. Many of them established their headquarters at Cheia high up in the Carpathians, while waiting for the inevitable outcome of the fray. Others took refuge at Snagov, and stored their treasure there. Most of them refused to collaborate with either Dracula or the Turks until the issues were clarified by the fortunes of war. Finally the boyars threw in their lot with Radu, Dracula's brother, but only when there could be little doubt as to Dracula's fate. As the Turks advanced into the country, all they saw was the desolate spectacle of smoke and ashes, vultures hovering in the sky, and howling wolves and coyotes at night.

Dracula's retreat was also accomplished with guerrilla tactics, where the element of surprise played the most vital part. His veterans knew the terrain well, generally maneuvering at dead of night under cover of the vast forests of Vlasie. In these "mad" forests were the lairs of the robber barons, who collaborated with Dracula's forces much as the Cossacks did with the Russian armies in the campaign of 1812. The signals used during the night attacks imitated the sounds of various animals or birds. For speed, which was essential, the best Wallachian horses were used.

The attack known in official sources as the "Night of Terror" particularly deserves inclusion here. In one of the many villages leading to Targoviste, near the forest encampment of the Turks, Dracula held a council of war. The situation of Targoviste was desperate, and Dracula presented a bold plan as a last-resort means of saving his indefensible capital. The council agreed that only the assassination of the sultan might sufficiently demoralize the Turkish army to effect a speedy withdrawal.

The outcome of this plan was admirably recorded by a Serbian Janizary, Constantine of Ostrovita, who experienced the whole impact of Dracula's audacious onslaught. His account describes the complex compound of a Turkish camp at night, with its vigilant Janizary guards occasionally called to order; the smell of lamb roasting over glowing fires; the noise of departing soldiers; the laughter of the women and other camp dependents; the wail of the muezzin; the plaintive chant of Turkish slaves; the noise of the camels; the countless tents, and finally the more elaborate gold-embroidered establishment of the sleeping sultan in the very heart of the camp. Mohammed had just retired after a heavy meal. Suddenly came the hooting of an owl—Dracula's signal to attack, followed by the onrush of cavalry, which penetrated deep into the various layers of guards, frantically galloping through the tents and half-sleeping soldiers, tearing all apart. The Wallachian sword and lance cut a bloody swath with Dracula always in the lead, carried along it seems by demoniac power. *"Kaziklu Bey!"*—

"The Impaler"—cried rows of awestruck Turkish soldiers, moaning and dying in the path of the Romanian avalanche. Finally Turkish trumpets called the men to arms. A body of determined Janizaries gradually formed around the sultan's tent. Dracula had calculated that the sheer surprise and impetus of the attack would carry his cavalry to the sultan's bed, and he came close to victory. But as he was within sight of the gold brocade tent, the bodyguard rallied, held the Wallachian offensive, actually began to push it back. Realizing the danger of being surrounded and captured, Dracula reluctantly gave orders for retreat. He had killed several thousand Turks, wounded countless more, created havoc, chaos, and terror within the Turkish camp; but he had lost a few hundred of his bravest warriors and the objective of the attack had failed. Sultan Mohammed had survived, and the road to Targoviste lay open.

The Wallachian capital presented a desolate spectacle to the oncoming Turks. Like the gates of some abandoned Foreign Legion fortress in a later era, those of the city had been left open, and a thick blanket of smoke shut out the dawning light. The city had been stripped of virtually all its holy relics and treasures; the palace was emptied of all that could be taken and the rest had been put to fire. Here, as elsewhere, all wells had been poisoned. As if to confirm the atmosphere of desolation, the only men who greeted the Turks on the outskirts of the city were Hamza Pasha, Bey of Nicopolis, and the Greek Catavolinos, their impaled bodies badly mutilated by the beaks of black-birds. Adding this awesome spectacle to his experiences of the night before, it is little wonder that Sultan Mohammed lost heart. His despairing comment has often been quoted: "What can we do against a man like this?" After a council of war, the sultan ordered retreat for the bulk of the Turkish army. Then he assigned a smaller contingent, in collaboration with the pro-Turkish boyars and Prince Radu (who had been brought to Targoviste and officially installed as prince), to pursue Dracula in his flight northward to his mountain castle, to capture him alive, and then to cut off his head and expose it at Constantinople as an example for all to see of the fate of those who dared flaunt Turkish power.

There was another, more compelling reason for the Turkish withdrawal. The plague had begun to make its appearances within the sultan's ranks, and the first victims of the dread disease were recorded in Targoviste.

Dracula's appeal for help from his kinsman Steven was answered with treachery. In the month of June, the Moldavian ruler attacked the crucial Wallachian fortress of Chilia from the north; simultaneously powerful Turkish contingents attacked it from the south. This extraordinary double assault was unsuccessful. The Turks abandoned the siege and marched on to their ultimate objective of Targoviste. As for Steven, he was wounded by the accurate Hungarian gunfire from the fortress and withdrew to Moldavia. (He did not renew the attack on Chilia until 1465, and this time captured it, while his cousin Dracula was safely in a Hungarian jail many miles farther up the Danube at Visegrad. Steven had certainly more justification in taking the fortress from Dracula's reigning brother, Radu, who had acquired the reputation of being a pliable tool of the Turks.)

Professor Giurescu explains Steven's betrayal of Dracula in terms of *raison d'état.* Steven did not think his cousin could hold the fortress against the Turks; he needed it to protect the flank of his own principality; and he was uncertain that the Hungarian members of Dracula's garrison, who were in a majority, could be trusted.

The last episode in the Turko-Wallachian war leads to Dracula's castle on the upper Arges, the prince's final place of refuge from the advancing Turks. Since the Janizary of Ostrovita (upon whom we have mainly relied for a description of the early phases of the campaign) returned to Constantinople with the sultan and the main bulk of the army, and since most of the western veterans abandoned Dracula and hence left no reports, the historian must once again rely for information on popular ballads from the castle region.

The peasants in the villages surrounding Castle Dracula relate numerous tales concerning the end of Dracula's second reign in the fall of 1462. All these stories end at the point where Dracula crossed the border into Transylvania and became prisoner of the Hungarian king. They start anew some 12 years later, when Dracula returned to Wallachia for his third reign. One of the more classic narrations of Dracula's last moments of resistance to the Turks in 1462 runs briefly as follows: After the fall of Targoviste, Dracula and a few faithful followers headed northward; avoiding the more obvious passes leading to Transylvania, they reached his mountain retreat. The Turks who had been sent in pursuit encamped on the Bluff of Poenari, which commanded an admirable view of Dracula's castle on the opposite bank of the Arges, and here they set up their cherrywood cannons. (At Poenari to this day there is a field known as *tunuri,* ''the field of cannon.'') The bulk of the Turkish Janizaries descended to the river, forded it at much the same place where the Tartars had crossed it a century before, and camped on the other side. A bombardment of Dracula's castle began, but had little success owing to the small calibre of the Turkish guns and the solidity of the castle walls. Orders for the final assault upon the castle were set for the next day.

That night, a Romanian slave in the Janizary corps—who according to local tale was a distant relative of Dracula and who perhaps was inspired by ethnic loyalty— forewarned the Wallachian prince of the great danger that lay ahead. Undetected in the moonless night, the slave climbed the Bluff of Poenari and after taking careful aim, he sped an arrow at one of the distant dimly lit openings in the main tower, which he knew contained Dracula's quarters. At the end of the arrow was a message advising Dracula to escape while there was still time. The Janizary witnessed the accuracy of his aim: the arrow extinguished a candle within the tower opening. When it was relit, the slave could see the shadow of Dracula's wife, and its faint indication that she was reading the message.

The remainder of this story could only have been passed down by Dracula's intimate advisors within the castle. Dracula's wife apprised her husband of the warning. She told her husband she would rather have her body eaten by the fish of the Arges than be led into captivity by the Turks. Dracula, of course, knew from his own experience at Egrigoz what that slavery would entail. Realizing how desperate their situation was and before anyone could intervene, Dracula's wife rushed up the winding staircase, and hurled herself from the donjon; her body rolled down the precipice, into the river Arges. Today this point of the river is known as *Riul Doamei*, ''the Princess' river.'' This tragic folktale contains practically the only mention of Dracula's first wife.

Dracula himself immediately made plans for escape: suicide, no matter how unfavorable the circumstances, was not part of the Dracula philosophy. He ordered the bravest leaders from the neighboring village of Arefu to be brought to the castle, and during the night they discussed the various routes of escape to Transylvania. It was Dracula's hope that Mathias of Hungary, to whom he had sent many appeals since that first letter in February 1462, would greet him as an ally and support his reinstatement on the Wallachian throne. Indeed, it was known that the Hungarian king, along with a powerful army, had established headquarters just across the mountains at Brasov. To reach him was a matter of crossing the Transylvanian Alps at a point where there were no roads or passes. It meant climbing to the summit of the Fagaras mountains, still a challenge to the most experienced Alpinist with the aid of special equipment. The upper slopes of these mountains are rocky, treacherous, often covered with snow or ice thooughout the summer. Dracula could not have attempted such an ascent without the help of local experts. The precise way of escape was mapped out by the peasants brought in from Arefu. Popular folklore still identifies various rivers, clearings, forested areas, even rocks, which were along the way of Dracula's escape route. We have tried to use them in reconstituting Dracula's actual passage, but the task has been difficult since many of the place names have changed over the years. As far as we have been able to reconstruct the escape, Dracula and a dozen attendants, his illegitimate son, and five men of Arefu left the castle before dawn by way of a staircase spiraling down into the bowels of the mountain and leading to a cave on the banks of the river. Here, the fleeing party could hear the noises of the Turkish camp located a mile to the north. Some of the fastest mounts were then brought from the village, the horses being equipped with inverted horseshoes so as to leave false signs of an incoming cavalry force.

During the night the castle guns continually fired to detract attention from the escape party. The Turks at Poenari replied in kind. Because of the noise of the gunfire, so the story runs, Dracula's own mount began to shy, and his son, who had been tied to the saddle, fell to the ground and in the confusion was taken for lost. The situation was far too desperate for anyone to begin a search, and Dracula was both too battle-hardened and too cold-hearted to sacrifice himself or his companions for his son.

This tragic little vignette has a happy sequel. The boy, not yet in his teens, was found next morning by a local shepherd from Arefu, who took him to his hut and brought him up as though he were one of his own family. Twelve years later, when Dracula returned as Prince of Wallachia, the peasant, who had found out the true identity of his ward, came to the castle. By that time the boy had developed into a splendid young man. He told his father all that the shepherd had done for him, and in gratitude Dracula richly recompensed the peasant with landed tracts in the surrounding mountains. It is possible that the son himself stayed on in the area and eventually became governor of the castle.

When the fleeing party finally reached the crests of the Fagaras mountains to the south, they were able to view the Turks' final assault, which partially destroyed Castle Dracula. To the north lay the castle and the city of Fagaras, where the armies of King Mathias, it was hoped, were maneuvering to come to Dracula's aid. At a place called *Plaiul Oilor,* "Plain of the Sheep," Dracula's party, now quite safe from the Turks, retired and made plans for the northward descent.

Summoning his brave companions, Dracula asked them how best he could recompense them for having saved his life. They answered in unison that they had simply done their duty for prince and country. The prince, however, insisted: "What do you wish? Money or land? (Part of the royal treasury had been taken along on this difficult climb.) They answered directly: "Give us land, Your Highness." On a slab of stone, known to this day as the Prince's Table, Dracula fulfilled their wishes, writing upon the skin of some hares caught the day before. He endowed the five peasants from Arefu with all the area to the south as far as they could see up to the plain, containing 16 mountains and a rich supply of timber, fish, and sheep—a tract containing perhaps 20,000 acres. He further stipulated in the deed that none of this land could ever be taken away from them by prince, boyar or ecclesiastical leaders; it was for their families to enjoy from one generation to the next.

Ancient tradition in the village of Arefu has it that these rabbitskins are still carefully hidden by the five men's descendants, but despite many efforts and inducements no peasant has been willing to shed light on the exact whereabouts of these alleged documents. Still we have reason to suppose that somewhere hidden in an attic, or buried underground, the Dracula rabbitskins still exist. One Romanian historian attempted to find these scrolls, but the peasants of the area have remained secretive and intractable. Even large sums of money would not persuade them to part with such precious souvenirs of Dracula's heroic age.

Dracula's seal. The inscription is in Old Slavonic and reads: *Vlad Voevod through the grace of God is Prince of Ungro-Wallachia.* "Voevod" signifies a warlord or warrior prince, not a prince who rules by inherited right.

CHAPTER

Castle Dracula

There are essentially two ways of going from Targoviste, in Wallachia, to the mountains of Transylvania. One of them proceeds north along the Dambovita to Campulung, then to Rucar at the Transylvanian border, and through the mountains, by way of the pass of Bran. This was the route traveled by Dracula during his raids against Brasov, which lay just across the mountains, on the edge of the Transylvanian plateau. The second route is slightly more cumbersome. It takes you west to the river Olt—another tributary of the Danube—north to the episcopal city of Ramnicul Valcea, and then into Transylvania, via the pass of Turnu Rosu (German, Rotherturm).

The first of these two routes is the more scenic. At Campulung, one finds a city of transition between the Germanic and Romanian worlds. It still has traces of what it was in the 13th century—a burgh of the Teutonic order, and in that sense it belongs to the civilization of Central Europe.

Among the medieval customs continued here is the celebration of the Feast

83

of St. Elias, when peasants come from neighboring areas to sell their wares and partake of the traditional entertainment. Dracula often sojourned at Campulung on his way to the north, but only a few local stories are linked to his name. This was largely due to the presence of the Germanic element, who were even more resented in Wallachia owing to the prejudices they brought to local trade.

There are many rustic villages on the route from Campulung to Bran, such as Cetateni din Vale. On a mountain overlooking Cetateni are the remains of a castle and a small church built inside a rock. This castle is not Dracula's, but was built according to popular legend by Wallachia's first prince, Basarab. Inside the grotto three monks still observe a ritual which has been held there at midnight since earliest times, an index to the ageless piety of the region. Peasants in gaily embroidered dress still come from as far as 50 miles away, often walking barefooted up the difficult ascent, to attend the midnight service in this musty, incense-filled, cavern-like place, where faded icons portray their martyrs and saints. One of the monks, who lost part of an arm while working in an aircraft factory, firmly believes that at each midnight mass his injured limb lengthens by an inch—yet another instance of faith-filled superstition. According to local legend Dracula himself climbed this mountain when fleeing from the Turks in 1462, and took sanctuary within the grotto before continuing on to his own castle.

The region between Campulung and Bran is the heart of Romania's historic area. Here a national life was born at the close of the 13th century. There is hardly a mountain, a river, a torrent, or any other landmark, natural or artificial, that in some way or other does not evoke the stormy past—so often recalled in the historical ballads of the peasants. Each village church, disintegrating castle, or fortified manor (*cula*), challenges the historian to seek the reason for its survival in an area where so much has been destroyed by hordes of invaders.

The peasants along this route are mostly *mosneni* (free peasants). Never having experienced serfdom, most of them are probably descendants of the warriors who fought in Dracula's and the other princes' armies—the bulk of Dracula's military forces having consisted of freeholders since they were more trustworthy than the boyars. Today's peasants proudly remain the owners of their soil, for collectivization has proved generally unworkable in the mountainous districts. Their wood houses are more ambitious than those found elsewhere: the scale larger; the styling somewhat Tyrolean in character; but the courtyards more extensive; and the porches, *pridvors*, more artistically carved. These peasants still tend cattle and sheep, and they take any surplus grapes, prunes, apples, and pears from their orchards to the market of Campulung once they have met their obligation to the state.

In Dragoslavele, the local priest, an amiable man by the name of Rautescu, has written an amazingly well-documented history of the region, in which he traces his own town and many others from Dracula's time.

Rucar is the border town, the ancient customs station, between Wallachia and Transylvania proper. Dracula's frontier guards, whose services he was often compelled by sheer lack of manpower to call upon in order to fight the Turks, had their headquarters in Rucar.

The Hungarian frontier was fairly peaceful in Dracula's time, and relationships with Buda cordial. In a sense, Hungarian-Romanian relations had to be correct. Struggling with the Turks on the Danube, Dracula was hardly able to challenge the formidable guns and fortifications of Castle Bran, which dominated the valley of the Dambovita.

Castle Bran was allegedly founded by the Teutonic knight Dietrich in the 13th century. Given the number of times it was besieged, burned, or partially razed, it is a miracle that so much of it is extant. In 1225 it came into the hands of the Hungarian kings, and then successively belonged to the Wallachian prince Mircea, King Sigismund, John Hunyadi, and his son King Mathias Corvinus. Dracula was undoubtedly a guest of Hunyadi at Bran.

With its vast halls, dark corridors, multi-level battlements, high water tower, numerous inner courtyards, Gothic chapel, and rustic Germanic furnishings of the period, Bran has an atmosphere which conveys, more than any other castle in Romania, the legacy of the age of Dracula. In the middle of the inner courtyard lies a well, and next to it, hidden by a covering of stone, is a secret passage. Through a winding staircase which sinks 150 feet down into the mountain one emerges into a cell near the bottom of the well. Beyond the cell is a heavy oak door, formerly locked, which opens to another passageway leading to the safety of a mountain knoll and farther on to the citadel of Brasov. The purposes of this intricate passageway were manifold: protection of the castle's water supply; a place of refuge; a place for torture and detention; and finally a secret means of escape. Dracula was apparently impressed by the features of this passageway, for very similar arrangements were later contrived in his own castle on the river Arges. After the death of his protector John Hunyadi, Dracula avoided Bran whenever he passed near it on his way to Transylvania.

After the reunion of Transylvania and Romania in 1918, Bran was given to Romania's Hohenzollern royal family; it was particularly pleasing to the princess who was wife of the heir to the throne, Ferdinand, and who later became the majestic Queen Marie. In fact, this romantic granddaughter of Queen Victoria preferred Bran as a summer retreat to the official royal residence at near-by Sinaia. One wonders if she chose Castle Bran as a royal residence because it accorded so well with Bram Stoker's description of Dracula's castle at the Borgo Pass. The analogies between Stoker's mythical Castle Dracula and the real Castle Bran are simply too close to be coincidental. Moreover, like Stoker, Queen Marie had a great love and understanding of Romanian folklore, which is so richly invested with the supernatural.

The second major route to Transylvania follows the valley of the river Olt, and via the pass at Turnu Rosu crosses the border into Dracula's favorite city of Sibiu. Turnu Rosu is often mentioned in documents concerning Dracula. The fortress here lies on a high bluff on the left side of the pass as one proceeds north and was built on a much

Castle Bran: exterior detail.   Castle Bran: secret underground passageway.

smaller scale than Bran. Only the ruins of its chief donjons are still visible. The fortress was built by the Saxon citizens of Sibiu around 1360, on the site of an old Roman castrum, to guard the southern approaches of the city and as part of an outward defensive network against Turkish attack. The name Turnu Rosu, derived from one of its donjons—the Red Tower, commemorates its heroic role in a specific battle, when its premises were reddened by the blood of barbarian assailants. Although the castle was almost entirely destroyed on this occasion, the Turks were never able to capture the Red Tower. Nor for that matter was Dracula.

Romanian historical chronicles (which if Stoker did consult he ignored for his own reasons) do not locate Dracula's castle on either of the two main routes from Wallachia into Transylvania. But aside from this, it seems highly unlikely that the wily Wallachian prince would erect his retreat in the shadow of either of the two formidable and sometimes unfriendly Germanic fortresses. In view of Dracula's taste for the inaccessible and his mistrustful nature, it is equally unlikely that he would build his eyrie on *any* well-traveled, commercial route. And, from the standpoint of defense, it would be unreasonable to assume that he would site his hideaway on a major route that could easily become a highroad for invasion by Tartars and Turks alike.

For all these reasons, Castle Dracula had to be sought elsewhere. Fortunately, the oldest Romanian chronicle and peasant oral tradition speak quite accurately on this point. The way to Dracula's castle lies somewhere *between* the two known routes, which follow along the river Olt and the Dambovita, and it does not include any accessible pass or traveled roads. The castle itself was located precisely at the source of the river Arges, which begins as a mere torrent here, collecting the melting snows of the Transylvanian peaks; then, gaining momentum little by little, painfully carves its way through the sub-Carpathian mountains into the Wallachian plain, and eventually flows into the Danube. To the south, the castle commanded a formidable view of the Wallachian plain; to the north, it looked to the snow-capped peaks of the Fagaras mountains. Isolated in this remote spot, Castle Dracula was virtually impregnable.

The road leading to the castle is far less scenic than the one we traveled from Campulung to Bran. The villages are both smaller and poorer; the inhabitants, less hospitable, rather suspicious of foreigners or strangers, much like those in Stoker's story; the houses, less decorative and the costumes not so gaily embroidered as in the usual mountain districts; and the churches, built on a more modest scale.

The road to the castle passes through Curtea de Arges (citadel of the Arges), site of the ancient cathedral, which no longer exists. Here Dracula's ancestors were anointed princes of the land by the head of the Wallachian Orthodox church in full presence of the boyar leaders. The ceremonies following such a religious exercise were normally held in the old princely church of this city, rather than at Targoviste. Generally, however, Dracula avoided the Citadel of the Arges and all it represented, for he got along no better with its church officials than he did with its boyars, who often intrigued against him in Targoviste. Castle Dracula, merely 20 miles to the north of this ecclesiastical capital, acted as a powerful deterrent to potential revolt. In fact, this center of church authority was generally submissive during Dracula's lifetime.

Wallachian chronicles, as well as popular folklore, place Dracula's castle high up on a rock on the left bank of the river Arges, and just beyond the small community of Arefu. By a strange irony, which will be explained, Castle Dracula is also known in the chronicles as the fortress of Poenari, the name of another village located on the opposite bank of the river. In fact, one of the oldest of these chronicles credits Dracula with just two accomplishments: "The 'Impaler' built the castle of Poenari, and the monastery of Snagov, where he lies buried." In this one sentence Dracula, a prince notorious throughout 15th-century Western and Eastern Europe, was summed up by chroniclers in his own land a hundred years after his death.Small wonder that there has been such difficulty in identifying the horrible tyrant and persecutor of the Germans with the castle-and-monastery founder recorded by the Romanians. Bram Stoker's novel, strange as it may seem, probably represents the first attempt at marrying Germany's demoniac to Romania's heroic character. Romanian histories, drawing upon the early chronicles, speak of "a castle known as Poenari, converted by Dracula into an impregnable retreat." Local tradition, however, disputes this idea of a *single* castle; maintaining that Dracula's castle was located on the left bank of the river Arges, and that the Castle of Poenari—a much older fortress, which has now disappeared—was located on the right bank. If this tradition is correct, one can only assume that the early chroniclers confused the two structures and later historians perpetuated the mistake.

It will take the work of the archaeologist to prove this matter one way or the other. For the time being, we are inclined to agree with tradition, and with the elders of Arefu and Poenari, that within the narrow gorges of the Arges, and at a distance of about one mile from each other, these were *two* castles. And we shall now hazard an explanation as to how the identification of one with the other came about.

Of the two villages, Arefu, where Dracula's castle actually is located, and Poenari, which the chroniclers have taken to be the actual site, the latter was by far the more important. In the Middle Ages, Poenari was a princely village; over the years the castle built within its confines gained control of all the neighboring villages, including Arefu. Deeds made by several princes to monasteries and individual boyars, both before and after Dracula's time, all speak of "land endowed to the Castle of Poenari." Moreover, Poenari is the only castle remembered in the documents of the 13th, 14th, and 15th centuries. Local peasant folklore tales clarified the historical problem their own way. The key to the confusion is that *Dracula's castle was literally built out of the bricks and stones of the Castle of Poenari.* Before describing this reconstruction, let us briefly survey our findings about the older Castle of Poenari.

Today, there are no visible remains of it, but peasants from Poenari told us about remains of a low-lying wall at the foot of the hill, which might have formed part of the

Ruins of Castle Dracula.

Mountain pass near Castle Dracula.

outward defense of a very ancient fortress. That fact could not, however, be scientifically corroborated. They also stated that when excavations were made not too many years ago in the local church, the workers came across bricks and stone that date back to the time of the Dacians. We were also led to some local mud houses, the chimneys of which contained stones remarkably like the ''Dacian'' stones found underneath the church. In addition, a small museum organized by the local priest displays an amazing array of stones, coins, weapons, and other artifacts, some of which date to Roman and pre-Roman times. None of this material has been scientifically examined by the Archaeological Institute at Bucharest. Pending such an analysis, however, the hypothesis presented by the local priest, Stanciulescu, seems quite plausible: Castle Poenari was built upon the site of the ancient Dacian fortress of Decidava. After all, the center of Dacian power, Sarmisegetuza, which was destroyed by Trajan's Roman legion in 106 A.D., was only 100 miles to the northwest. In accordance with this theory, Decidava was rebuilt by Romanian princes at the close of the 13th century to resist Hungarian and Teutonic incursions from the north, and given the name of the village which surrounds it—Poenari. It thus figures as a princely foundation with extensive land holdings and occupied a strategic point on the Transylvanian frontier. As a minor fortress, Poenari continued to survive until Dracula's time though it was badly battered by Turkish and Tartar invaders. In 1462, when pursuing the Wallachian prince, the Turks stumbled across the decaying fragments of the fortress and completed its destruction. What is left of Poenari is likely to be found in the foundation of the village church, in peasant chimneys, in the local museum, and in the remaining walls and donjons of Castle Dracula itself.

We must turn now to a further complication in the story of Dracula's mountain retreat. In a strict sense, Dracula was not its founder. When he came to the throne in 1456, the ruins of *two* fortresses faced each other across the river Arges: on the right bank, the ruins of the ancient medieval fortress of Poenari; on the left, the remnants of

93

the Castle of the Arges. One of the two structures deserved to be rebuilt. Dracula chose to rebuild the Castle of the Arges, which had greater strategic advantage, being sited at a higher point along the river. Tradition has it that this particular fortress was founded by one of the early Basarab princes a century before Dracula's time. A few historians claim that the initial fortress was even older than that, and that it belonged to the network of Teutonic fortresses, such as Bran, built to defend the Hungarian frontier at the beginning of the 13th century. If so, since the castle lies across the mountains, directly opposite the Teutonic castle of Fagaras, its usefulness would have been that of a sentinel warning the home base of the presence of hostile forces on the southern slopes of the Carpathians. Here, as elsewhere, local tradition often predates the chronicles and the historians' ordinary sources. The Castle of the Arges (Castle of Agrish, as it was initially known in Hungarian documents) was, in our view, founded by the earliest Romanian princes coming from Transylvania and was definitely not a Teutonic fortress. In a sense it represents one of their first bastions on Wallachian soil. Structurally it bears little resemblance to the much more formidable Germanic fortresses, such as Bran or Hunedoara, located in Transylvania proper. In fact, like Wallachian castles at Cetateni, it is built on a modest scale and bears some of the features of Byzantine fortifications.

There are local tales to the effect that Prince Basarab withdrew to his citadel on the Arges following his encounters with the Turks around 1330. It was considerably fortified by his successors and, like so many other castles in the region, had a stormy history even before Dracula's time. A particular incident in that history requires mention here. On one occasion at the close of the 14th century, the Tartars, who had penetrated the heart of Wallachia—pillaging, burning, and looting on the way—reached the ecclesiastical see of Curtea de Arges farther down the river. The Prince, his bishops, and boyars fled to the Castle of the Arges. In pursuit along the right bank of the river, the Tartars reached the village of Capatineni within sight of the castle, crossed the river, and encamped in a clearing on the left bank (to this day called Plasea—''hilt of a sword''). Next morning they began bombardment with their cherry-wood cannon. When they eventually stormed the fortress, they found not a man within its walls. The prince, his bishops, and boyars had fled through a secret passage, still existing in Dracula's time, leading to the banks of the river. The Tartars in their vengeance left the castle severely damaged. This story has been related because it provides the vital clue to the link between the Castle of the Arges, built by Basarab, and the Castle of Poenari. The Tartars had, in fact, so badly mauled the earlier fortification of Prince Basarab that it was in need of reconstruction. This reconstruction, which could be viewed as virtually new construction, was Dracula's distinctive contribution. On that basis, Dracula might also be named, as local tradition, indeed, has named him, the founder of the Castle of the Arges. Historical chronicles are incorrect only in confusing the names.

To sum up what is surely a complicated matter: Castle Dracula was a reconstruction of the Castle of the Arges, partially with materials from the Castle of Poenari, which itself seems to have been built on the site of the ancient fortress of Decidava.

The story of the construction (call it reconstruction) of Dracula's castle is very succinctly described in one of the ancient Wallachian chronicles:

So when Easter came, while all the citizens were feasting and the young ones were dancing, he surrounded and captured them. All those who were old he impaled, and strung them all around the city; as for the young ones together with their wives and children, he had them taken just as they were, dressed up for Easter, to Poenari, where they were put to work until their clothes were all torn and they were left naked.

A second chronicle states that they worked ''until their clothes fell off their backs,'' a description that has often been quoted. As much as any Romanian document, this one

95

has established Dracula's reputation for cruelty, for these enslaved workers were neither Turkish nor Saxon fiends, rather Dracula's own Wallachian subjects.

As often in this narrative, the chroniclers' story will have to be enlarged, explained, and ultimately accounted for by reference to popular folklore, which is both more colorful than the historian's language and probably closer to the historical truth than documents written a century later. From the village of Arefu come two different tales explaining Dracula's reason for this drastic abuse of his boyar subjects. One of them can be readily dismissed because the offense it relates seems far too trivial, even by Dracula's standards, to justify so severe a punishment. It states that Dracula's brother had been spurned to the point of ridicule by the daughters of a powerful boyar. To clear the family's honor, Dracula took vengeance on the particular faction to which the young ladies' family belonged. The other narrative is far more plausible in view of the circumstances surrounding Dracula's accession to the throne, and his basic hostility toward, and legitimate suspicion of, the boyar class. It runs as follows:

Shortly after assuming power in Wallachia, Dracula investigated the circumstances surrounding the death of his father, Dracul, and particularly those concerning the assassination of his favorite elder brother, Mircea, a gallant hero of war. He found out that Mircea, caught by the boyars with his father at Tirgsor, was dragged to Targoviste and secretly buried alive. He had already been convinced of the boyars' duplicity, in the famous court scene resulting in the impalement of hundreds of boyars outside his palace at Targoviste. The discovery of this later boyar act filled his cup of indignation to the brim, and his servants witnessed a scene of mad rage which must have paralleled those of Ivan the Terrible. However, there was always great cunning in his dementia, and he now planned a revenge worthy of the crime.

Earlier in the course of his journey from Transylvania, Dracula had made a personal survey of the region of the two castles on the upper Arges and was struck by its commanding strategic position, particularly in regard to the Castle of Agrish. The punishment of the boyars and the reconstruction of the castle on the left bank immediately became linked in his mind. ''Thus, on Easter Day,'' states a ballad of Arefu, ''our new Prince Dracula assembled both the high and the low of birth for the occasion, with little concern for rank, in this day of peasant democracy, for all to join in the festivities.'' On the night before, all attended the Easter vigil service, the most important religious celebration of the year. The following morning, there were to be festivities in the princely gardens surrounding the city walls, including a lavish banquet. In addition to the roasted lambs, sweetened cakes, and wines provided by the palace both boyars and humble merchants were to bring provisions of their own.

On Easter morning the boyars came to the meadows, mounted on their fine horses and riding in carriages. The merchants followed in carts or on foot. The Metropolitan and bishops wore their imposing ecclesiastical robes. The boyars imitated the Hungarian nobleman's dress, though a few preferred the more ornate Byzantine style. Turkish dress in those days was as yet unknown. The high headgear with an ostrich feather held by a cluster of costly diamonds, the ermine cape, and the silk embroidered shirt were almost *de rigueur.* The merchants and artisans dressed more simply, some of them wearing peasant dress essentially identical to that still worn today. The men wore the Dacian costume, an embroidered shirt, trousers held by a wide leather belt, a woolen-lined and embroidered vest, and soft pigskin laced sandals. The boyars' wives gathered in small circles, usually in accordance with their rank or court function, and had brought handsome Persian carpets to rest on. Gypsy fiddlers organized both the music and the mirth.

The merchants, craftsmen, and guild representatives were equally conscious of rank and formed small groups of their own. Unperturbed by the feast of the wealthy boyars, the middle estate carefully instructed their apprentices how to settle their less expensive carpets, how to handle their wine, how to serve a table in genteel fashion. On such occasions, they had entertainment of their own at a more modest level. They also came with food and wine.

After the feast, as was customary, the children enjoyed the swings, carousels, and various games provided by a specifically organized fair, their elders rested on the grass, and the younger folk, both boyars and artisans, joined in the *hora*, a traditional Romanian folk dance, while local groups of minstrels and jesters sang or played for the Prince, the boyars, and their ladies. In this fashion, the evening wore on until the sun had set behind the Carpathians.

Observers relate that Dracula was preoccupied throughout the day, rarely conversing with the boyars, nor joining, as was his wont, in the dances. While the partying was at its height, he conversed secretly with the captains of the yeomen guard, issuing instructions, and posting men under trees and bushes surrounding the meadows. As dusk turned into evening, harsh words of command were issued. Within seconds, Dracula's soldiers isolated from the rest of the partying community most of the boyars, their wives and their children, all of whom were easily identifiable by their more gaudy dress. Some 300 of them were enclosed in a prepared paddock, and then manacled to each other.

The operation had been so well organized that few boyars had the time to flee and seize weapons. In any case, because of the heavy quantities of wine consumed, many of them were in a state of torpor. The occasion could not have been better chosen. Dracula was intent upon teaching his boyars a lesson in submission they would not ever forget—if they survived the ordeal.

Persuaded of the unreliability of his own capital of Targoviste, Dracula had determined to build a new castle; it would be closer to Transylvania—on some secure elevation far from any well-traveled highway, or any of the traditional passes, or any powerful Germanic fortresses. The slopes of the Arges satisfied him on all these points. Logistically, he had made up his mind to rebuild the castle of the Arges with the bricks and stone from the Castle of Poenari. Moreover, the outer walls of the new complex were to be doubled in thickness. Castle Dracula was to be made virtually impregnable, able to resist the heaviest cannon fire of either Tartars or Turks. The boyars thus became the instruments of a dual and devilish plot, which combined a punitive operation with the securing of free labor for the construction of a powerful mountain retreat. This situation also neatly solves the problem of identifying Poenari as Castle Dracula. In a sense, it is quite correct to state that Castle Dracula was built "out of the brick and stone of the Castle of Poenari," even though its location lay on the site of the Castle of the Arges on the left bank of the river. This is the obvious way of reconciling both views in an ancient polemic.

The boyar trek from Targoviste—no less than 50 miles—was a painful one, particularly for the women and children. Those who survived it were allowed no rest until they reached Poenari. The region here was particularly rich in lime deposits and possessed good clay, and on Dracula's orders ovens and kilns for the manufacture of bricks had already been prepared. The "concentration camp" at Poenari must have presented a strange sight to the local peasants (one bears in mind that the boyars arrived in what was left of their Easter finery). As construction began, some of the boyars formed a work chain relaying the bricks and stones from Poenari to the Arges castle. Others worked up the mountain; yet others made bricks. The story does not tell us how long the reconstruction took, nor the number of those who died in the course of it. People were fed simply to keep them alive; they rested just long enough to restore their energies; they toiled until their tattered clothes literally, as the chronicler would have it, fell off their bodies, then continued to work in the nude. Months later, Dracula had succeeded in both of his aims: the powerful boyar class had been savagely humiliated, and he now had his castle retreat.

The path leading from Arefu to the top of the mountain where Castle Dracula is located is not, by any standards of modern Alpinism, a difficult one. The actual climb takes about one hour. The first element of surprise, as one reaches the small wooden bridge over a sheer precipice which leads to the main gate, is the smallness of the structure, particularly when compared with the vast areas occupied by Castle Bran or Castle Hunedoara. However, the plan of Castle Dracula was limited by the perimeter of the mountain top. The view is superb, almost majestic, both in the southern and east-west directions. One can see dozens of villages scattered among the hills immediately surrounding the valley of the Arges. Behind, barely visible in the sunscorched Wallachian plain, is the city of Curtea de Arges. To the north, lie the snow-capped mountains of the Fagaras, dividing Transylvania from Wallachia proper. It is perhaps inevitable that Dracula's eyrie reminds today's visitor of Hitler's high retreat at Berchtesgaden.

The extent of the castle's destruction and decay is already apparent on the way up; one sees a trail of fallen bricks from the top of the mountain down to the river Arges, which is slightly reddened at one spot, not with the blood of Dracula's victims as the local peasants would have it, but with the bricks on the floor of the crystal-clear water.

Castle Dracula is built on the plan of an irregular polygon—the shape of the narrow plateau at the summit of the ridge: approximately 100 feet wide from east to west, and 120 feet long from north to south. One can detect the remains of three of the five original donjons and their connecting walls despite a heavy overgrowth of every variety of Carpathian wild flower, greenery, and fungi. The central tower, probably the oldest, and built by Prince Basarab, was prism-shaped. The other two, probably built by Dracula, are in the classical cylindrical form. The fortress structurally attempts to combine some of the best features of Teutonic fortifications with the more intricate Byzantine style. The thickness of the walls, which were reinforced with brick on the outside, confirms the tradition that Dracula doubled the width of the walls of the earlier fortress. In due course, they were able to withstand the worst cannon fire of the Turks. These walls, protected by conventional battlements, originally were quite high, and from afar give the impression of being part of the mountain itself.

The five original donjons and other elements could have housed not more than 200 soldiers and an equal number of retainers and servants. Within the courtyard, it would have been difficult to drill over 100 men. In the middle of the courtyard the remains of a well are barely discernible. This was the source of the fortress' water supply. An arrangement remarkably similar to one at Castle Bran has also been detected: a secret staircase leading from the well into the bowels of the mountain, and connecting with a tunnel that emerges in a grotto on the bank of the river Arges. This was the escape route that Dracula used successfully in 1462. The grotto on the riverbank is referred to in popular tradition as *pivnit*, which in Romanian means cellar—in this case, perhaps, the cellar of the castle. In the courtyard, a few feet away from the entrance to the secret passage or well, there remains a vault, indicating the presence of a chapel at one time.

Of whatever else there was within the fortress, there is not a trace today. The houses of the attendants, the stables, the animal pens, the various outhouses that were customarily erected in small fortifications of this nature, now have to be imagined. So, too, the drawbridge which preceeded the present slender wooden bridge. We know that the donjons had some openings, probably under the battlements on top, for the peasants' ballads speak of candlelight being visible from a distance at night.

Following Dracula's escape to Transylvania in 1462, the Turks partially dismantled the castle. It was never used by Radu the Handsome, the new Wallachian incumbent, since the place was still haunted by souvenirs of his hated rival and brother. But it was enjoyed as a hunting retreat by Radu the Great, Dracula's cousin, the builder of the Monastery of the Hill. The records at the time speak of a princely governor, a boyar by the name of Gherghina, who was, it seems, a relative of Dracula—perhaps one of Dracula's bastards, or possibly that son who had miraculously escaped the Turks in 1462 and been brought up by a peasant from Arefu. The castle enjoyed renewed prestige under the rule of Dracula's only legitimate son (by his second wife), Prince

Mihnea. However, even that half-Hungarian prince could not have felt strong ties to a retreat that was associated with his father's first wife and where a half-brother may have been governor. Shortly after Gherghina's death, the castle was totally abandoned, and during the 16th century the neglect that was ultimately to destroy it set in. By that time, the center of Wallachian power was gradually moving toward the Danube—toward Bucharest. A castle which had existed primarily to survey the boyars in the ancient capitals had virtually lost all meaning. Its location away from all the commercial routes leading into Transylvania deprived it of any strategic value. And even as a hideaway, it had become too remote. For all these reasons, the castle was never used again. Physically, it became entombed in a morass of Alpine overgrowth.

The peasants of the area often talk about it but rarely dare visit it. In the eyes of the superstitious, the spirit of Stoker's "undead hero" still dominates the place. The peasant guarding the castle at night is never seen without a tattered Bible; he reads it constantly while on duty, to ward off, so he indicated, the evil spirits that linger around.

These spirits, in the vivid imagination of the peasantry, take the shape of various animals. Among the actual creatures that are found at this ruin is the Wallachian eagle, which has an enormous wing span, and which was always symbolized in the ancient national crest. The cursed bat, another element of woe in Romanian folklore, dominates the battlements at night. Romania's bat is larger than its North American counterpart though not quite so large as the vampire bat of South America, and is considered dangerous by the peasants. They relate strange tales of people with bat wounds becoming demented and wishing to bite others, and usually dying within a matter of a week. These are the symptoms of hydrophobia. They also concord remarkably well with the Dracula vampire myth and provide a rational explanation of Stoker's horror tales.

The eagles that nest in the castle area are probably attracted by the number of smaller animals. Within the ramparts, rats and mice abound; snake holes are evident, probably nesting the dangerous Carpathian viper; occasionally a stray sheep or mountain goat gets entrapped within the overgrowth of vines; foxes are in large supply; and the Romanian mountain bear is an occasional visitor as well as the mountain lynx. But the most dangerous visitor by far is the wolf. In his novel, Stoker mentions wolves howling while accompanying Dracula's carriage. They will attack men during the winter, driven by sheer despair. Wild dogs often howl here at night— particularly, as legend would have it, during a full moon—sending a spine-tingling shiver through the heart of the most valiant. These are some of the legitimate reasons why spending a night on the site of Dracula's castle has become a sport commanding a high fee. Bets of that nature have been made by the more venturesome, but only one person of our acquaintance has survived the ordeal.

Although the sophisticated, adventuresome students from the University of Bucharest and elsewhere are occasionally willing to try their luck and brave the spirit of Dracula, one can hardly blame the superstitious peasants of the area for shunning it. As Stoker also described it, when a stranger approaches them to ask directions to the castle, they usually turn away and emphatically refrain from giving help. If the tourist persists, they simply shrug their shoulders in quiet disbelief that anyone should be so bold as to tempt the spirit of evil, or they mutter *"nu se poate,"* an approximation of the German *verboten.*

Beyond their superstitions, if such they are, is a strange belief somewhat reminiscent of the medieval German obsession that the great Barbarossa would someday arise again to save the German race. Here, in times of stress, the peasants feel that the spirit of Dracula will be born again, or to put it more accurately, that he never really died; he is just "undead." This feeling is expanded even to the prediction that someday when he does rise again, he will save Romania from its outside enemies as he saved the country from the Turks in the 15th century.

Present-day visitors to the castle prefer to view it from a safe distance, usually from the opposite knoll where the Castle of Poenari once stood. From this perspective, too, most of the sketches, oil paintings, and watercolors of Castle Dracula have been made. Such a distance brings into relief not only the castle itself, but the picturesque mountain scenery surrounding it. Because of the abrupt ridge and the heavily forested area, it is almost impossible to photograph the castle from close by, except when you are actually on top of it. The first painting of the castle was done in 1865 by Hensic Trenk, a Swiss artist, and now belongs to the Romanian Academy.

In spite of the overgrowth, the brick on the outer walls and the three main towers is still quite visible. As late as 1912, a visitor to the castle reported seeing the sunken well already covered with wild vines and fungi, and spoke of other interior details which are now gone. One year later, January 13, 1913, around 9:15 in the morning, the peasants in the area reported a violent earth tremor in the whole Arefu region. To the superstitious, it seemed that the spirit of the "Great Undead" had suddenly awakened from centuries of slumber. At noon, when the tremor was over, the main tower of the castle was no more. Its bricks and stones had toppled down the precipice into the river Arges. This earthquake wrought far more destruction to the castle than either the Turks or ages of neglect had accomplished. In 1940, a severe earthquake affected not only Bucharest, but also the mountainous region. This completed the destruction of the castle.

Because of the tourist interest generated by Bram Stoker's Dracula, the identification of the historical Dracula, and the authors' identification of the castle itself, the Romanian government has appropriated a sum for the castle's restoration. When this is done, Castle Dracula may well become the chief tourist attraction of Romania, vying with the Black Sea towns for foreign visitors. Fortunately our visit to the castle preceded this commercialization. The spirit of Dracula is best preserved the way it is— with sunken stones, Alpine weeds, snake holes, and the trails of brick falling down the banks of the river Arges.

Die facht sich an gar ein grauseñ

liche erschrockenliche hystorien von dem wilden wütric Dracole wayde. Wie er die leût gespist hat. vnd geprate vnd mit den haûbtern.yn einem keffel gefoten. vñ wie er t leût gefchunden hat vñ zerhacken laffen als ein kraut. J er hat auch den mütern ire kind geprate vnd fy habes mi fen felber effen.Vnd vil andere erfchrockenliche ding die diffem Tractat gefchriben ftend.Vnd in welchem land geregiret hat.

CHAPTER

NOTE: The Appendices at the back of the book contain translations of the Germanic St. Gall Manuscript; several tales, including a few variants, from Romanian folklore; and the oldest Russian manuscript about Dracula.

Dracula Horror Stories of the 15th Century

More fascinating in a way than official archives, which lead to political and diplomatic history, is what the French refer to as *"la petite histoire,"* the more intimate history of a subject, which in the case of Dracula is especially found in the contemporary German pamphlets. In modern parlance, these German pamphlets not only created a "bad press" for Dracula in due course but also became "best-sellers" in the extensive medieval Germanic world from Brasov to Strasbourg. The Saxons' desire for vengeance was realized, at least after Dracula's death, by defaming his character for centuries to come. Although this is a controversial topic, the experiences of, and stories told by, Transylvanian-Saxon refugees may well lie at the basis of all the accounts of Dracula's misdeeds.

About the wild bloodthirsty berserker, Dracula Voevod. The pamphlet in which this page appears was published by Ambrosius Huber, 1499, Nuremberg. The text above the impalement scene states:

Here begins a very cruel frightening story about a wild bloodthirsty man, Dracula the voevod.

How he impaled people and roasted them and with their heads boiled them in a kettle, and how he skinned people and hacked them to pieces like a head of cabbage. He also roasted the children of mothers and they had to eat their children themselves. And many other horrible things are written in this tract and also in which land he ruled.

It is, of course, impossible to know exactly how the stories in these pamphlets were initially conceived, by what manner the Saxons left Transylvania, and how they eventually came to the West. To date no less than 14 accounts about Dracula have been found, in locations as diverse as the Public Archives of Strasbourg and the Benedictine Monastery of St. Gall (today the Stiff Library), in Switzerland. Most are printed, a few are in manuscript form, and some are illustrated with crude woodcuts. These pamphlets with their woodcuts were the principal medium of the 15th century for transmitting stories and images to the general public. One is tempted to compare this use of the woodcut with television today, not only the screening of late-night monster films but also newscasts.

The Germanic language varies, ranging from Transylvanian-Saxon to High German. Most of the stories concerning Dracula are tales of horror with some sort of a moral for the reader. Though an element of distortion and exaggeration is probable (after all, it is a part of human nature to exaggerate one's plight) the amazing coincidence of the stories, and the virtual impossibility of one model inspiring all of them, leads to some acceptance of their factual basis. For reasons that will be demonstrated, the German stories about Dracula can be considered a reliable historical source, and constitute a much more intimate account of Dracula's life and times than do the formal and diplomatic dispatches, which often tend to be written for posterity's sake. One might well imagine some monk—serving the chapel of St. Jacob at Brasov, or possibly the Monastery of Carta located at the foot of the Fagaras mountains—compelled to seek refuge in the West and relating there the story of his woes. We know the name of one such monk, Brother Jacob, from the monastery of Gorion, which has been variously located in Transylvania, Wallachia, Serbia, or Bulgaria where there evidently were more numerous Catholic and Saxon foundations than at one time suspected. It stands to reason that this monk once having reached safe haven at some place like St. Gall in Switzerland or Beuron in Bavaria was quick to relate what he had either personally experienced or heard of. That others copied what, to say the least, in this age of religious literature was lively material and that this process was repeated across generations is quite probable. In time there was an obvious degree of distortion, and it is safe to assume that a 15th-century manuscript was more accurate than one recopied a hundred years later. The details of Dracula's horrors, his depravity, insanity, as well as his motivation, will be discussed further. What matters here is the authenticity of the Dracula tales.

The most persuasive element by far is the remarkable coincidence of all Germanic manuscripts and pamphlets with other contemporary sources. For, after all, Dracula was not merely a subject of great interest in the Germanic world. In the 1480's, a Russian ambassador reported various Dracula anecdotes to the Grand Duke of Moscow. At Constantinople, the representatives from Venice wrote lengthy reports to the Doge of that city republic concerning not only Dracula's valor but also his misdeeds. The Vatican archives still hold secret reports sent by the papal legates to Pius II. The Byzantine chroniclers Chalkokondyles, Sphrantzes, Doukos, and Critoboulos of Imbros recorded Dracula's formidable military reputation. The Turkish historians spoke of Dracula as *Kaziklu Bey.* The wily Genoese and pilgrims and travelers from France, England, and the Italies, fearful but admiring, attributed to him essentially the same traits.

Perhaps most picturesque of all are the local legends of the Romanians themselves, handed down by word of mouth, usually in the form of children's tales. The present authors are the first to have made a comprehensive assemblage of the Romanian folkloric elements concerning Dracula. These have been gathered in villages with Dracula associations, usually from the elder citizens, who best preserve historical ballads—and who are, we believe, a dying breed. A number of local teachers and priests, aware of this threatened extinction, have in recent years been busy collecting such tales, not only concerning Dracula but other heroes and villains of old. The

Folklore Institute at Bucharest finally has become concerned lest the fascinating historical tradition be permanently lost, and has organized a number of official expeditions in ''Dracula Country.'' The fact we shall stress at this time is that the Dracula tales collected so far from oral Romanian tradition have an amazing coincidence, even in regard to details, with Slavonic and Germanic stories. In the case of the Romanian sources there evidently could have been no possibility of a common model or pattern. If connections between a fleeing 15th-century Saxon monk Jacob and a 15th-century Russian ambassador Kurytsin are already difficult to maintain, those between a 15th-century Saxon monk and a 20th-century Romanian peasant are impossible to establish. In the last resort the proof of the historicity of the Dracula stories lies in their remarkable coincidence of both character and plot.

The two oldest manuscripts containing Dracula horror stories were written in Low German dialect around 1462, shortly after Dracula's imprisonment at Buda, the Hungarian capital. One, mentioned earlier, is located in the famous 6th-century Celtic Benedictine monastery of St. Gall (St. Gallen) in Switzerland; the other, in the Lambach monastery in Austria. A more elaborate horror story, which fills in many details and brought the account to Dracula's actual imprisonment, was authored by Michel Beheim, a famous 15th-century German troubadour, who narrated Dracula monstrosities in poetic form; it was probably written shortly after Dracula's imprisonment in the winter of 1462 or the spring of 1463. Very similar anecdotes circulated in Central Europe, in the Germanic world, and in Italy. The most authoritative account was undoubtedly one by King Mathias' official court historian, Antonio Bonfinius; the most famous name linked to Dracula memorabilia is that of the *bon vivant* Renaissance pope, Pius II, whose memoirs refer to certain crimes that he may have heard of from his legate at Buda, Nicholas of Modrussa, who had met Dracula and who himself has left us a remarkably accurate literary portrait of the tyrant. Both the legate's and the pope's accounts were written in Latin; the pope's memoirs were initially published in 1584.

The following excerpt from the title page of a German pamphlet indicates the lurid preview of what lay in store for the reader:

The shocking story of a MONSTER and BERSERKER called Dracula who committed such unchristian deeds as killing men by placing them on stakes, hacking them to pieces like cabbage, boiling mothers and children alive and compelling men to acts of cannibalism.

By way of further enticement, the anonymous pamphleteers promised many other shocking revelations, plus mention of the country over which Dracula ruled. For dramatic purposes, the frontispiece of several pamphlets included a woodcut depicting the tyrant Dracula dining happily amid a forest of the impaled. Others simply showed Dracula's face, but with distorted features. One printed in 1494 has a woodcut portraying a bleeding, suffering Christ. Given the fact that the literature disseminated at a time closely coincident with the invention of the printing press was almost exclusively religious matter, one can't help suspecting that the horror plot centering on a lay figure generated enormous interest, even as reading material in monasteries, and provided a welcome diversion from spiritual exercises. It is conceivable, too, that the Dracula "horror stories" were to the 15th century what Stoker's vampire novel was to the 19th century, what horror films are to the age of the cinema.

The deeds attributed to Dracula in the German narratives are so appalling that the activities of Stoker's bloodsucking character seem tame by comparison. The following excerpt is an example of "Dracula's unspeakable tortures unequaled by even the most blood-thirsty tyrants of history such as Herod, Nero and Diocletian."

Once he had a great pot made with two handles and over it a staging device with planks and through it he had holes made, so that a man could fall through them with his head. Then he had

111

a great fire made underneath it and had water poured into the pot and had men boiled in this way.

Dracula's principal means of inflicting cruel death was, as we know, impalement. The victim was usually pulled apart by two horses, after a stake firmly held by attendants had penetrated the rectum and entrails. Care was customarily taken to have the stake rounded at the end and oiled lest it cause instant death.

The German woodcuts graphically demonstrate that there were other methods of impalement: the stake penetrating the navel, or as vampires would express it, piercing the heart, which would of course be instantly fatal. The ''berserker'' was not deterred by age, sex, nationality, or religion. The German pamphlets mention the killing of native Romanians, Hungarians, Germans, Turks, and Jews; and gypsies, it seems, incurred Dracula's wrath on frequent occasions. Catholics, the Orthodox, Moslems and ''heretics'' perished. Mothers and even sucklings were executed; sometimes children's heads were impaled on their mother's cut breasts. There was, it seems, a stake in constant readiness in the courtyard of the palace at Targoviste.

The German writers relate that aside from impaling his victims, Dracula decapitated them; cut off noses, ears, sexual organs, limbs; hacked them to pieces; burned, boiled, roasted, skinned, nailed, and buried them alive; exposed them to the elements or wild animals. If he did not personally drink blood or eat human flesh, he compelled others to practice cannibalism. His cruel refinements included smearing salt on the soles of a prisoner's feet and allowing animals to lick them for indefinite periods. If any relative or friend of an impaled victim dared remove the body from the stake, he himself was apt to hang from the bough of a neighboring tree. With the cadavres of his victims left at various strategic places until beasts or the elements had reduced them to bones and dust Dracula terrorized the entire countryside.

How credible are these Dracula horror stories? Were they based on concrete historical fact, or were they the product of sadistic-minded 15th-century pamphleteers seeking to awe or amuse, or to relieve the monks from the daily fare of religious literature? Or, as some critics of these anecdotes have suggested, were they in fact contrived, on orders of the Hungarian court, to destroy Dracula's reputation and justify the harsh treatment subsequently meted out to him in a Hungarian prison? It would follow from this hypothesis—a Hungarian plot to defame Dracula—that a common model inspired all the 15th-century Dracula narratives, whether German or not.

The Hungarian court seems to have had strong reasons for discrediting Dracula and having him safely removed from power; aside from other factors, his strong one-man rule threatened Hungarian hegemony in Transylvania and Wallachia. However, even granting that a common anti-Dracula model inspired the accounts by the Hungarian chronicler Bonfinius, by Pope Pius II, and by the German pamphleteers (who by a stretch of the imagination might be conceded as ''in intelligence'' with the aims of the Hungarian king Mathias), one finds it hard to account for the similarity of the many other Dracula anecdotes published in a variety of languages and circulated over widely scattered geographic and political regions. For instance, there is the Russian Dracula manuscript first written in 1486; it closely coincides with the German stories, yet to assume that it was a translation of them is to credit the 15th century with 20th-century standards of transmission efficiency. In addition the Russian story is sufficiently different in terms of ethics and political theory to allow a single source. One major argument against the theory of a ''common horror stereotype'' is provided by the oral ballads and traditions of the Romanian peasants concerning Dracula. Although more reverential and apologetic toward ''the impaler,'' they contain anecdotes similar to those mentioned elsewhere, but the Romanian peasants could neither understand German or Slavonic, nor read or write even their own language. For that matter, no literary language existed in Romanian lands in Dracula's time.

113

Dracula stories in his lifetime were simply transmitted orally from one person to another, very much as the Viking sagas were. Not until the 20th century were they formally committed to print, and it is safe to assume that a few Romanian Dracula anecdotes still go unrecorded.

One can pursue the argument against a single source for all Dracula anecdotes by pointing out that stories about Dracula appeared in Turkish in the works of official chroniclers; others in Greek penned by Byzantine historians; yet others in the Italian, Hungarian, and Czech accounts written by travelers.

It seems reasonable to suppose that German refugees from Transylvania somewhat embellished the story of their "escape" from Dracula country, as political refugees are apt to do, with the thought that the more sensational their pamphlets were, the better they would sell. The factual basis of their accounts, however, must be taken as generally true. To the determined skeptic, an additional yardstick of credibility might be provided by the serious reports of foreign diplomats stationed in various capitals surrounding Dracula country. Diplomats reporting to their home governments have no material wares to sell; they are usually wary of embellished facts and their reports have to be terse and to the point. Let us quote from the papal legate at Buda, Nicholas of Modrussa, reporting to the Vatican on the subject of Dracula's crimes in 1464. Concerning a specific massacre in which Dracula killed 40,000 men and women of all ages and nationalities, the papal legate wrote:

He killed some by breaking them under the wheels of carts; others stripped of their clothes were skinned alive up to their entrails; others placed upon stakes, or roasted on red hot coals placed under them; others punctured with stakes piercing their head, their breast, their buttocks and the middle of their entrails, with the stake emerging from their mouths; and in order that no form of cruelty be missing he stuck stakes in both the mother's breasts and thrust their babies unto them. Finally he killed others in various ferocious ways, torturing them with many kinds of instruments such as the atrocious cruelties of the most frightful tyrant could devise.

Another papal nuncio, the Bishop of Erlau, who was certainly not prone to fabrications, reported in 1475 that by that date Dracula had personally authorized the killing of 100,000 people. This figure is equivalent to at least one-fifth of the total population of Dracula's principality, which did not exceed 500,000. (Robespierre's notorious reign of terror, 1793-94, was responsible for 35,000-40,000 victims and France had a population of approximately 18,000,000 at the time.)

How did the German Dracula stories reach Western Europe? The German troubadour Michel Beheim reveals in his very poem how he obtained many details of his Dracula story. In the winter of 1462, while residing at the Imperial court of Frederick III at Wiener-Neustadt, Beheim met Brother Jacob, a Capucin monk from the monastery of Gorion (probably located in Serbia) who had obviously fled from Transylvania. Dracula had specific grudges against Catholic monasteries in his lands: many of them were ruled internally by foreigners and all of them were controlled by the Church of Rome, a "schismatic" church in the view of the Orthodox. Dracula's treatment of these enclaves of the papacy was severe. Brother Jacob, and undoubtedly other refugees from Transylvania, knew the area's history well, and were impressive in their mention of not only specific dates but also names of historic personages. The meticulous geo-political descriptions of Transylvania witness further to the basic historicity of these accounts. Many of the ethnic groups in Transylvania at that time are mentioned, as are the religions. The larger Transylvanian towns of Kronstadt (Brasov) and Hermannstadt (Sibiu), administrative units such as the Bursenland (Tara Birsei), the southeastern district surrounding Brasov where many German Saxons live to this day, figure prominently in the German stories. With pinpoint accuracy a German pamphlet published in Nuremberg, 1499, refers to individual sections of

Hie facht sich an gar ein graussem
liche erschröckenliche hystorien. von dem wilden wü
trich Dracole weyde Wie er die leüt gespist hot vnd
gepraten vñ mit den haüßtern yn einē kessel gesotten

Nach Cristus geburt M.cccc
Lui. hat ð Dracole vil erschröcke
liche wünderliche vnd grausamliche ding gethön.

Tem der alt gubernator zů Vngern hot den
alten Dracole lassen todten. Vñ der dracole
vnd sein brüder haben ab getreten von yren
glaüben vñ haben verheissen vñ geschworn den Cri
stengelauben zů beschirmen vnd ouch zů halten ouch
dor eyn zů treten.

¶ Item des selben jars ist er gesetzt worden zů einem
herrn in der walchey zů hand ließ er todten den Laß
la wey de der do selbs herr ist gewesen.
¶ Pald dornoch hot er in siben Bürgen ouch in würtz
land mit namen beglendorff lassen verbrennē ouch
frawen vnd man iung vñ alt Etlich hot er mit im
heym gefürt in die walchey an eysnen ketten vnd die
all gespist.
¶ Item er hot alle iung knaben die yn sein landt ge
schickt seyn worden von lernung wegē der sprach die
hieß er yn ein stüben sperren vnd lyes sy do alle ver
brennen der sein vierhundert gewesen.
¶ Item er hot ein fried gesetzt in dem selben hot er vil
kauffleüt vñ fürleüt vß würtzen land lassen spissen.
Er hot ouch ein groß geschlecht vß reytten lassen vnd
spissen võ dem minstē byß zů dē meistē iung vñ alt.
¶ Er hot ouch sein volck etlich nacket lassen eyn gra
ben biß zů dem nabel vñ hot zů yn lassen schiessen.er
hot ouch etlich lassen praten vnd schinden.

A iij

*About the wild bloodthirsty berserker, Dracula
Voevod.* Impalement scene and text page from a
15th-century German pamphlet published by
Matthias Hupnuff in Strasbourg, 1500.

Kronstadt:

And he led away all those whom he had captured outside the city called Kranstatt near the chapel of St. Jacob. And at that time Dracula . . . had the entire suburb burned. Also . . . all those whom he had taken captive, men and women, young and old, children, he had impaled on the hill by the chapel and all around the hill, and under them he proceeded to eat at table and get his joy that way.

As noted earlier, a woodcut enables us to identify this area as the Tampa Hill section even though the chapel of St. Jacob no longer exists there. The ''Church of St. Bartholomew,'' which Dracula burned, after ''stealing the vestments and chalices,'' is a 13th-century structure that was built in the heart of the old city and survives to this day.

The mention of smaller townships, even individual villages, monasteries, and fortresses, further strengthens the historicity of the accounts. Although identification is at times difficult since most German names in use during the 15th century have been replaced by Romanian ones and some ancient townships have now disappeared, it has been possible with the help of 16th-century maps to retrace Dracula's path of destruction through Transylvania. In the Hermannstadt (Sibiu) region ''he had villages by the name of the monastery of Holzmenge (Holtznetya) completely burned to ashes''; in Beckendorff (Wuetzerland), ''those men, women and children large and small whom he had not burned at the time, he took with him in chains and then had them impaled.'' In these incidents one can identify Holzmenge, where presumably a convent existed at one time, as the Romanian village of Hosmanul a few miles to the northeast of Sibiu (Nocris district); and Beckendorff as being in the vicinity of the village of Benesti. Other Transylvanian villages variously terrorized by Dracula according to the German stories were: Neudorff (the present village of Noul Sasesc,

Brasov district), Zeyding (the fortress of Codlea to the southeast of Brasov); Talmets (Talmetch, near Sibiu). Fugrach can easily be identified as the town of Fagaras, a Dracula fief where a castle at one time owned by the Bathorys still stands; Humilach, another Dracula possession in Transylvania, is the present town of Amlas.

Shylta is the Germanic version of Nicopolis, a powerful fortress on the Danube; Konigstein (where Dracula was arrested in 1462) on the Wallachia-Transylvania frontier is Piatra Craiului (literally meaning ''the stone of the king''), where a small fortress at one time existed. A few villages mentioned in Michel Beheim's account—for instance, Thunow and Bregel—could not be traced with any accuracy and presumably were completely destroyed. We know from an authoritative Romanian source that at least two other villages, Sercaia and Mica in the Fagaras district, had been so completely decimated by Dracula's raids that they had to be repopulated after his death.

Among the sources that the historian can turn to for verifying the authenticity of the German accounts is the rich primary documentation in the archives of Brasov and Sibiu, two towns which figure prominently in all the German accounts. It includes, among other items, a number of missives by Dracula himself, three of them bearing the awesome signature DRAKULYA (normally he signed himself Vlad).

As the criminal investigator when seeking the truth about a suspect looks for motivation, so the historian testing the veracity of these German stories looks for motives that could reasonably have led Dracula to commit his horrible deeds. Un-doubtedly, there was a mad streak in the prince, but we have found all along that this madness was accompanied not by incompetence, rather with keen awareness and enormous cunning. Some of the causes for his acts are suggested below, and very briefly illustrated.

Revenge. The killing of Dracula's father, Dracul, and of his brother Mircea, related in the first episode of the St. Gall manuscript, is an authentic historical fact. The double assassination occurred in December 1447: Romanian sources state that the father was killed in the marshes of Balteni, near Bucharest, and the son was dragged to Targoviste and buried alive by the boyars and merchants in the vicinity of that town. This action may well have prompted Dracula's enslavement of the aristocrats of Targoviste for the construction of Castle Dracula.

The execution in 1456 of Vladislav II (episode 2 in the St. Gall version), who was Dracula's predecessor (1447-56), can also be credited to revenge since Vladislav, along with Hunyadi, was responsible for Dracul's assassination, and also was a member of the rival Danesti faction.

Inter-family feuds. The struggle between the two rival factions of the Wallachian princely family—Draculas versus Danestis—was little less than a struggle for survival, and helps account for many of Dracula's Transylvanian massive raids and individual murders. One German story gives a specific date, 1460, for the assassination of a particular member of the Danesti clan: Dracula allowed him to go through his priestly function and when the service of the dead was completed, he had Dan dig a grave according to Christian custom and had his body slaughtered by the grave.

Political enmity. Because of their defection and subversion in supporting his political enemies, Dracula destroyed two of his own enclaves, Fagaras and Amlas.

Protection of Transylvanian commerce. Most of Dracula's vindictiveness against the German Saxon population of Transylvania, which climaxed between 1459 and 1460, was due to an ill-defined but rising sentiment of nationalism, directed in this instance against the commercial monopoly exercised by the Transylvanian Saxons in all Romanian provinces. This monopoly tended to hamper or retard the development of native trade and industry, which Dracula encouraged in a manner reminiscent of current Romanian policies. A specific incident from the German stories illustrates this intensive jealousy of "national sovereignty." In 1460 Dracula arrested 30 German carriages "on a holiday" from Wurtzland and 400 Saxon trainees (mere boys who had come to Wallachia "in order to learn the language . . . and *other things*"). He had them assembled in a room and burned alive. Dracula undoubtedly saw these persons less as tourists and trainees than as spies sent by the Saxon merchants of Brasov and Sibiu to learn about native methods of production.

Establishment of personal authority. When Dracula first came to rule, in 1456, his native province of Wallachia was beset by internal anarchy, boyar intrigue, rival factions, and Hungarian political pressure. In that same year there occurred at Targoviste the most famous instance of mass boyar impalement; described in Beheim's poem and recounted in other sources. The killings resulted from the somewhat jocular answers of the boyar council to Dracula's question: "How many reigns have you my loyal subjects personally experienced in your lifetime?" Thus Wallachia was immediately and horribly instructed that the princely title, and all that it implied, was not to be taken lightly. Moreover, the property of the victims was distributed to Dracula adherents, who may well have formed a new nobility with a vested interest in the survival of the regime.

Affirmation of national sovereignity. Dracula's motives in his atrocities against the Turks are easily arrived at. Some were surely personal in nature, the result of his imprisonment by the Turks, in Egrigoz, when he was a young boy. But he was impelled by national concerns, too. When his reign as prince of Wallachia began in 1456, Turkish aggression had brought Constantinople and almost all of the Balkans under the sultan's control. In the next year, the Turks began supporting the claim of Radu, Dracula's more pliable younger brother, to the Wallachian throne.

Records state that Dracula refused to make his yearly submission at Constantinople; was slow in paying the tribute; unwilling to supply the yearly levy of 500 children for the Turkish infantry corps; and while the Turkish sultan was busy elsewhere, made frequent incursions on the line of the Danube, raiding villages on the Bulgarian side. It is, therefore, not unreasonable to believe that Dracula's defiance also included the famous scene in the throne room of Targoviste, when Turkish representatives failed to remove their turbans, contrary to Romanian custom at court. When they explained that this was contrary to Moslem law, Dracula's response was "I will hammer in your law." Immediately their headgear was secured to their scalps by "small iron nails." This story, concluding with Dracula's moralizing about the impropriety of imposing Turkish customs upon another nation, clearly indicates his intention of affirming full national sovereignty over limited sovereignty.

The motives that have been assigned to Dracula here by no means exhaust the possibilities. Nor are the illustrations of them limited to the ones we have mentioned.

Another indication of the veracity of the German stories is what they omit. For example: Beheim's poem includes an invaluable, detailed description of Dracula's last days of freedom in the fall of 1462, right after his failure against the Turks, his appeal to the Hungarian king for help and protection, flight to his mountain retreat, and so on. It does not include an account of Dracula's subsequent imprisonment in Hungary: an understandable omission since German Transylvanian witnesses could hardly have been present in Buda. Beheim's poem also does not mention Dracula's liberation in 1474 nor his third reign in 1476; but it could not, for it was written before these events.

In addition to anecdotes which can clearly be placed in a geographic or chronological historical context are a number which cannot be connected with any specific place or date, but which are nevertheless mentioned in the various German texts and form an integral part of the story. The most famous of these episodes can be identified as follows:

1. The foreign ambassadors
2. The nobleman with a keen sense of smell
3. The two monks
4. The lazy woman

5. Dracula's mistress
6. The Florentine merchants
7. The golden cup
8. Dracula's treasure
9. The burning of the sick and poor

The authenticity of such anecdotes can be substantiated essentially by four considerations: They occur for the most part in all three variants, German, Slavonic, and Romanian and, for reasons explained above, could not have derived from a common literary model. In terms of content, moral and political philosophy, and even specific methods of punishment, they coincide fairly closely with those anecdotes that do have historic validity. They reveal characteristics of Dracula which correspond with traits indicated in the other anecdotes. They describe events and policies which are susceptible to credible explanation. Let us look at two of these anecdotes.

1. There was a famous fountain in a deserted square of Targoviste where travelers habitually would rest and refresh themselves. Dracula had ordered a golden cup to be permanently located at this place for all to use. Never did that cup disappear throughout his reign.

2. A foreign merchant who spent the night at an inn left his treasure-laden cart in the street, being aware of the reputation of Dracula's country for honesty. Next morning, to his amazement, he found that 160 gold ducats were missing. He immediately sought an audience with the prince. Dracula simply replied: ''Tonight you will find your gold.'' To the citizens of Targoviste he gave the ultimatum: ''Either you find the thief or I will destroy your town.'' Certain of success in advance, Dracula further commanded that 160 substitute ducats plus one extra one be placed in the cart during the night. Duly the thief and the original ducats were found. Having proved the honesty of his capital, Dracula desired to test the ethics of the foreigner. Fortunately,

the foreigner was honest and admitted to the additional ducat. While impaling the thief, Dracula told the merchant that such would undoubtedly have been his fate had he proved dishonest.

Both of these stories are in keeping with contemporary references to Dracula's attempt to set a strict code of ethics in his land—a most difficult thing to implement in a society known for its Byzantine cynicism and absence of moral standards, but not an impossible one since Dracula enforced public morality by means of personally directed terror.

Throughout the various sagas of Dracula's crimes, there is a sadistic sexuality: the ritual and manner of impalement, a husband's enforced cannibalism of his wife's breasts, and similar horrors. Here, too, one encounters Dracula imposing morality with morbid measures. The extent of Dracula's indignation against an unfaithful wife almost surpasses belief. Dracula ordered her sexual organs to be cut. She was then skinned alive and exposed in public, her skin hanging separately from a pole or placed upon a table in the middle of the marketplace. The same punishment was applied to maidens who did not keep their virginity, and to unchaste widows. In other instances, Dracula was known to have the nipple of a woman's breast cut off, or a red-hot iron stake shoved through the vagina until the instrument penetrated the entrails and emerged from the mouth.

What explanation might successfully reconcile Dracula's apparent attraction to women with the savagery of his sexual crimes? One obvious conjecture—the very ritual of the penetration of the stake suggests it—is some sort of sexual inadequacy, most likely partial impotence.

There are other, general considerations which must be kept in mind when evaluating Dracula's criminality. One is the proverbial concern of viewing a man's actions according to the standards of his time. Dracula's age is that of the Spider King Louis XI (1423-83); Ludovico Sforza "the Moor" (1452-1508); the Borgia Pope,

123

Alexander VI (1431-1503); Sigismondo Malatesta (1417-68); Cesare Borgia (1476-1507). One could go on and on in enumerating brutal contemporaries. The point is that the Renaissance, for all its humanism, was marked by extraordinary inhumanity.

Concerning impalement, though never before (or since) in history practiced on so wide a scale, it was not a Dracula invention. It was known in Asiatic antiquity and practiced by the Turks. (The only recorded instance in the West is attributed to John Tiptoft, Earl of Worcester, during the War of the Roses; he had learned it from the Turks.)

Dracula's cruel traits were, in addition, not unique in his family. We know too little about his father, but it seems safe to say that his deeds must have earned him the cognomen "Devil." Moreover, one of Dracula's own sons is remembered as Mihnea the Bad. It should also be borne in mind that Dracula spent more years in prison than he did on the throne; his first imprisonment, by the Turks, began when he was no more than 15, and it involved both physical and moral abuse. But most of his experiences seemed to reinforce one fact: life is insecure—and cheap. His father was assassinated; a brother was buried alive; other relatives were killed or tortured; his first wife killed herself; subjects conspired against him; his cousin, a sworn friend, betrayed him; Hungarians, Germans, and Turks pursued him. *Tout comprendre est tout pardonner?* In reviewing Dracula's life—what he suffered and what he caused others to endure—it makes more sense to say that to know all is to reflect on how horror begets horror.

CHAPTER 6

The Historical Dracula: 1462-76

King's Prisoner

Dracula's 12 years of imprisonment in Hungary (1462-74) constitute the most obscure phase of his extraordinary career. Romanian oral and written sources are understandably silent about the prince's experiences at that time, since they took place far from the Transylvanian-Wallachian region connected with his name. Turkish chroniclers had no means of being appraised of Dracula's fate, since technically the Turks were in a state of war with Hungary. The German publicists, having triumphed in their anti-Dracula cause, were no longer interested in the subject: Dracula was safely removed from the Wallachian throne, which is all they desired. As for the official Hungarian historians, apart from being generally silent on Wallachian affairs, they maintained discretion in matters of political prisoners.

Despite all this, it is possible to construct some picture of what Dracula's life was like during 1462-74. His presence in Buda when his positive achievements in the Turkish campaign were still fresh in people's mind certainly did not pass

Solomon's Tower, Visegrad; one of the places where Dracula was confined while a prisoner of King Mathias during the years 1462-74.

unnoticed. Kurytsin, the envoy of the Grand Duke of Moscow, and the Italian diplomats and papal envoys all wrote lengthy dispatches about the imprisoned prince to their home governments.

Dracula spent his first year of imprisonment at a royal fortress in the ancient city of Buda, on the left bank of the Danube. Then, according to the Russian ambassador, he was transferred to Solomon's Tower within the site of the palace of Visegrad, some 20 miles away. This palace was built high on a hill, with a commanding view of the Danube; Solomon's Tower, where political prisoners were held, was located at the foot of the site, on the river's edge. Within this vast complex—today the scene of careful archaeological investigation and partial reconstruction—the flowering culture of the Hungarian Renaissance was focused. Judged by the countless artistic treasures recently discovered in the palace, Mathias appears to have been a true patron of learning and art.

The Hungarian government is interested less in reconstructing the entire palace than in preserving what is left of it. Solomon's Tower, however, has been virtually rebuilt. The cells are tiny; some have barred openings with a view of the Danube. All prisoners were carefully secluded at night, though during the day they were allowed to exercise in the courtyard.

The Russian chronicle of Ambassador Kurytsin relates that Dracula was on good terms with his guards, who kept him regularly supplied with small animals: birds, mice, rats, and other creatures. These he tortured, either by cutting them up into pieces, or by impaling them on minute sticks and arranging them in rows—as was his wont with human victims—around his cell. It is said that he derived particular satisfaction from plucking chickens bare and then watching them run around in circles, finally slitting their necks. These episodes related by the Russian ambassador form additional proof of Dracula's taste for blood—one so obsessive that apparently he was unable to repress it even in a prison cell. In Stoker's novel, the character Renfield had a similar sadistic pleasure in small animals.

Dracula's ultimate liberation and his marriage into the Hungarian royal family make it logical to assume that Mathias kept in personal contact with his prisoner and in time allowed him to be present at court. Possibly King Mathias—like Archduke Ferdinand II of the Tyrol, who enjoyed entertaining his guests with eccentric personages—could not resist the desire of the curious to meet the legendary demon who had impaled Saxons and the hero who had defeated the Turks. In any event, Dracula did become acquainted with one of the king's sisters, and a romance leading to marriage developed, possibly as early as his first year of imprisonment.

Dracula was at that time, insofar as we can judge from the oil portrait at Castle Ambras, a rather handsome man: the Saxon woodcuts seen on the cover of some of the German pamphlets are crude in technique and doubtless distorted and deformed his true features. A second oil painting, a miniature in Vienna, to which we have already referred, reveals the face of a powerful man. The large dark green eyes have an intense expression; the nose is long and has thin nostrils; the mouth is large, ruddy, thin-lipped. Dracula appears clean-shaven except for a long drooping mustache, and so far as we can judge, his hair was dark and slightly grayed and his complexion deadly, almost sickeningly white. In the painting, he is wearing the Hungarian nobleman's tunic with an ermine cape and a diamond-studded Turkish-style fur-lined headdress.

The literary description left by Nicholas of Modrussa, the papal legate who met Dracula at that time, corresponds fairly well with the painting. ''He was not very tall, but very stocky and strong, with a cruel and terrible appearance, a long straight nose, distended nostrils, a thin and reddish face in which the large wide-open green eyes were enframed by bushy black eyebrows, which made them appear threatening. His face and chin were shaven but for a mustache. The swollen temples increased the bulk of his head. A bull's neck supported the head, from which black curly locks were falling to his wide-shouldered person.''

Marriage of this man to Mathias' sister inevitably involved not only the political facts of life, but also matters of religion. To Mathias, a descendant of St. Stephen, it would never do for a Roman Catholic princess of Hungary to marry an Orthodox "schismatic." Though union between Orthodoxy and Catholicism had been established by the Council of Florence, it had always been more apparent than real. Now the rivalry between the two churches, notwithstanding the Turkish danger, had once again incurred a fruitless polemic and broken into open hostility.

To Dracula, baptized in the Orthodox faith as his forebears had been, the question of conversion to Catholicism, which was clearly entailed in any marriage contract with the Hungarian crown, posed no particular problem. Like Henry Bourbon in 1593, he may well have calculated that the throne of Wallachia, implicit in his Hungarian marriage, was fully worth a Catholic mass.

Dracula's conversion to Catholicism, however, incurred the wrath of the Orthodox world—and understandably so in a period when religion was closely linked to national identity. The Orthodox world of the 15th century had been threatened not only by Islam, but by a tide of Catholic crusaders. Now Dracula's conversion to Catholicism was an additional threat, implying the convert's reestablishment on the throne of Wallachia, hence loss of that principality to Orthodoxy. The Grand Duke Ivan III of Moscow calculated that Moldavia at least ought to be safely linked by marriage to the Orthodox world. Accordingly, another marriage contract, this time sealed at Jassy in 1463, offered a Ukrainian princess, Evdochia, to Dracula's Moldavian kinsman Steven. To strengthen the new Orthodox alliance, Steven's daughter Elena married Demeter, the heir to the Russian throne.

Prince Restored

From the moment that Dracula's marriage was secretly celebrated at Visegrad (the precise date is unknown), his return to Wallachia was a foregone conclusion. Even from the Hungarian point of view it was timely. The Danestis, and their German sponsors, had thoroughly discredited themselves by continued petty intrigues in Transylvania. Radu the Handsome, who ruled in Wallachia, was no more than the instrument of the sultan. Steven of Moldavia was considered unreliable, if only because of his Russian entanglement. The mutual suspicions of the still independent powers of eastern Christendom; the rivalry between Poland, Bohemia, Moldavia, and Hungary; the religious problems posed for the Hungarians by Ivan's pan-Orthodox crusade—all these favored Dracula's candidature. Moreover, as a man capable of giving military leadership in the event of renewal of an anti-Turkish crusade, Dracula was a natural choice. Dracula, now safely married into the royal family of Hungary, could be trusted as King Mathias' man. Even Steven of Moldavia, safely identified with Orthodoxy but apparently heedless of any Russian pressure, recalled the old vow that he and Dracula had made years before that whichever of them should be on the throne should help the other gain his legitimate succession. Thus, to the amazement of the Hungarians, Steven sent emissaries from Suceava to Budapest, urging King Mathias to hasten Dracula's return to Wallachia and promising Moldavian military support.

In 1474, after conversion, marriage and 12 years of imprisonment, Dracula was finally liberated and became the official candidate for the Wallachian throne. The Transylvanian duchies of Almas and Fagaras, within the gift of the Hungarian crown, were the first constituencies to be handed back. In preparation for his future role, the Wallachian claimant accompanied Mathias on official journeys to Central and Eastern

Europe. It was probably in the course of one of them that the existing portrait of Dracula at Castle Ambras was painted.

Beyond the fact that Dracula accompanied his brother-in-law on a military expedition against the Turks in Croatia, we have few details about his activities from 1474 to 1475. We know he received a house at Pest, that he lived there with his Hungarian wife, and that she bore him a son initially baptized Milhail and later known as "Mihnea the Bad." The Russian ambassador reported one other incident: Dracula's taking justice into his own hands by killing a guard who had entered his house.

After a short stay in Pest, Dracula settled in Sibiu, in Transylvania. From here he began his campaign to regain the throne of Wallachia from the Turks and his rival Basarab Laiota. We are in possession of more internal documentation on this period of Dracula's career than any other. It is possible to follow his route from Sibiu to Bucharest month by month, sometimes week by week, since he wrote numerous letters to the Hungarian king. In a letter dated August 4, 1475, written from Arghiz, Transylvania, Dracula asked the burgomasters of Sibiu to allow construction of a house for him and his family, and interestingly enough he signed himself Wladislaus Drakulya.

Prince Steven Bathory of Transylvania was officially commander-in-chief of the expedition; the Wallachian contingent was supported by Moldavian foot soldiers; the bulk of the army was composed of Hungarians and Transylvanians. As news of Dracula's liberation leaked out, some of the boyars abandoned Basarab Laiota and defected, as was their wont, to the power which seemed on the ascent. On July 25, 1476, Dracula and Bathory held a council of war in Turda. By July 31 they reached the Medias in central Transylvania. In October the citizens of Brasov, where Dracula had committed so many of his crimes, were wooed into subservience by extensive commercial concessions. A splendid reception was offered to the incoming commanders by the harried burgomaster at the city hall. Services were held in all the churches, and prayers were said for the success of the new campaign. The Danesti claimant, who had long sheltered in Brasov, fled the city as Dracula's cohorts entered.

Wallachia itself was reached by way of the pass at Bran during November. Finally the army encamped in the valley of the Prahova river, from where the road led into the Wallachian plain. This time Dracula's aim was less Targoviste, which was besieged and captured by November 8, than the city of Bucharest—the citadel of the Dambovita—fortified by Dracula during his second reign, and now the seat of Prince Radu's power. On November 16 the battle was fought and won in the vicinity of the fortress. Most of Wallachia was once again under Dracula's control.

In mid-November, as a few boyars stood by, the Metropolitan at Curtea de Arges reinvested Dracula as Prince of Wallachia—a prince unacceptable to the Orthodox; feared as a merciless criminal by both Saxons and boyars; intrigued against by supporters of the Danesti claimant; hated by the Turks and Prince Radu, who had vowed to kill him. Thus, when Bathory's Hungarian force and Steven's contingent left the country, Dracula was clearly exposed to great dangers for he had had little time to consolidate his strength. The fact that he was aware of these dangers is suggested by his failure to bring his wife and son with him to Wallachia. It was an irony, and in a sense Steven's expiation for his previous infidelity, that the only contingent which Dracula could now completely trust was a small Moldavian bodyguard two hundred strong.

An Unusual Corpse

According to Romanian tradition, Dracula fought his last battle just outside the city of

Bucharest—possibly close to the place of his father's assassination.

The accounts of his death differ in details. One story has it that at this battle the Turks were beginning to break ranks, and Dracula, confident of victory, climbed a hill in order to observe his army cutting the Turks down. However he was temporarily isolated from his men and to maintain his safety disguised himself as a Turk. Unaware of this subterfuge, one of his followers came upon him, and thinking he was a Turkish leader, struck him with a lance. Dracula defended himself with his sword as well as he could, killing five assailants, but he soon fell victim to his own men. Another version states that it was a force of boyars and other personal enemies who confronted him and—despite the efforts of the loyal Moldavians—killed him. Thus death came to ''the impaler'' when he was 45 years old, and when his third reign had spanned barely two months.

We know that Dracula was decapitated—perhaps in the battle, perhaps by the Turks after their arrival on the scene. His head was sent to the sultan at Constantinople, where it was openly displayed on a stake—proof perfect and gruesome to the world of Islam that *Kaziklu Bey* was dead.

Island Grave

Monks from the Monastery of Snagov secretly gathered up Dracula's headless body and took it to the monastery. Fearing reprisals from Dracula's enemies, they laid it in an unmarked grave.

Snagov is an island in one of the lakes surrounding Bucharest, and is located in the heart of the Vlasie forest. The island is about a mile in length, and a half mile in width. Today, a small brick chapel is all that remains of the ancient monastic complex. This chapel, one of three that originally belonged to the monastery, was rebuilt in 1517. It is here that tradition assigns Dracula's grave. There are other legends associating Dracula with Snagov, and it is difficult for the historian to know how many are founded on fact, how many are fanciful creations of the superstitious peasants nearby, some of whom have envisaged Dracula's ghost rising from the waters of the lake. In this area today, as one sees the motor launches, sailboats, lovely villas—the full paraphernalia of 20th-century relaxation—it is difficult to think back to the bloody era of Dracula; within the walls of the chapel itself with its faded Byzantine murals, it is another matter: as one listens to the stories of the monks, one seems to go back in time.

As in the case of Castle Dracula, one may safely presume that the island monastery with its secure strategic position was originally built on an extensive scale, either by Dracula's grandfather, Prince Mircea of Wallachia, or by one of the boyars at his court. From official documents we do know that Mircea often resided at the monastery and that he endowed it with vast tracts of land from the surrounding villages. Relatively few official documents mention this monastery in Dracula's reign, but in the 16th century a Wallachian prince, in an act of endowment, confirmed those estates bestowed upon the monastery by Dracula. In addition, we know that between 1436 and 1447 Dracula's father endowed Snagov with more land than any other monastery of the realm, and that in 1464 Radu the Handsome endowed it with three additional villages: Vadul Parvului, Calugareni and Stroesti. These along with gifts from other members of the family lead to the conclusion that Snagov is *par excellence* a Dracula ecclesiastical establishment.

In Dracula's time, Snagov undoubtedly was one of the three largest and most important monasteries in Wallachia. Instead of the small church one can see today, the original complex must have reached the full length of the island. It was heavily fortified; the walls extending to the edge of the lake were for additional protection since it

View of Snagov today.

136

Carved door from ancient church at the monastery of Snagov. A storm destroyed the church, and this remnant then was used at a nunnery.

is known that in times of peril both princes and boyars stored their treasures here. In addition to the chapels, there were cloisters for the monks, farms and outbuildings for the boyars and their mounts, and according to tradition a prison.

Dracula's son Mihnea the Bad repaired the monastery after extensive damage had been done to it by the Turks, and also had some of his boyar victims interred there. Vlad the Monk, Dracula's half brother, who defrocked himself to become briefly prince, may have attempted to atone for some of the family crimes by becoming abbot of Snagov. Vlad's second wife, Maria, became a nun and lived at Snagov. One of her sons, ''Little Vlad,'' spent all his early years at the monastery before becoming prince in 1510. His son, yet another Vlad, who ruled between 1530 and 1532, may well have drowned in the lake at Snagov and is known logically enough in Romanian history books as Vlad the Drowned.

Though we know very little about the tragedies of Snagov in Dracula's time, or even during the lifetime of the immediate members of his family, a great deal has been written about the violent history of the monastery since that period. A small portion of the tragedy of Snagov is enshrined in its walls and on the cold stone floor of the present small church. One can still read the terse inscriptions in the original Slavonic giving the names of the victims each successive century has contributed to the initial list compiled by the Draculas. Death came to these princes and boyars in different ways and for various reasons, but chiefly they were politically motivated.

In spite of the monks' ongoing prayers the monastery was not spared punishment. It was burned and partially destroyed by the Turks shortly after Prince Radu's inauguration in 1462, and at that time Dracula's treasure is supposed to have been sunk in the lake by the monks, who were in fear for their lives; it is reputed to lie close to the island in one of the deeper spots. In addition to destruction wrought by man, natural disaster added to the tragedy of Snagov. Shortly after Dracula's death, a violent storm erupted with winds of hurricane velocity. Of the two churches then existing, the

137

one built by Dracula's grandfather, the Church of the Annunciation, was torn, steeple and all, from its very foundations and blown into the lake, as was the bell tower. Local tradition has it that only the heavy carved oak door floated on the waters of the lake and that it was blown to the opposite bank, where it was found by some nuns who had established a place of their own. They simply used this providential gift to replace a much less decorative door of their nunnery. The Snagov door has since been deposited at the Bucharest Art Museum. As for the submerged tower, peasants to this day say that whenever the lake is unduly agitated one can hear the muffled sound of the bell.

At the close of the 17th century, the monastery had a fine reputation as a place of learning. It contained one of Romania's first printing presses, the result of the labor of one of the erudite monks of the period, Antim Ivireanu, who printed Romanian and Arabic versions of the Testaments. Because of Antim's excellence as a teacher two famous 17th-century travelers came to the island—Paul of Alep and his father, Patriarch Macarie of Antioch. Writing in Arabic, these men compiled the first scientific ''travelogue'' of Snagov, which tells of two churches there and of a bridge to the mainland. From their account one might almost believe that Snagov had finally become exempt from tragedy and was launched on a brilliant new cultural phase. This presumed change of fortune, however, was never to occur. Antim, for reasons still obscure, was compelled to leave Snagov and was poisoned and died in exile. His books were dispersed, and the printing press taken to Antioch.

The 18th century period of Greek rule gave Snagov some respite. It was not placed under the custody of the Greek Patriarchates, which at that time were taking over many of the country's ancient ecclesiastical foundations, rather it remained under the jurisdiction of the Romanian Orthodox Church. Even so, the local populace became unsympathetic to Snagov, for many Greek monks served there and all Greeks were regarded with suspicion—particularly because of the vast sums of money that their princes were sending abroad. This may partly account for the peasants burning the wooden bridge linking Snagov to the mainland, making communications to and from the monastery difficult since no permanent replacement of the bridge was ever built. The worst indignity to the monastery, however, was yet to come.

General Kiselev, the Russian-born governor-general of Wallachia in 1830, decreed the conversion of Snagov into a prison for minor offenders. The monks were allowed but a small portion of the monastery for worship. Even in the capacity of a prison, Snagov experienced tragedies. On one occasion as chain-bound criminals were crossing over to the island on a flimsy pontoon bridge, it broke under the weight and sent 59 helpless victims to the bottom of the lake.

Pillage is another, lengthy chapter in the story of Snagov. Since Dracula's time, the monastery had been reputed to store many princely and ill-begotten boyar treasures within its vaults: artistic legacies, valuable religious books printed by the Monk Antim, and a large number of valuable ikons and other religious items. The bait was there, not only for the robber barons, or haiducs, of the Vlasie forest, but also for peasants and priests from the village communities nearby—and the monks were really without means of defense.

At the end of its prison history, which lasted barely 20 years, Snagov, which had always housed a few monks, was virtually abandoned, and by 1867 it formally closed down. The few remaining monks left; no abbot was appointed. Only Sunday services were occasionally said by priests from neighboring villages. During this time vandalism and thievery occurred on a more massive scale, and all joined in—professional thieves, villagers, and government officials. The peasants used the bricks and stones of the remaining outside walls, stole all the wood they could find, and tore doors from their hinges. Roofing material disappeared; stained-glass windows were broken. Inside, the church suffered equally, if not more; pews, pulpits, not to mention holy vases and other religious items, were removed. Tombs were opened, inscriptions torn off, remains of boyars combed for valuables. Abbots and priests from neighboring villages joined in the collection of valuable Bibles and manuscripts, allegedly to save some of them from destruction. In the name of religion, they were sharers in the loot. This pillage could hardly have gone unnoticed by ecclesiastical authorities, and it is inconceivable that the looting of an historic edifice located only a few miles away from the capital was unknown to the government.

In 1890 the administrator of state domains described the ancient monastic complex as reduced to a partially dismantled roofless church. By 1897, the same year Stoker published *Dracula* in London, concerned Romanians—lovers of the antique, historians, and archaeologists—began the difficult task of saving what was left of the neglected Dracula chapel.

The battle to save Snagov as an historical monument, strange as it may sound in this age of national self-consciousness, was as difficult as any single disaster that the monastery has endured—simply through the apathy of the government and of individual ministers. The necessary sums were finally voted and the restoration of the present church began only at the turn of the century—a restoration which, unlike that of many other churches, was done in good taste. The local architects and engineers as well as historians reconstructed the monastery exactly the way it was supposed to have been in the days of Dracula, without the frills of other restored sites. The restoration of Snagov is still being carried out. Like any puzzle long abandoned, there are pieces missing. It is conceivable that the government may someday decide to reconstruct the whole monastery and rebuild the second church as it was in the days of Dracula.

In 1940, during the famous earthquake in Bucharest, when many historic buildings were sent toppling to the ground, the tremor tore the nave of the chapel at Snagov in two. In the eyes of the superstitious peasants, the spirit of Dracula, the great undead, is still there, inviting retribution.

Today, as one surveys the church where Dracula is supposed to be interred, a strange calm surrounds the monastery. Only an abbot, two monks, and a peasant woman attendant pace its grounds. The abbot is a learned man who knows the history of the 15th century and Dracula's connection with the monastery. He has done his homework so well that the Romanian government yearly sends him to Curtea de Arges to train the tourist officials in the complexities of the medieval period. One of his monks, who strangely does not wear the religious garb, spends much time deeply and penitently in prayer inside the church. When questioned as to the absence of religious dress, he confessed that he had committed a ''crime'' and been assigned by the Patriarch to the island monastery for expiation. Old traditions here, as elsewhere, die slowly.

This story brought to life once again the ancient princes and boyars in similar grief—exiled here to wipe away sin. The life of a penitent at Snagov is still rugged since he suffers long periods of total isolation during the winter months, when the ice on the lake is not quite firm enough to traverse on foot. Provisioning, which has to be done by boat, seems to be the main problem. In summer, flocks of tourists are brought twice a day by steamer and innumerable excursionists come by canoe or rowboat to disturb the mystery of Snagov. This daily intrusion in itself is a hardship.

Snagov . . . a place of prayer and prisoners, famous names and infamous acts. Even if one does not believe the popular tradition that Dracula lies buried here, the very atmosphere of this antique site forms an ideal setting for the last phase of the search for Dracula.

The Consequences by Goya. In this plate from the *Disasters of War,* Goya has imaged war as a strange winged creature, part vulture, part vampire, sucking blood from the breast of man.

142

CHAPTER

7

Vampirism

Old World Folklore

Transylvania has sometimes been described simply as "the land beyond the forest." Even today many Americans, indeed many Europeans, would be hard put to speak precisely about this province. In fact, all of Romania seems to be a place of indeterminable geography, unpronounceable names, and (in the view of film-makers) innumerable violins. As for its people, our knowledge of them is similarly vague. Before going on to look at their vampire folklore, we shall look at them.

They live not in R*u*mania, but in R*o*mania—a fact stressed by their present government to make clear the land's ties to ancient Rome. Most of them claim to be of Roman descent, but this claim in itself is ambiguous. What does it mean to be a Romanian? There are no specific ethnic characteristics. The people are not all blond with blue eyes, nor all dark-haired with dark eyes; they are not all light-skinned, not all dark-skinned. The chief factor in national identity is that most of the people speak a language which is called Romanian. Even so, one can still

143

hear a kind of Low German dialect in areas like Brasov and Sibiu; one can hear Hungarian in the west near Oradea, or close to the center of Romania at Tirgu Mures. Both Eastern and Western influences affect this culture and give it unique variety and depth.

The people of Romania are still almost 60 per cent rural, and although this basically peasant society is working hard to break into the urban 20th century, its oral traditions are still more powerful than the written word.

Finally, it should be noted that the majority of Romanians are affiliated with, or exposed to the influence of, the Eastern Orthodox Church. This factor, as we shall see, strongly affects the native customs and beliefs concerning vampires.

The notion behind vampirism traces way back in time—to man the hunter, who discovered that when blood flowed out of the wounded beast or a fellow human, life, too, drained away. Blood was the source of vitality! Thus men sometimes smeared themselves with blood and sometimes drank it. The idea of drinking blood to renew vitality became transferred from the living to the dead, and thereupon the vampire entered history. To the vampire, indeed, ''The blood is the life''—as Dracula, quoting from Deuteronomy 12:33, tells us in Stoker's novel.

Vampires have left their mark in all of recorded history. They are cited among the dead in Ancient Egypt. They are defined in 20th-century dictionaries as bloodsucking, walking dead whom some persons still believe in.

Any credence in vampires of course requires conviction that in the afterlife the deceased has a physical body, hence a need for sustenance. According to Eastern Orthodox belief the body of anyone bound by a curse will not be received by the earth—will not decay. The bodies of those who die under ban of excommunication are doomed to remain ''incorrupt and entire.'' Such undead ramble at night and spend only daytime in their tombs until absolution is granted. All this goes a long way toward explaining why vampirism has been so credible in Orthodox countries.

144

Most Romanians believe that life after death will be much like life now. There is not much faith in any purely spiritual world. So it is reasonable that after death an undead will walk the earth in much the same way as a living person. The walking dead does not always have to be a vampire with a thirst for blood. In fact, the Romanian term *moroi* (undead) is more prevalent than the stark term ''vampire'' (blood-drinker). But both the undead and the vampire are killed in the same ways. One must drive a stake through their hearts or else one must burn their bodies.

Another Romanian term for vampire is *strigoi.* Strigoi are demon birds of the night. They fly only after sunset, and they eat human flesh and drink blood. In other parts of the Balkans they are sometimes called *vukodlak* or *brukolak.*

Historically, plagues are often blamed on vampires. And sometimes a fir tree is plunged into the body of the vampire in order to keep it in the grave. A sophisticated example of this is the fir-tree ornament which one finds over graves in Romania today.

The belief in vampires is still prevalent in Dracula country. Today at the foot of Castle Dracula, in the small village of Capatineni, lives a gypsy named Tinka. She is the local *lautar* or village singer, and is often called up to sing old stories at weddings, balls, and funerals.

In the autumn of 1969 Tinka told one of our authors two stories about the undead (the moroi). One of them concerned her father. When he had died 30 years ago, he was duly laid out, but the next day the villagers discovered that the old man's face was still ruddy, and his body still soft, not rigid. The people knew that he was an undead. A stake was driven through his heart so as to prevent him from becoming one of the walking dead.

The other story concerned an old woman in the village. After her death many of her close relatives died. So did various animals around her home. Because of these things, the people realized that she was an undead. They dug up her coffin. When the lid was removed, they found that her eyes were wide open and that her body had rolled over in

145

the grave. They also noticed that the corpse had a ruddy complexion. The people of the village burned her body.

Belief in the walking dead and the blood-sucking vampire may never entirely disappear. It was only in the past century—1823, to be exact—that England outlawed the practice of driving stakes through the hearts of those who had committed suicide. Today, it is in Transylvania that the vampire legends have their strongest hold. As one looks over the following superstitions, it is chilling to imagine their potency and that of similar ones 600 years ago.

In Eastern Europe vampires are said to have two hearts, or two souls; since one heart, or one soul, never dies, the vampire remains undead.

Who can become a vampire? In Transylvania, criminals, bastards, witches, magicians, excommunicated people, those born with teeth or a caul, and unbaptized children can become vampires. The seventh son of a seventh son is doomed to become a vampire.

How can one detect a vampire? Any person who does not eat garlic or who expresses a distinct aversion to garlic is suspect.

Vampires sometimes strike people dumb. They can steal one's beauty or strength, or milk from nursing mothers.

In Romania, peasants believe that the vampires and other spectres meet on St. Andrew's Eve at a place where the cuckoo does not sing and the dog does not bark.

How does one kill a dragon? St. George killed the dragon with a lance. One must impale the dragon, as one must impale the vampire.

Vampires are frightened by light, so one must build a good fire to ward them off, and torches must be lit and placed outside the houses.

Even if you lock yourself up in your home, you are not safe from the vampire, since he can enter through chimneys and keyholes. Therefore, one must rub the chimney

Scene with vampire by Gustave Doré; published
1847 among Doré's illustrations for Dante's
Divine Comedy.

and keyholes with garlic, and the windows and doors as well. The farm animals must also be rubbed with garlic to protect them.

Crosses made from the thorns of wild roses are effective in keeping the vampire away.

Spread thorns or poppy seeds on the paths leading to the village from the churchyard. Since the vampire must stop to pick up every one of them he may be so delayed that he cannot reach the village before sunrise, when he must return to his grave.

Take a large black dog and paint an extra set of eyes on his forehead with white paint—this alienates vampires.

According to Orthodox Christian belief, the soul does not leave the body to enter the next world until 40 days after the body is laid in the grave. Hence, the celebrations in Orthodox cemeteries 40 days after the burial. Bodies were once disinterred between three to seven years after burial and if decomposition was not complete a stake was driven through the heart of the corpse.

If a cat or other "evil" animal jumps or flies over someone's dead body before it is buried, or if the shadow of a man falls upon the corpse, the deceased may become a vampire.

If the dead body is reflected in a mirror, the reflection helps the spirit to leave the body and become a vampire.

One of the most common ways of locating a vampire was to choose a boy or girl, young enough to be a virgin, and seat such person on a horse of a solid color, all white, brown or black, which was also a virgin and had never stumbled. The horse was led through the cemetary and over all the graves. If it refused to pass over a grave, a vampire was thought to lie there.

Usually the tomb of a vampire has one or more holes roughly of the size through which a serpent can pass.

How to kill a vampire? The stake must be driven through the vampire's body and

148

The Vampires by Estienne Csok, Salon 1907.

Vampire Nightmare by Max Klinger. This illustration and the preceding one are typical of the horrifying vampire images created during the period between 1897, when Stoker published his novel *Dracula,* and 1919, when Murnau began directing the film *Nosferatu.*

into the earth in order to hold him securely in his grave. The stake should be made from a wild rosebush, or an ash or asp tree. In some areas, red-hot iron rather than wood is used for the stake. The vampire's body should be burned or else reburied at the crossroads.

If a vampire is not found and rendered harmless, it first kills all members of its immediate family, then starts on the other inhabitants of the village and its animals.

The vampire cannot stray from his grave too far since he must return to it at sunrise.

If not detected, the vampire climbs up into the belfry of the church and calls out the names of the villagers—who instantly die. Or, in some areas, the vampire rings the death-knell and all who hear it die on the spot.

If the vampire is allowed to go undetected for seven years, he can travel to another country or to a place where another language is spoken and become a human again. He or she can marry and have children, but they all become vampires when they die.

Did the peasants of the 15th century consider Vlad Tepes, or Dracula, a vampire? Those who renounce the Eastern Orthodox faith can become vampires after death. Since the historical Dracula converted to Roman Catholicism while in Hungarian captivity and apparently died in that faith, it is conceivable that the peasants might once have considered the possibility of his becoming a vampire. But no evidence of any such notion has survived. Dracula or Vlad was referred to as *wütrich* or "bloodthirsty monster" in the 15th-century German horror stories (*see* frontispiece). As we shall discuss further in the next chapter, this word presumably suggested "vampire" to Stoker. However, we find no reason for thinking this old German epithet was so construed in the 15th century; probably it simply meant "slaughterer" for it can also be translated as "berserker."

As for the views of the vampire in Eastern Europe during the 15th century, one can only infer them from the living folk traditions recorded there in the 19th century.

Current beliefs in the vampire were investigated by the authors. In the region around Castle Dracula, for instance, McNally actually questioned the peasants; he found that there is now no connection between Vlad Tepes and the vampire in the folklore. For that matter, the peasants there are not even aware of Stoker's modern Dracula. They do believe passionately, however, in the vampire and the undead.

Most of our culture has an urban bias against the peasants' belief in vampires. This is reflected in our use of the word "urbane" to describe something positive, broadminded, and rational; and the word "provincial" to designate something negative, narrow-minded, and superstitious. We tend to look down on peasants and their cultures. To us, peasants are primitive and "unscientific." Even Karl Marx conceded that capitalism at least had saved a majority of the population from "the idiocy of rural life."

But the fact is that so-called primitive, peasant people are not incessantly preoccupied with doubt and fear. They spend most of the day in very practical pursuits which are necessary for them to subsist. They use natural explanations to accomplish these daily tasks.

Some evolutionists have assumed that primitive people have no real capacity for natural explanations. The basis for this assumption is that since primitive man lives at a low technological level he must have a thought process which is opposite to that of modern man. To them, primitive, rural man is "prelogical," a kind of child.

But just as primitive man has some beliefs that are vague and uncertain, so does modern man in an urban, technological society. The point is, attitudes toward death and life have been complex for *all* men—hate and love, attraction and repulsion, hope and fear. The belief in vampires is a poetic, imaginative way of looking at death and at life beyond death.

Primitive beliefs are not any stranger than modern scientific beliefs. Nightly on our TV sets, there is some variation of the man in the white coat who stands up amid

The vampire bat. Found only in Mexico and
Central and South America, this small creature
feeds on the blood of cattle but has been known to
attack humans.

bunsen burners and test tubes and declares, ''Scientific tests have proved that in 9 out of 10 cases. . . .'' whereupon everyone in the audience genuflects to the new god science. If it is scientific then it must be *true*, and only the scientifically proven fact *can* be true. Is this any more absurd than primitive peasant beliefs?

The vampire possesses powers which are similar to those belonging to certain 20th-century comic-book characters. During the day he is helpless and vulnerable like Clark Kent or Bruce Wayne. At night, just as the mild-mannered Clark Kent becomes Superman and the effete Bruce Wayne becomes Batman, so the vampire acquires great powers and springs into flight.

Dracula, the vampire-count or the count-vampire, is a kind of father figure of great potency. He, of course, like any good father, is powerful at night. In mythology, opposite to God the Father with his flowing white beard is the father figure in the form of a black satan. Significantly, Satan is usually portrayed with huge bat-like wings.

The connection among Dracula, the devil, the bat, and the vampire becomes clear. In Romanian folklore the devil can change himself into an animal or a black bird. When he takes wings, he can fly like a bat. During the day he lives in hell—quiet there, like the bat in its refuge; when day is done, the night is his empire—just as it is with the bat.

The bat is the only mammal who fulfills one of man's oldest aspirations: it can really fly all by itself, defying gravity like Superman.

The bat is not a flying rat. The ''wings'' of this small animal are actually elongated, webbed hands. The head of the bat is erect like a man's head. Like man, the bat is one of the most versatile creatures in the world.

New World Bats

Why is the vampire image linked to that of the so-called ''vampire bat'' in particular? Vampire bats do not exist anywhere in Europe. Yet it is there that belief in the vampire itself, a night-flying creature which sucks the blood of the living, has flourished.

When Cortes came to the New World, he found blood-sucking bats in Mexico. Remembering the mythical vampire, he called them "vampire bats." The name stuck. So a word which signified a mythical creature in the Old World became attached to a species of bats peculiar to the New World.

The vampire bat, the *Desmodus rotundus*, is marvelously agile. It can fly, walk, dodge swiftly, turn somersaults, all with swiftness and efficiency. Generally it attacks cattle rather than men. The victim is not awakened during the attack. The vampire bat walks very softly over the victim and, after licking a spot on the flesh, neatly inserts its two front incisor teeth. As the blood spurts out, the vampire bat licks it into its mouth. That the vampire bat subsists on blood alone is a scientific fact.

The vampire's existence is a frightening tragedy, *sans* goodness or hope, repose or satisfaction. In order to survive, he must drink the blood of the living. And the option of not surviving is closed to him. He should decompose, but he cannot do so. Thus he continues: wanting to live, wanting to die; not truly alive and not really dead. The folklore about him is not based on science, yet it is essentially true. Ten out of 10 vampire legends and customs attest what no one doubts; man fears death, and man fears some things even *more* than death.

A Real Blood Countess

To many people, the events and personages in vampire legends may appear to be pure inventions or distorted details of actual happenings and in either case the work of simple peasants. We have, however, official documentation concerning an authentic seventeenth-century countess, Elizabeth Bathory, which reveals her to have been a

Elizabeth Bathory. This portrait of the Blood Countess is now lost.

living vampiress. In the view of some persons today, and in that of most of her contemporaries, she was the most fearsome living vampiress of all time. Here is her story:

Elizabeth Bathory was born in 1560 in a part of Hungary edging the Carpathian mountains. The Bathorys were one of the oldest and wealthiest families in Transylvania; one of Elizabeth's relatives was a cardinal, several were princes of Transylvania, and her cousin Count Gyorgy Thurzo was prime minister of Hungary. Undoubtedly, the most famous Bathory was King Steven of Poland, 1575-86. But along with religion and affairs of state, the family had other interests—one uncle was a diabolist, an aunt a lesbian, and a brother a satyr.

As a child, Elizabeth was betrothed to Count Ferencz Nadasdy. She was 15 and he was 26 when they were married on May 8, 1575. King Mathias II of Hungary sent them a wedding present. The bearded Count Ferencz added her surname to his, and thus the countess continued to be known as Elizabeth Bathory.

Elizabeth and Ferencz went to live at Castle Csejthe in the Nyitra country located in northwestern Hungary. The count was rarely home, as he was usually off fighting. A great soldier, he eventually became known as "The Black Hero of Hungary."

It appears that Elizabeth's manservant Thorko introduced her to the occult. In a letter to her husband the countess wrote: "Thorko taught me a lovely new one. Catch a black hen and beat it to death with a white cane. Keep the blood and smear a little of it on your enemy. If you get no chance to smear it on his body, obtain one of his garments and smear that instead."

Elizabeth temporarily eloped with a dark stranger, but upon her return home, the count forgave her unfaithfulness.

Back at the Csejthe Castle, Elizabeth chafed under the dominance of her mother-in-law, whom she hated. Aided by her old nurse Ilona Joo, Elizabeth began torturing some of the servant girls at the castle. Her other accomplices included the major-domo Johannes Ujvary, her manservant Thorko, a witch Dorottya Szentes, and a forest

Bathory Castle.

The Blood Countess by St. Csok. This late 19th-century painting is now lost.

witch named Darvula.

During the first 10 years of her marriage to Count Nadasdy, Elizabeth bore no children. But within the next four years she gave birth to three boys and a girl. In 1600, Ferencz died. Elizabeth's epoch of real atrocities was about to begin. First, she sent her hated mother-in-law away, then she turned to running the household for her own pleasure.

Elizabeth was afraid of becoming old and losing her beauty. One day a maid accidentally pulled her hair while combing it. Elizabeth instinctively slapped the girl hard—so hard that she drew blood which spurted onto her own hand. It immediately seemed to Elizabeth as if her skin in this area took on the freshness of that of her young maid. Blood—here was the key to an eternally beautiful skin texture. The countess then summoned Johannes Ujvary and Thorko. They stripped the maid, cut her, and drained her blood into a huge vat. Elizabeth bathed in it to beautify her entire body.

Over the next 10 years Elizabeth's henchmen provided her with new girls for the blood-draining ritual and her literal blood baths. But one of her potential victims escaped and informed the authorities about the gruesome goings-on at Castle Csejthe.

Upon hearing the news, King Mathias of Hungary ordered action. Elizabeth's own cousin Count Gyorgy Thurzo, governor of the province, led a band of soldiers and guards in the raid of Castle Csejthe on the night of December 30, 1610. What a sight they saw within the castle! In the main hall they found one girl dead, drained of blood, and another alive whose body had been pierced with tiny holes; in the dungeon they discovered "a number" of other living girls, some of whose bodies had been pierced. Below the castle, the authorities exhumed the bodies of some 50 girls.

Elizabeth was placed under house arrest in her castle. A trial was held at Bitcse during January and February of 1611. Elizabeth never appeared in the courtroom. She refused to plead either innocent or guilty. A complete transcript of the trial, made at the time it took place, survives in Hungary today and is the major document concerning this horrifying history.

Johannes Ujvary, the countess' major-domo, testified at the trial that as far as he knew, about 37 unmarried girls had been killed, six of whom he had personally lured to the castle with promises of jobs as serving girls. These victims were bound and then slashed with scissors. Sometimes Dorottya and Ilona tortured these girls, otherwise the Countess Elizabeth did it herself. Ilona Joo, Elizabeth's old nurse, testified that about 40 girls had been tortured and killed.

Everyone implicated in the killings, except for Countess Elizabeth, Ilona Joo, and Dorottya Szentes, was beheaded and cremated. The latter two accomplices had their fingers torn out individually and were burned alive. Countess Elizabeth was never formally convicted of any crime.

Instead, stonemasons were brought to Castle Csejthe; they walled up the windows and doors of the bedchamber, with the countess inside, leaving only a small hole through which food could be passed. At first, Mathias II, King of Hungary, had demanded the death penalty for Elizabeth, but because of the entreaties of her cousin the prime minister, he agreed to the indefinitely delayed sentence, which meant solitary confinement for life. In 1614, four years after she had been walled in, one of the guards posted outside her chamber wanted a look at this woman whose beauty was renowned far and wide. He saw her lying face down on the floor. Elizabeth Bathory, the "Blood Countess," was dead.

The extent of the ties between the Bathorys and the Draculas is not known. It is certain, however, that the commander-in-chief of the expedition that helped Dracula regain his throne in 1476 was Prince Steven Bathory. In addition, a Dracula fief, Castle Fagaras, became a Bathory possession during the time of Elizabeth. It is interesting to note that the dragon motif is common to both families. The awesome Bathory crest displays three wolf's teeth encircled by a dragon biting its tail. Finally, in some circles it is believed that the story of the Blood Countess was known to Stoker.

159

The Bathory crest, showing three wolf teeth beneath a crown. Not shown here is the encircling motif: a dragon biting its tail.

CHAPTER 8

*Bram Stoker
and the Vampire
in Fiction and Film*

The time has come to talk of terror and horror. Strictly speaking, they are two different things—but, of course, we seldom speak strictly!

Both are responses to the frightful thing, person, deed, or circumstance. But terror is the extreme *rational* fear of some accepted form of reality, whereas horror is extreme *irrational* fear of the *utterly* unnatural or the supernatural. Moreover, there is realistic horror—the unnatural or supernatural fright presented in the guise of the normal.

Terror is also the dread of the use of systematic violence; horror the dread of something unpredictable, something that may have a potential for violence.

When a mad bomber is on the loose in a city, the inhabitants become terrified; they are aware of the capacities of a seriously deranged person; they understand the devastating effects of a bomb. The nature of the danger is clear, and any attendant mystery is susceptible to rational solution. But if a ghost is heard walking at night, the inhabitants of the house are in horror. What *is* a ghost?

161

Portrait of Bram Stoker as William the Conqueror. Part of an historical mural at the London Stock Exchange.

What might *this* one do: What *can* it do? And finally, there is the realistic horror: perhaps a man in a tuxedo—he looks and acts very natural at the country club—yet we go into shock when we see him flying over a blood-stained corpse on the seventh green. Horrible . . . mysterious. In short, it is some fundamental, forever unexplainable mystery that distinguishes horror from terror.

Bram Stoker's novel *Dracula* is one of the most horrifying books in English literature. It was published in May 1897, was an immediate success, and has never since been out of print. In America, where it has been published since 1899, it is still a best seller.

In selecting a setting for Dracula, Bram Stoker hit upon Transylvania because it was, and is still, a far-away never-never land in the view of most Englishmen and Western Europeans, a ''land beyond the forest'' where anything can happen, a perfect setting for a vampire. Even in the recent musical *My Fair Lady*, ''the prince of Transylvania'' is regarded as coming from a wholly imaginary land.

Stoker chose to tell his story through the diaries of the Englishman Jonathan Harker and his fiancee, Mina Seward; the letters of Mina and her friend Lucy; Lucy's journal; and the testimony of Dr. John Seward on a phonograph record—this last, a rather novel touch for the time. The basic story line is simple:

Harker, a real-estate agent, travels to far-off Transylvania in order to arrange for the purchase of Carfax Abbey, an English property, by a certain Count Dracula. As a guest in the count's castle, he finds ''doors, doors everywhere, and all bolted and locked,'' and rooms in which there is not a single mirror. Almost at once he becomes aware that Dracula is a vampire living with a harem of female vampires—and that he himself is a prisoner. He also learns that the count is planning to leave soon for Carfax Abbey, taking with him 50 coffins. Dracula's ultimate intent: the conquest of England.

The count boards a Russian schooner, the *Demeter,* at Varna on the Black Sea. En route to England, he kills the crew. After arriving in England, he attacks Lucy Westerna, who is on vacation with Harker's fiancee Mina.

Dracula gradually drains Lucy of her blood, and infuses his own blood into her body. She "dies" and becomes a vampire. Dr. Abraham Van Helsing, an expert from Amsterdam, tries to save her from vampirism but fails. The undead Lucy attacks children in Hampstead. When Van Helsing drives a stake through her vampire heart, her corpse finds eternal repose.

Dracula also victimizes Renfield, a patient in an insane asylum who has a taste for small animals.

Meanwhile Harker has miraculously escaped to London, and Van Helsing persuades him to help seek Dracula's many coffins. There is a thrilling search for Dracula's corpse, culminating in its destruction just in time to save Mina, whom Dracula has also attacked in his bloodthirsty campaign to spread the vampire cult throughout England.

In actual fact, Dr. Abraham Van Helsing—whose first name is identical with that of Abraham ("Bram") Stoker—is the real hero of *Dracula*; Count Dracula himself is the underdog. Van Helsing has all the cards stacked in his favor. He knows that Dracula is powerless during the day, and at night Van Helsing can ward him off with garlic or the cross. Abraham Van Helsing may be Abraham Stoker's substitute self. He unites the scientific with the occult. He is all-wise and all-powerful. His mind pierces everyday reality to the reality beyond. Van Helsing is also courageous and relentless when confronting the ignorance of other scientists and rationalists and when up against the vampire himself.

Just a few days before Stoker's vampire novel was published, the character Dracula appeared on stage for the first time, in a play entitled *Dracula or the Un-Dead*; it was solidly based on the book and its playing time was something more than four hours. Its performance on May 17, 1897 was the only one which Stoker ever witnessed.

163

In 1921, almost a quarter of a century later, F. W. Murnau, a young German film director, decided to make the first horror movie about Dracula. (That same year, Henrik Galeen also adopted the Stoker novel for the cinema.) Though Murnau gave full credit on the screen to Stoker's novel, he had failed to get permission to use it. So he changed the setting from Transylvania to the Baltic area, and he also added a final erotic scene. His silent film entitled *Nosferatu* was released by Prana Films in Berlin in 1922. By this time Stoker had died; his widow, Florence Stoker, brought suit against Murnau and won. Murnau's company folded. Although the courts had ordered that the negative and prints of *Nosferatu* be destroyed, this fortunately did not happen. The film opened in London in 1928 and in the United States in 1929. Since then, *Nosferatu* has continued to be shown in the art cinema theatres of the world.

The central locale in *Nosferatu* is the port of Bremen in northern Germany. Here Dracula has an agent named Renfield, who sends Jonathan Harker to Transylvania so that he can discuss with Dracula the rental of a home in Bremen. During Harker's stay with him, Dracula sees a medallion of Harker's beloved Mina, and becomes attracted to her. He attacks Harker, then leaves by ship for Bremen.

During the voyage, he kills the entire crew. Upon his debarkation in Bremen, the fear arises that the plague has arrived in the city. Dracula installs himself in a house across the road from Mina. Harker, who had slowly recovered from the vampire's attack, has also returned home. He warns Mina against the stranger from Transylvania. At the movie's end, Mina realizes that she must spend the night with Dracula—must keep him at her side until daylight—in order to save Jonathan and her fellow humans. She does it. As the morning sunlight falls upon Dracula, he disintegrates. Jonathan now enters the room and Mina expires in his arms. This bizarre ending was invented by Murnau, and it shows a strange, Teutonic attitude toward the use of sexual attractiveness. It takes real guts to go to bed with a vampire in order to save mankind.

Max Schreck as Count Orlock in *Nosferatu*. This frame from the film shows the count on board a ship arriving in Bremen with a cargo of coffins.

Death of Count Orlock in *Nosferatu*

An Irish actor-manager, Hamilton Deane, who had read Stoker's *Dracula* around 1899, tried for many years to persuade some playwright to write a Dracula play. Finally, Deane himself took over the task in 1923. His play, entitled *Dracula,* was performed in June 1924 at the Grant Theatre in Derby. It was an immediate success. On February 14, 1927, it came to London, where it had one of the longest runs of any play in English theatrical history.

For the New York stage, Deane revised *Dracula,* collaborating with the American writer John L. Balderston. It opened at the Fulton Theatre, in October 1927, with an unknown Hungarian actor named Bela Lugosi in the vampire role. The show ran for a year on Broadway, and for two years on tour—breaking all previous records for any modern play touring the States.

While the stage versions were becoming such huge successes in England and the United States, the film director Tod Browning decided to make his own Dracula movie. Accordingly, in 1930 Universal Pictures bought the motion picture rights to the Deane-Balderston version. Browning's film presents Dracula the vampire as an accepted fact of existence.

Bela Lugosi, the stage Dracula, played the lead in this famous American film, which was released on St. Valentine's Day in 1931. The actor had been born Bela Lugosi Blasko in the town of Lugoj, which is in the Banat region of Romania and once was part of Hungary. Most film critics agree that he was a natural for the role. His deep, thick Hungarian accent and slow manner of speaking, his aquiline nose, high cheek bones, and six-foot frame all seemed perfect attributes for the part. The eerie effect of his almond-shaped, crystal-blue eyes was heightened in the film by focusing light on them through two small holes in a piece of cardboard. This Dracula film became Universal's biggest money-maker in 1931.

In the Tod Browning film, Renfield, an agent for a London firm, comes to Transylvania to get a lease signed by Dracula for Carfax Abbey. On the way, the peasants warn Renfield about Dracula's vampirism. He meets Dracula at his castle, and is attacked by him there.

Dracula travels by boat to London, accompanied by Renfield, who is now his slave. Needing blood, Dracula kills all the sailors on board. In London, Renfield is placed in an insane asylum. At the opera Dracula meets both Lucy and Jonathan Harker's fiancee Mina. Lucy is fascinated by him, and Dracula later makes her into one of his entourage of female vampires. He also begins the process of converting Mina into one. Along the way, he kills other Londoners.

Then Professor Van Helsing, an expert on vampires, arrives on the scene. He declares, ''Gentlemen, we are dealing with the undead, Nosferatu, the vampire.'' He notes that Count Dracula throws no reflection in a mirror. He repels him with a cross. In the course of this film, the character Van Helsing becomes the archetype of the fearless killer of vampires. Van Helsing convinces Mina's father and Jonathan that they must find Dracula in his grave during the day and kill him with a stake in order to save Mina from his dire control. Together they discover Dracula's coffin at Carfax Abbey. Van Helsing drives the stake into Dracula's heart. He is destroyed forever. Mina recovers from her shock. She is saved.

The American horror film became popular because of the almost simultaneous release of two remarkable creatures: Dracula the vampire (1931) and Dr. Frankenstein's monster (1932). It is interesting to speculate on whether there is any correlation between the popularity of these creatures and the period in which they were released—the Great Depression. The optimistic Dr. Frankenstein created a monster which ultimately destroyed him, just as many optimistic investors created a market situation which in 1929 destroyed them. Dracula drained away the life of his victims, an effect comparable to that of the economic disaster.

Lugosi's only rival as the horror king was, of course, Boris Karloff, who played Dr. Frankenstein's monster. In 1938 the film *Dracula* was reissued; there followed a long

Scene from Dreyer's *Vampyr* (1932), one of the
greatest Dracula films.

Christopher Lee in the role of Vlad Tepes. This
scene from *In Search of Dracula* was filmed inside
the real Castle Bran.

line of horror films in which Lugosi participated, *The Return of the Vampire*, *House of Dracula*, and so on; similarly, the Frankenstein film spawned a series. Lugosi toured in the role of Dracula both in America and in England. He was addicted to drugs, and by 1955 was in a state institution. He had taken morphine, he said, during his filming of the 1931 Dracula story for relief from pains in his legs. In August 1956, Bela Lugosi, the vampire king, the living embodiment of Dracula, died at 73 years of age. Although Dracula and other horror roles had netted him more than $600,000, he had only $3,000 left at the time of his death. In accordance with his request, Lugosi was buried in his black Dracula cloak lined with red satin.

In 1958 the British scriptwriter Jimmy Sangster produced a new Dracula, for Hammer Films, which was based wholly on Stoker's story line. He made Dracula into a realistic monster in technicolor. Some film critics found the film to be "too realistic." Its director was the now famous Terence Fisher. The erotic element predominated: women were attracted to Dracula; they eagerly awaited his kisses and bites—and kiss them and bite them he did in full view. Christopher Lee, a tall thin macabre-faced figure, played Dracula. The new Dracula movie opened in May 1958 in both London and New York. In less than two years it made eight times its original cost. Several take-offs on this theme have been made, the latest being *Dracula Has Risen from the Grave*. (You can't keep a good man down!) And still more take-offs on the Dracula theme in film come out almost every year. The current Hammer films about Dracula are terror, not horror, films, for any real sense of mystery has been lost.

There are four truly great horror films: *Nosferatu* (1922), *Dracula* (1931), *Vampyr* (1932), and *The Horror of Dracula* (1958).

Presently the leading vampire-Dracula productions come from Hammer Films in Great Britain, and the most impressive Dracula actor is Christopher Lee. A filmography of this genre of films, covering 1896-1971 and including commentary, may be found in the final section of this book. In addition, 1972 will see even more startling variations.

About two years ago Harry Allan Towers, a producer at Britain's Tigon Studio, commissioned the Italian director Jesus Franco to film a definitive version of Bram Stoker's novel for issue by Commonwealth United Releasing Corporation. The film was largely shot in Spain; Christopher Lee played Dracula. Commonwealth United Releasing Company folded and American International bought it out, but due to a legal hassle the Dracula film has not been shown in Spain or the United States. However, the film has played in much of Europe with great success; was especially successful in Paris during the spring and summer of 1972. The film is entitled *The Nights of Dracula*; in France, *Les Nuits de Dracula*, and in Italy, *Count Dracula*. It reputedly encompasses the atmospheric horror of Stoker's *Dracula*.

Another current film is *Vampir*, a documentary about the making of *The Nights of Dracula,* directed by Pedro Portobello. This film shows how the classic horror effects are achieved with such means as the fog and cobweb machines, lighting, and makeup, and how the stake is driven through the heart. *Vampir* was screened in 1971 at the Cannes Film Festival, where it received fine reviews; at the Museum of Modern Art in February 1972 as part of the museum's Cineprobe series; and at the Olympia Theatre in New York on May 5, 1972 at midnight. It has recently been picked up by Roninfilms, a small company which usually distributes Japanese films.

A film entitled *Dracula vs. Frankenstein* is to be released by Independent International. An all-black modern version of Dracula called *Blacula* (American International) is also being made. The noted Shakespearean actor William Marshall will play the title role, and Denise Nicholas of *Room 222* will portray the heroine.

On American television in 1972 a film with one of the highest ratings was ABC's *Night-Stalker* about a reporter who realizes that a vampire is loose in Las Vegas. All the officials make fun of the reporter, thinking that he is simply looking for a sensational story. In the end there really is a vampire, a Transylvanian count who never speaks in the film but has fantastic physical power. The reporter, who destroys the vampire, is hounded out of town by the officials.

In Search of Dracula was produced in 1972 by Aspekt Films, Sweden; director, Calvin Floyd; screenplay by Yvonne Floyd. The authors of the present book served as historical consultants. This film is an entertaining documentary about the real Dracula and Transylvanian folklore, shot on location in present-day Romania. It is the first film to deal with both the fictional vampire Count Dracula and the genuinely historical Vlad the Impaler. Clips from famous Dracula films are interwoven with scenes from Transylvanian folklore about vampires. Christopher Lee is the narrator, and appears as Count Dracula and, in native Romanian costume, as Vlad the Impaler.

This fad for Dracula the vampire all began with Bram Stoker. But how did *he* get the idea? How did he come to be the creator of this modern horror story?

Stoker was born in Dublin on a November day in 1847. He was named Abraham after his father—an employe at the Chief Secretary's Office in Dublin Castle, but he was affectionately called "Bram" throughout his life. His mother was Charlotte Matilda, daughter of a Captain Thornley.

As a child, Bram was so sick and feeble that he was confined to bed for the first eight years of his life. This was a period as critical in the development of Bram Stoker as was life in "the Land of Counterpane" for the young and sickly Robert Louis Stevenson. During Bram's years of confinement, the Reverend William Woods, who had a private school in Dublin, was brought in to instruct him. He continued as his principal teacher until Bram entered college at age 16. But it was Mrs. Stoker who particularly influenced Bram's early childhood and his fantasy life. Her warm love for this son provokes remembrance of Freud's dictum about the success assured to those sons who are especially loved by their mothers. Charlotte Stoker often declared that she loved her boys best and "did not care a tuppence" for her daughters. She told young Bram not only Irish fairy tales but also some true horror stories. An Irish woman from Sligo, she had witnessed the cholera epidemic there in 1832, and later in life Bram recalled her accounts of it. The vampire pestilence in his novel is comparable to the frightful, relentless spread of cholera.

Bram entered Trinity College, Dublin, in 1864. But his interest lay more in the drama than in his studies for a career in the Irish Civil Service. He regularly attended the Theatre Royal, the city's one large, regular theatre. One evening in August 1867 *The Rivals* was performed there, with Henry Irving as the star. Bram was enthralled by the famous actor.

When Henry Irving returned to Dublin in a comedy entitled *Two Roses*, Stoker was in the audience along with another young unknown Irishman, a 15-year-old agent's clerk named George Bernard Shaw. Like Shaw, Bram decided to be a drama critic. His first review appeared in the *Dublin Mail* in November 1871. At this time Stoker's interest in Sir Henry Irving was to be joined with an interest in vampirism.

A Dublin author with the unlikely name of Joseph Sheridan Le Fanu (1814-73) had just written the short novel ''Carmilla,'' one of the greatest vampire stories of all time. Stoker read it and began thinking about writing his own tale of a vampire. In Le Fanu's work, the heroine Laura welcomes a strange girl named Carmilla into her father's castle and they become close companions. Laura senses, however, that she has seen Carmilla in her childhood nightmares. The author creates an aura of Romantic horror about the almost lesbian relationship between the blond Laura and the beautiful dark Carmilla, and so successfully achieves suspense that not until the story's end does one know whether Carmilla is a vampire or simply a victim of one. Finally, in the chapel of Karnstein, the grave of the Countess Mircalla is opened. Carmilla turns out to be the dead countess, whose ''features, though a hundred and fifty years had passed since her funeral, were tinted with the warmth of life. Her eyes were open; no cadavrous smell exhaled from the coffin.''

Le Fanu followed vampire mythology closely by asserting that her ''limbs were perfectly flexible, the flesh elastic; and the leaden coffin floated with blood. . . .'' To destroy the undead countess:

The body . . . in accordance with the ancient practice, was raised, and a sharp stake driven through the heart of the vampire . . . the head was struck off . . . body and head were next placed on a pile of wood, and reduced to ashes.

Le Fanu's description of how a person becomes a vampire is also based upon folk belief in Eastern Europe:

Assume, at starting, a territory perfectly free from that pest. How does it begin, and how does it multiply itself: I will tell you. A person, more or less wicked, puts an end to himself. A suicide, under certain circumstances, becomes a vampire. That spectre visits living people in their slumbers; they die, and almost invariably, in the grave, develop into vampires.

Stoker found in ''Carmilla'' the basic ingredients for the vampire aspects of Dracula. Enchanted, he began delving seriously into vampire mythology.

In the winter of 1876 Henry Irving was in Dublin again, and Stoker described him in the role of Eugene Aram with phrases that give a foretaste of Dracula: ''The awful horror . . . of the Blood avenging spite''—''eyes as inflexible as Fate''—''eloquent hands, slowly moving, outspread, fanlike.'' Stoker tells us, in fact, that he became hysterical at the performance.

Bram began working in a part-time capacity for the great actor. Two years later, in 1878, he left his job in the Irish Civil Service and with his new wife, Florence Anne Lemon Balcombe, went to London. Irving had just taken over the Lyceum Theatre there and needed his friend's help full-time. The Stokers settled down in Cheyne Walk in Chelsea, where their neighbors included Dante Gabriel Rossetti; and James Mc-

173

Neill Whistler.

In all, Bram worked as the actor's private secretary and confidant for 27 years, which are described in his *Personal Reminiscences of Henry Irving.* He called their friendship "as profound, as close, as lasting as can be between two men." But there was more to the relationship than that. Irving held such fascination for Bram that he achieved an extraordinary dominance over him. Indeed, in life Irving was to Stoker, as in fiction Dracula is to Renfield.

Although much of Bram's time was taken up in arranging tours for Irving and his company, he continued to investigate vampirism. He also explored the Gothic novel, a development in English literature which traces back to the 18th century. The Gothic novel was initially a tale of spooks and had a medieval atmosphere highly charged with emotion. In time such stories—particularly those of Ann Radcliffe—were given *rational* endings: all of the mysteries turn out to have natural causes; the supernatural elements prove to be only illusions; the horror is explained away.

When Mary Godwin Shelley (1797-1851) wrote *Frankenstein* (1817), there was a new, *realistic* development in the Gothic novel. Mrs. Shelley achieved horror and mystery through the use of science, or, if you will, pseudo-science. The agent of horror in her book was no spook, no supernatural being, nor the illusion of such. It was a real monster manufactured by the technical expertise of a Dr. Frankenstein.

Both the vampire and the Frankenstein monster were created at the same time in English literature and at the same place. The coincidence occurred during the summer of 1816 in Geneva, Switzerland, where Mary Shelley with Percy Bysshe Shelley, her stepsister Claire, Lord Byron, and his personal physician John Polidori had gone on vacation. The group first stayed at the Hotel d'Angleterre, then rented adjacent villas along the shores of Lake Geneva. Mary later wrote that it was a "wet ungenial summer," and the rain "confined us for days." In order to amuse themselves, this gifted group decided to read German tales of horror. Then, one night in June, Byron said, ''We will each write a ghost story.''

Before the end of the summer, the 18-year-old Mary, inspired by a philosophical discussion and a nightmare, had written entirely on her own the novel *Frankenstein.* When it later appeared in print, some book reviewers thought that her husband was really its author.

Mary Godwin Shelley wrote her Frankenstein story to show in a sympathetic way the failure of a would-be scientific savior of mankind. The public turned it all upside-down, and her creation came to inspire an endless run of stories about the ''mad scientist'' who tries to go *beyond* nature's laws, unlike ordinary, God-fearing mortals. In so doing, he unwittingly creates a monster rather than a superman. Eventually, the unholy creature destroys its own creator.

Not to be outdone by any woman, Byron sketched out at Geneva a plan for a tale about a vampire, but he never finished it. Instead, the 20-year-old Polidori (1795-1821), an Englishman of Italian descent and a former student of medicine at the University of Edinburgh, took over Byron's idea, and using it as a basis he wrote a story called ''The Vampyre.''

In April 1819, Polidori's tale appeared in the *New Monthly Magazine* under Byron's name, through a misunderstanding on the part of the editor. Goethe swallowed the story whole and declared it to be the best thing that Byron had ever written. Years before, Goethe himself had given substance to the vampire legend in his *Braut Von Korinth*, published in 1797.

In Polidori's ''Vampyre'' a young libertine, Lord Ruthven, a character modeled loosely on Byron, is killed in Greece and becomes a vampire. He seduces the sister of his friend Aubrey, and suffocates her on the night following their wedding. This story never caught on with the public, and two years after its publication Polidori, un-successful at both literature and medicine, took poison and died. However, the vampire myth itself remained popular. Other writers tried their hands at creating a

175

fascinating vampire figure, and Stoker profited from their attempts.

Alexandre Dumas Père composed a drama entitled *Le Vampire*. In 1820 Nodier's *Le Vampire* was translated into English by J. R. Planche. In 1830 Planche's melodrama *The Vampire* was published in Baltimore.

In *Melmoth the Wanderer*, published by the eccentric Irish clergyman Robert Maturin in 1820, the hero is a meld of a wandering Jew and a Byronic vampire. The character interrupts a wedding feast and terrifies everyone. Soon after the event the bride dies, and the bridegroom goes mad. The vengeance of the vampire is complete.

In 1847, Thomas Preskett Prest published *Varney the Vampire or The Feast of Blood*, which was well received and was reprinted in 1853. Before writing it, the author had studied the vampire legends in detail. His story is set in the 1730's during the reign of George II. It concerns the Bannesworth family and its persecution by Sir Francis Varney. Varney sucks the blood of Flora Bannesworth, captures her lover, and insults her family. Oddly, the author presents Varney as a basically good person who is driven to evil by circumstances. He tries often to save himself, but at the end of the story he is in utter despair and commits suicide by jumping into the crater of Mount Vesuvius.

It was soldily in the realistic horror-story tradition of Mary Godwin Shelley, Maturin, and Prest that Bram Stoker wrote his own horror story. Like them, he presented the vampire as an actual phenomenon. His Dracula is, and remains, a vampire—quite different from, say, the horror in a Gothic novel who seems to be a bloody ghost and then turns out to be a wounded human being. Stoker's novel indeed made no attempt to explain away the vampire. Moreover, Stoker made Dracula a contemporary, a vampire who lived in, and walked the streets of, Victorian England. This, too, differed from the early Gothic romances, which employed historic figures and settings.

Stoker had come to London in 1878, and during the next 10 years he published

Cover of an installment of *Varney the Vampire.*
The first installment of this popular Gothic novel
appeared in 1847.

among other works a book entitled *Under the Sunset*, in which there is a King of
Death. He also met Sir Richard Burton, the prominent orientalist. Burton had
translated into English the *Arabian Nights,* in which there is a vampire tale, and in
1870 some 11 tales about vampires from Hindu sources. It is fascinating to note that in
his reminiscences, Stoker wrote how impressed he was not only by Burton's accounts
but also by his physical appearance—especially his canine teeth. Additional food for
Bram's imagination was supplied by Jack the Ripper, who terrorized London from
August to November in 1888. In reporting Jack's murders, the *East London Advertiser* stated:

It is so impossible to account, on any ordinary hypothesis, for these revolting acts of blood that the mind turns as it were instinctively to some theory of occult force, and the myths of the Dark Ages arise before the imagination. Ghouls, vampires, blood-suckers . . . take form and seize control of the excited fancy.

As the idea of writing a vampire story increasingly preoccupied him, Bram searched for a ''matrix'' that would give it an air of authenticity. Around 1890, he met with a Hungarian scholar, Professor Arminius Vambery, whose travel talks were already known to him. In the 1890's Vambery was famous in Eastern Europe for his *History of Hungary*, his autobiography, and his writings about his travels through Central Asia. The two men dined together, and during the course of their conversation, Bram was impressed by the professor's stories about Dracula ''the impaler.'' After Vambery returned to Budapest, Bram wrote to him, requesting more details about the notorious 15th-century prince and the land he lived in. Transylvania, it seemed, would be an ideal setting for a vampire story.

Unfortunately, no correspondence between Vambery and Stoker can be found today. Moreover, a search through all of the professor's published writings fails to reveal any comments on Vlad, Dracula, or vampires.

Whatever information did come from Vambery supplemented items about Dracula that Stoker found in some old books in the British Museum Reading Room. There was, for instance, the Romanian legend stating that ''In Wallachia, Vlad the 5th, son of Vlad the Devil, cut his way to the throne, sabre in hand, and maintained it by the greatest terrorism and tyranny''; and that ''Vlad was created for the part he played; he hated foreigners, he hated the boyars! He hated the people! He massacred, empaled, killed without distinction for his own pleasure and security.''

The Vlad in this legend appeared to be ''der streng a tyrannisch man Dracula'' who reigned simultaneously with Mathias Corvinus, according to a 16th-century work, Munster's *Cosmographia*, which Stoker also found in the museum's library.

178

Seeking material on Transylvania, Stoker gathered all the guide books and survey maps he could find about Eastern Europe. He also explored the folk tales concerning Dracula.

Another important source in his years of preparation was E. Gerard's *Land Beyond the Forest* (1888), which included a discussion of Romanian superstitions. Gerard recorded that:

Even a flawless pedigree will not ensure one against the intrusion of a vampire into their family vault, since every person killed by a Nosferatu (a vampire) becomes likewise a vampire after death, and will continue to suck the blood of other innocent persons 'till the spirit has been exorcised by opening the grave of the suspected person and either driving a stake through the corpse or else firing a pistol shot into the coffin.

So Stoker had his themes and the setting for his story: the dominating figure of the cruel ruler, the vampire cult, and Transylvania. It was time to begin writing.

When *Dracula* was completed, there were references in it to an ''Arminius''— Stoker's way of acknowledging his debt to Professor Arminius Vambery. Of more importance to us, they suggest what information and conclusions the professor had passed on to Stoker. In the novel, the character Dr. Van Helsing—an expert on vampires (with an uneven command of English)—says of Count Dracula:

''. . . when we find the habitation of this man-that-was, we can confine him to his coffin and destroy him, if we obey what we know. But he is clever. I have asked my friend Arminius, of Buda-Pesth University, to make his record; and, from all the means that are, he tell me of what he has been. He must, indeed, have been that Voivode Dracula who won his name against the Turk, over the great river on the very frontier of Turkey-land. If it be so, then was he no common man; for in that time, and for centuries after, he was spoken of as the cleverest and

the most cunning, as well as the bravest of the sons of the 'land beyond the forest.' That mighty brain and that iron resolution went with him to his grave, and are even now arrayed against us. The Draculas were, says Arminius, a great and noble race, though now and again were scions who were held by their coevals to have had dealings with the Evil One. They learned his secrets in the Scholomance, amongst the mountains over Lake Hermanstadt, where the devil claims the tenth scholar as his due. In the records are such words as 'stregoica'—witch, 'ordog,' and 'pokol'—Satan and hell; and in one manuscript this very Dracula is spoken of as 'wampyr.' ''

Shortly before Stoker wrote his famous book, the British Museum had purchased one of the German pamphlets printed in 1491 which related horror tales about Dracula. Surely Stoker must have discovered it there, or been directed to it by Vambery, who was familiar with a similar pamphlet in the library of the University of Budapest. Although the pamphlet does not describe Dracula as a ''wampyr,'' it does call him a cruel tyrant and *wütrich,* an old German term for ''berserker'' or, more literally, ''blood-thirsty monster.'' This presumably was Stoker's cue for transforming Dracula into a vampire. In addition, we learn through Van Helsing's conversation that Vambery was the source for the link between Dracula and ''the Evil One,'' the devil. And, finally, the conversation indicates that Vambery had made the association between the brave, heroic Dracula known through one tradition and the horrifying tyrant known through another.

Dracula begins with the words, ''3 May, Bistritz.'' In the entry that follows, Jonathan Harker records, ''I found that Bistritz, the post town named by Count Dracula, is a fairly well-known place . . . a very interesting old place.'' The town marks, as described in the novel, the beginning of the Borgo Pass, which leads into Moldavia—a true description of a real location. (Indeed, after *Dracula* was published, Stoker was complimented for his accurate, *firsthand* descriptions of a country which he had never actually seen.)

180

The link between Stoker's Dracula and the region of Bistrita is not wholly imaginary. There was an old Szeckler family in this region. The family was called Ordog, which is a Hungarian translation of the word *Dracul,* or devil. In the novel the people of the Bistrita region speak the words ''Ordog, Satan'' before Jonathan Harker takes off in the carriage to the Borgo Pass.

The major elements of Bram Stoker's ritual acts against vampires correspond with Eastern European folk beliefs. According to James G. Frazer: ''Among the Romanians in Transylvania . . . in very obstinate cases of vampirism it is recommended to cut off the head and replace it in the coffin with the mouth filled with garlic; or to extract the heart and burn it, strewing the ashes over the grave.'' In *Dracula,* as in Romanian folklore, garlic has the power to protect men against vampires and a vampire can be killed by decapitation and a stake driven through the heart.

In Stoker's novel Dracula appears in the form of mist or phosphorescent specks; the Romanian vampire of folklore also sometimes comes as points of light shimmering in the air. Stoker's vampire can turn into a wolf or a bat, particularly the latter. The Transylvanian Szeklers, self-supposed descendants of an East Asian race older than the Magyars, link the bat with vampirism in their folklore. Following Slavic folklore, Stoker's vampire moves only at night, casts no reflection in a mirror, and is repelled by the sign of the cross.

These and many other details reveal the range and accuracy of Stoker's research. The persistence with which Stoker worked is expressed via Van Helsing's remark ''I have studied, over and over again since they came into my hands, all the papers relating to this monster.''

Bram Stoker, creator of Count Dracula, re-creator of the devilish-and-heroic Prince Dracula, died in 1912. Sir Henry Irving had predeceased him by some years, leaving Bram at a loss. The death certificate lists the official cause of Stoker's death as ''exhaustion.''

Seal of the town of Lugoj, Hungary, birthplace of Bela Lugosi.

CHAPTER

9

Beyond the Grave

Where is the precise location of Dracula's tomb within the Monastery of Snagov? Does it, in fact, lie there as popular tradition will have it?

In 1931, George Florescu and the archaeologist Dinu Rosetti were officially assigned by Romania's Commission on Historic Monuments to dig around the monastery and elsewhere on the island. Their findings, published in a fascinating monograph, *Diggings Around Snagov*, included various artifacts showing that the island was the site of an ancient pre-Dacian settlement; also a great number of skulls, tending to confirm popular traditions about the crimes committed at Snagov from the 15th century onward; and numerous gold and silver coins of all kinds, indicating the use of Snagov as a secret treasury and mint for boyars and princes alike since Dracula's time.

One of the sites investigated by the Florescu-Rosetti team was a stone beneath the altar, which, according to tradition, marked the place where Dracula lay buried. Popular legend had various explanations as to why this was

183

Stone over the Dracula tomb near altar.

Existing church at Snagov, 1933.

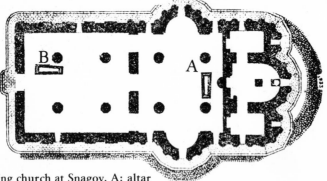

Floor plan of existing church at Snagov. A: altar
tomb. B: grave on north side.

the location of his grave. First, it was claimed that the monks had the remains of his body placed close to the altar so that his troubled soul could have the advantage of perpetual prayers. Secondly, this particular tombstone, though not of princely proportion and lacking an inscription, was more ambitious than that of several others. The stone was finally removed, but in the large grave below, no headless skeleton was found, instead only ox bones and various Dacian artifacts.

Further exploration—this time just inside the entrance on the northern side of the church—revealed an unopened grave of exactly the size of the altar tomb. When opened, it was found to contain a casket still partially covered by a purple shroud embroidered with gold. Both coffin and covering were mostly rotted away. Within the coffin lay a badly deteriorated skeleton; fragments of a faded red silk garment suitable for a person of at least boyar rank, with a ring sewn onto one sleeve; a golden crown ornamented with cloisonne and having claws clasping a jewel; and a necklace with the barely perceptible motif of a serpent. All of the grave's contents have unfortunately, and mysteriously, disappeared from the History Museum of Bucharest, where they were deposited.

Rosetti told us that he believed that this second grave, if it was not the original site of Dracula's burial, was at least the final resting place. The two graves had the same proportions—the stone of the one below the altar seeming to fit exactly the grave near the north entrance of the chapel. The necklace with the serpent device resembled others found in the Nuremberg area, and undoubtedly was some insigne of the Order of the Dragon, to which Dracula belonged. The red silk fragments were in accord with the Hungarian-style shirt worn by Dracula in the Ambras portrait. The lost ring could have been either a princely ring or a romantic token. During Dracula's time, one of the dying customs of courtly love in Western Europe was the practice of a knight, when going forth to joust in a tournament, to wear on his sleeve his lady's ring. Dracula could well have known this custom from his youthful years in Germany. But

185

whose ring was it? His Hungarian wife's, or some now unknown lover's? Whoever bestowed this tender token of courtly love, it is a strange item to find in the grave of such a prince.

The absence of a headless skeleton and the presence of the animal bones in the grave near the altar are the most mystifying findings of all. They have provoked a debate among the experts that continues today. As in the case of the mysterious disappearance of the body of Alexander I of Russia, dozens of opinions have been voiced, sometimes almost violently. We are inclined to accept the *original* grave as being the one near the altar, the one approved by local folklore, which has succeeded in giving a clue to many enigmas connected with Dracula. At various times village traditions about tombstones have led to the identification of historic personalities. In the old church of Curtea de Arges, for example, it was long observed that the faithful persisted in standing at a certain place to the right of the altar for no other reason than that it was the place where their elders worshipped. They also lit their candles there. An enterprising young archaeologist excavated that particular spot and discovered the unmarked tomb of one of Wallachia's early princes. At Snagov the peasants for many years were similarly accustomed to stand close to the altar. According to legend, they took their places there to express contempt for the tyrant by walking over his grave.

How and when the remains might have been transferred is suggested by a local priest from the neighboring village of Turbati, the Reverend G. Dumitriu. According to him, at the close of the 18th century a Wallachian Metropolitan by the name of Filaret, under the pretext of some repairs on the church, ordered the desecration of Dracula's body. The body and the other items mentioned above were then transferred from the more exalted position near the altar and reinterred in an unmarked place near the entrance of the church where all could trample upon them. The Greeks were not particularly concerned, as were the Romanians, in praying for Dracula's soul. All inscriptions were removed, and a plain slab was substituted for the engraved one. As

ɔmb traditionally assigned to Dracula. This ɪmb is near the altar of the existing church at ιagov. Photo made in 1933 at time of exvations.

General view of graves—not including Dracula's—excavated at Snagov.

an additional gesture of contempt, the ox bones were substituted for Dracula's skeleton, thereby compounding a hoax with a sacrilege. "Thus," adds the priest in an article in which he published his theory, at the rear of the chapel of Snagov "lie the earthly remains of Dracula . . . without trace of either an inscription or memento, under some cold stone that gets yearly trampled by the weight of the tourists." All this to wipe away forever the memory of that degenerate prince.

Had the tomb not been desecrated in the particular way related by the Reverend Dumitriu (and his theory does jibe with the dates of certain repairs made in the altar area during the late 1700's), one could still safely conjecture that since the tomb of Dracula looked more ambitious than most it was bound to have been opened and pillaged by the peasants during the period of neglect and abandonment that followed the closing of Snagov as a state prison.

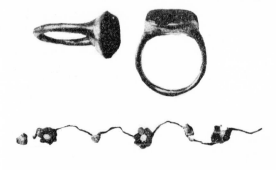

Items found in Dracula's "second grave": pieces of man's silk vest; fragments of gold crown; lady's ring that was sewn to sleeve fragment.

188

Historical commonsense suggests that Dracula, who in spite of his misdeeds was after all a prince, would be assigned an important burial place in the church—therefore, one close to the altar—and that his tomb should be a little more ornate than that for other mortals. Thus, on all these grounds we are inclined to accept the traditional location of Dracula's grave as the original.

There is really no need, however, to strain after explanations for the possible transfer of graves or, if the second grave is not Dracula's, the disappearance of his body. They almost seem to suggest themselves. Given Dracula's invidious reputation, the general horror in which his name was held in the Orthodox world, and the desecrations committed on the island at various times, it may even be unreasonable to expect that his tomb would have survived intact. Yet, after all the explanations about Dracula's tomb have been considered, somehow the mystery lingers on.

We have attempted to recreate the *REAL* Dracula as scientifically as the available sources will allow. We have worked diligently and hard. We have consulted every domestic source of the period available. We have ploughed our way through German, Slavonic, Byzantine, and other foreign documentation. We have studied the traditions of the people, closely collaborated with historians in Bucharest and historians at the local level. Now, having fathered the first massive compilation on Dracula—a body of information which ought on all accounts to have resolved many of the riddles that we began with—we must confess that we have not entirely succeeded in bridging the gap between myth and reality, in reconstructing the full personality of Dracula, in clearing up the numerous ambiguities which stand in the way of absolute historical character. So why not, at the end of our story, take refuge in the myth rather than in the historical reality?

Freed from his monastery or castle, traveling in the shape of man during the day, flying like a bat at night, Dracula rises again to terrify and exercise his vampirical powers. Thus liberated with his powers for evil, the vampire crosses the frontier of his own country and attempts, as he did in Stoker's novel, the conquest of England itself. His frontiers have become infinitely extended. It is this Dracula, the man of fiction, not the historical Dracula, who has conquered the imagination of the Western world. Without him, the real Dracula would be greatly reduced in size, tyrannical and bloodthirsty as he was. The ultimate fascination of the Dracula story lies in its myth, not in its reality. Blood is in fact the only valid connection between the two.

The mystery of Dracula endures. It lives in the vampire fictions, which someday may encourage another Harker to make the scenic journey to the town of Bistrita in northern Transylvania in the direction of the Borgo Pass, or impel some zoologist to study the incidence of large bats in the Carpathian mountains. It continues in Dracula's own castle, where none dare trespass at night and where the peasants have unfolded stories of the plaintive voice of Dracula's first wife at a place in the river Arges reddened by a vague subterranean object. The mystery of Dracula persists in the question of whether he exemplifies some spirit of evil that all men encounter—of whether Professor Van Helsing was an expert as much on human experience as on vampires when he said:

"My friends . . . it is a terrible task that we undertake, and there may be consequence to make the brave shudder. For if we fail in this our fight he must surely win; and then where end we? . . . to fail here is not mere life or death. It is that we become as him; that we henceforward become foul things of the night like him—without heart or conscience."

The warnings of the peasants about the perils of seeking the "great undead" may derive from more than a pedestrian sense of caution—may be warnings from the spirit of Dracula himself. For us a signal finally came through as we were on the point of reaching the last few yards separating us from the castle. Fortunately, it was restrained, spelling a broken hip and six months in hospital for one of our members—it could have spelled death. Was it Dracula's way of saying that despite the ruins of his castle, he still rules in some other, unearthly domain?

APPENDIX I

GERMAN STORIES

Translation by Raymond T. McNally of Manuscript No. 806 at the Monastery Library of St. Gall, Switzerland.

1. Once the old governor had the old Dracul killed; and Dracula and his brother, having renounced their own faith, promised and swore to protect and uphold the Christian faith. [*Reference is to assassination of Dracula's father.*]

2. During these same years Dracula was put on the throne and became lord of Wallachia; he immediately had Ladislaus Waboda [*Vladislav II*] killed, who had been ruler of that region. [*The killing of Vladislav II occurred in 1456.*]

3. After that Dracula immediately had villages and castles burned in Transylvania near Hermannstadt [*Sibiu*], and he had fortifications in Transylvania and villages by the name of the monastery Holtznuwdorff, Holtznetya [*Hosmanul*] completely burned to ashes.

4. He had Berkendorf [*Benesti*] in Wuetzerland [*Tara Birsei*] burned; those men, women, and children, large and small, whom he had not burned at the time, he took with him and put them in chains and had them all impaled.

5. Dracula imprisoned merchants and carriage-drivers from Wuetzerland on a holiday and on that same holiday he had many impaled. [*Confirmed by internal Romanian sources.*]

6. Young boys and others from many lands were sent to Wallachia, in order to learn the language and other things. He brought them together and betrayed them. He let them all come together in a room and had them burned. There were four hundred in the room. [*Confirmed by internal Romanian sources.*]

7. He had a big family uprooted from the smallest to the largest, children, friends, brothers, sisters, and he had them all impaled. [*Execution of Wallachian boyar family by name of Albu is confirmed elsewhere.*]

8. He also had his men bury a man naked up to the navel, then he had them shoot at him. He also had some others roasted and some skinned alive.

9. He also captured the young Darin [*Dan*]. Later on he allowed him to go through his priestly function, and when he had completed it all, then he had him make a grave according to the custom of Christians, and he had his body slaughtered by the grave. [*Dan's execution is a historical fact confirmed elsewhere.*]

10. Ambassadors, numbering fifty-five, were sent to Wallachia to Dracula from the king of Hungary and from the Saxons and in Transylvania. There Dracula had the lords held captive for five weeks and had stakes made for their hostel. And they thought that they would all be impaled. Oh, how greatly troubled they were! He held them so long, so that they might betray him. And he set off with all his army and went to Wuetzerland. Early one morning he came to the villages, castles, and towns. All those whom he overcame, he also destroyed and had all the grain and wheat burned. And he led away all those whom he had captured outside the city called Kranstatt [*Kronstadt; Brasov*] near the chapel called St. Jacob [*Tampa Hill*]. And at that time Dracula rested there and had the entire suburb burned. Also as the day came, early in the morning, all those whom he had taken captive, men and women, young and old children, he had impaled on the hill by the chapel and all around the hill, and under them he proceeded to eat at table and get his joy in this way. [*Undoubtedly these ambassadors were men sent by King Mathias to learn Dracula's precise relationship with the Turks.*]

11. Once he had St. Bartholomew's Church [*in Brasov*] burned, then he also stole and took away the vestments and chalices. Once he sent one of his captains to a great village called Zeyding [*Zeinding; Codlea*] to burn it, but that same captain could not burn it, because the villagers resisted. Then he went to his lord and said: "Lord, I was not able to bring myself to do what you ordered me to do." Then he took him and hoisted him up on a stake. [*Attack on this church and*

execution of the Wallachian captain who was unable to capture fortress of Codlea are historical facts appearing in other sources.]

12. Once he impaled all the merchants and other men with merchandise, the entire merchant class from Wuetzerland near to Thunow and to Pregel, six hundred of them with all their goods and he took the goods for himself.

13. Once he had a great pot made with two handles and over it a staging device with planks and through it he had holes made, so that a man could fall through them with his head. Then he had a great fire made underneath it and had water poured into the pot and had men boiled in this way. He had many men and women, young and old, impaled.

14. Also he came again to Siebenburgen [*means the seven fortresses of Transylvania*] to attack Talmetz [*Talmetch, near Sibiu*]. There he had men hacked up like cabbage and he had those whom he took back to Wallachey [*Wallachia*] as captives, cruelly and in various ways, impaled.

15. Once he had thought up terrifying and frightening and unspeakable tortures, so he had mothers impaled and nursing children, and he had one-year or over two-year-old children impaled. He also had children taken from their mothers' breasts and also the mothers from the children. He also had the breasts of the mother cut off one from the other and pushed the children's heads through and impaled them. And he caused many other sufferings and such great pain and tortures as all the bloodthirsty persecutors of Christendom, such as Herod, Nero and Diocletian and other pagans had never thought up or made such martyrs as did this bloodthirsty berserker.

16. Once he had humans impaled, usually indiscriminately, young and old, women and men. People also tried to defend themselves with hands and feet and they twisted around and twitched like frogs. After that he had them also impaled and spoke often in this language: "Oh, what great gracefulness they exhibit!" And they were pagans, Jews, Christians, heretics, and Wallachians.

17. Once he caught a gypsy who had stolen. Then the other gypsies came to him and begged Dracula to release him to them. Dracula said: "He should hang, and you must hang him." They said: "That is not our custom." Dracula had the gypsy boiled in a pot, and when he was cooked, he forced them to eat him, flesh and bone.

18. Once a nobleman was sent to him, who came to him among the people whom he had impaled. There, Dracula walked under them and gazed upon them, and there were as many as a great forest. And he asked Dracula why he walked around under the stench. Dracula asked: "Do you mind the stink?" The other man said: "Yes." So Dracula immediately had him impaled and hoisted him up high in the air, so that he would not smell the stench.

19. Once a priest had preached that sins could not be forgiven until one made good the injustice done. Then Dracula had that same priest invited to his house and set him at his table. Then the lord had simmel bread put into his food. The priest took the broken bread up with his tablespoon. Then the lord spoke about how he had preached about sins, etc., etc. The priest said: "Lord, it is true." He said: "Why then do you take from me my bread, which I have broken into the food?" And he immediately had him impaled.

20. Once he invited all his landlords and noblemen in his land to his house, and when the meal was over, he turned to the noblest men and asked them how many voevods or lords they remembered who had ruled that same land. One answered him as many as he could think of. So did the other lords, both young and old, and each among them asked how many lords they could recall. One answered fifty; another, thirty; one, twenty; similarly, twelve, so that none was so young as to remember seven. So he had all those same lords impaled, and there were five hundred of them.

21. Once he had a mistress who announced that she was pregnant, so he had her looked at by

another woman, who could not comprehend how she could be pregnant. So he took the mistress and cut her up from under to her breast and said: "Let the world see where I have been and where my fruit lay." He also had similar things cut or pierced and did other inhuman things which are said about him.

22. In the year 1460, on the morning of St. Bartholomew's Day, Dracula came through the forest with his servants and had all the Wallachians of both sexes tracked down, as people say outside of the village of Humilasch [*Amlasch*], and he was able to bring so many together that he let them get piled up in a bunch and he cut them up like cabbage with swords, sabers and knives; as for their chaplain and the others whom he did not kill there, he led them back home and had them impaled. And he had the village completely burned up with their goods and it is said that there were more than 30,000 men.

23. In the year of Our Lord 1462 once Dracula came to the large city of Schylta [*Nicopolis*], where he had more than 25,000 people of all kinds of ethnic groups killed, Christians, pagans, etc. Among them were the most beautiful women and maidens, who had been taken captive by his courtiers. They begged Dracula to give them to them as honorable wives. Dracula did not want to do this and ordered that all of them together with the courtiers should be cut up like cabbage. And that he did because he had become obliged to pay tribute to the Turkish sultan, who had demanded tribute from him. Immediately Dracula let his people know that he wished to give over the tribute personally to the sultan. The people there were overjoyed, so he let his people come to him in large groups one after the other and he let all his courtiers ride with him. And then he had these people all killed. Also he had the same region called Pallgarey [*Wulgerey*] completely burned. He also had others nailed by their hair and in all there were 25,000 not counting those whom he had burned.

24. Once messengers from Hermannstadt saw the dead and impaled in Wallachia like a huge forest, aside from those whom he had roasted, boiled, and skinned.

25. Once he rounded up an entire region called Fugrasch [*Fagaras*], women, men and children, and led them to Wallachia where he had them impaled. Similarly, he had the heads cut off his men who had helped him to bury his treasure.

26. Once he had several lords beheaded and took their bodies and had food cooked up with them. After that he had their friends invited to his house and he gave them something to eat from that food and said to them: "Now you are eating the bodies of your friends." After that he impaled them.

27. Once he had seen a worker in a short shirt and said to him: "Have you a wife at home?" He said: "Yes." Dracula said: "Bring her here to me." Then he said to her: "What do you do?" She said: "I wash, cook, spin, etc." He immediately had her impaled, because she had not made her man a long shirt, so that one could not see the seam. Dracula at once gave him another wife and ordered that she should make a long shirt for her man, or he would also have her impaled.

28. Once he had a donkey impaled and on the earth above it a Franciscan monk whom he had met.

29. Once some three hundred gypsies came into his land; he thereupon took the best three out and had them roasted and made the other gypsies eat, and said to them: "Thus each of you must eat the others until there are none left," or he sent them against the Turks, and fought with them. They were very willing to go there, where he wanted them to go. Then he did something: he clothed them all in cowhide, and similarly their horses as well. And as they came upon one another, the Turkish horses shied away and fled because of the cowhide clothing which their horses did not like and the Turks fled to some water and the gypsies after them, with the result that they all drowned.

30. Once he also had the poor people who were in his land invited to his house; after they had eaten there, he had them all burned in a small city. There were two hundred of them.

31. Once he had young children roasted and forced their mothers to eat them. He cut the breasts off women and forced their husbands to eat them; after that he had the men impaled.

32. Once several Wahlen [*Western ambassadors*] were sent to him. When they came to him, they bowed and took off their hats and under them they had brown and red berets or caps, which they did not take off. So he asked them why they had not taken off their caps or berets. They said: "Lord, it is not our custom. We never take them off before our ruler." He said: "Well, I wish to strengthen you in your custom." And as they thanked his grace, he had them take good strong nails and had them nailed around the caps into the head, so that they could not take them off. In this way he strengthened them in their custom. [*In most versions, including Romanian, the victims are Turkish ambassadors.*]

APPENDIX II

RUSSIAN STORIES

Translation by Raymond T. McNally of the oldest Russian manuscript about Dracula: MS 11/1088 in the Kirillov-Belozersky Monastery Collection at the Saltykov-Schredin Public Library, Leningrad. First translation of this document into a Western language.

Among the very few authentic signed documents which have been preserved from the late 15th century is the Russian "Story about Dracula." Copies of it were made from the 15th to the 18th century in Russia. It is one of the first instances of belletristic writing in Russian literature, and the historian Nicholas Karamzin has called it his country's "first historical novel."

This manuscript was written by the monk Efrosin from the Kirillov-Belozersky Monastery in northern Russia in the year 1490. In it the monk states that he copied the story from another manuscript penned in 1486. No one knows who the author of that earlier manuscript was. Most scholarly opinion has focused upon a Russian diplomat who was at the Hungarian court in the 1480's, Fedor Kurytsin; he could have picked up the tale there since Dracula had been a captive of the Hungarian king from 1462 to 1474; moreover the monk states that the earlier author had seen one of the sons of Dracula.

Whoever the original author was, he was more disturbed by the prince's abandonment of Orthodoxy than by his cruelties. While in prison Dracula "forsook the light" of the Orthodox Church and accepted the "darkness" of the Roman Church because he was too attracted to the "sweetness" of this earthly life and not motivated enough by concern for the next one. Thus, the story has a marked religious tone.

The manuscript supports the notion of a "cruel but just" autocrat in its presentation of Dracula. All that this tyrant had done, however cruel it may have appeared by the standards of the average person, was necessary for the good of the state. In order to ward off not only the Turkish invaders but also the continual threat of opposition from the aristocratic boyars in his own land, Dracula had to take harsh measures. Obviously, the manuscript was written to indicate support of the autocratic ruler in Russia at the time, Ivan III, known as Ivan the Great. Here is the text:

1. There lived in the Wallachian lands a Christian prince of the Greek faith who was called Dracula in the Wallachian language, which means devil in our language, for he was as cruelly clever as was his name and so was his life.

   Once some ambassadors from the Turkish sultan came to him. When they entered his palace and bowed to him, as was their custom, they did not take their caps from their heads and Dracula asked them: "Why have you acted so? You ambassadors have come to a great prince and you have shamed me." The ambassadors answered, "Such is the custom which our land has, Lord." And Dracula told them, "Well, I want to strengthen you in your law. Behave bravely." And he ordered that their caps be nailed to their heads with small iron nails. And then he allowed them to go. He said, "Go tell your lord, for he is a cultured man: let him accept this shame from us. For you seem to think that we are not cultured. Let him not impose his customs upon other rulers who will not accept them, but let him keep his customs in his own land." [*This episode confirmed in Romanian and German sources.*]

2. The Turkish sultan was angered and he set out with an army against Dracula. He invaded his land with overwhelming force. Dracula gathered his whole army and attacked the Turks during the night, and he killed a great many of them. But he could not conquer them with his few men against an army so much greater than his, so eventually Dracula drew back.

   He examined those who had fought with him against the Turks. Those wounded in the front he honored and made them heroes and gave them gifts. But those who were wounded in the back he ordered to be impaled from the bottom up and said: "You are not a man but a woman." And when he set against the Turks once again, he spoke to his entire army in this way, "Whoever wants to think of death, let him not come with me but let him remain here." And the Turkish sultan, hearing of this, retreated with great shame. He lost innumerable men, but he never dared again to set out against Dracula. [*The night attack is confirmed by an eye-witness report.*]

3. The sultan sent an ambassador once to Dracula, in order that he be given the yearly tribute. Dracula greatly honored this ambassador and showed him the whole treasury which he had. And said, "I not only wish to give the sultan the yearly tax, but I also wish to go in his service with my whole army and with my whole treasury. I shall do as he commands and you shall announce this to your emperor, so that when I shall place myself at his disposal, he will give orders in his whole land that no harm should come to me or to my men. And I shall come to my sultan, my liege, quickly after you get back. And I shall bring him the yearly tribute, and I shall personally place myself at his disposal."

When the sultan heard from his ambassador that Dracula wished to come into his service, he honored the ambassador and gave him gifts, and was happy because at that time the Turkish sultan was at war with many of the eastern countries. Immediately the sultan sent to all his fortresses and towns and throughout his land the message that when Dracula comes, no one should do him any harm. On the contrary, they should honor him. Dracula set out with his whole army. With him were his various yeomen. And he was greeted and greatly honored by the emperor. And he traveled throughout the Turkish empire for about five days. But then suddenly instead of helping the sultan, he began to rob and attack the towns and the villages. And he captured many prisoners whose heads he cut off. Some he impaled, others he cut in two, and others he burned. The whole country which he penetrated was laid to waste. He allowed no one to remain alive, not even the babes in the arms of their mothers. But others, that is, those who were Christian, he spared and set them up in his own lands. After taking much booty, he returned to Wallachia. And he set a few prisoners free and said, "Go and tell your sultan what you have seen. As much as I could, I have served him. If my service was pleasing to him, I shall serve him again with as much power as I can." And the sultan could do nothing against him and fled in shame. [*This episode confirmed by historical documents.*]

4. Dracula so hated evil in his land that if someone stole, lied or committed some injustice, he was not likely to stay alive. Whether he was a nobleman, or a priest or a monk or a common man, and even if he had great wealth, he could not escape death if he were dishonest. And he was so feared that the peasants say that in a certain place, near the source of the river, there was a fountain; at this fountain at the source of this river, there came many travelers from many lands and all these people came to drink at the fountain, because the water was cool and sweet. Dracula had purposely put this fountain in a deserted place, and had set a cup wonderfully wrought in gold and whoever wished to drink the water, had to drink it from this gold cup and had to put it back in its place. And so long as this cup was there no one dared to steal it. [*Romanian folklore stresses Dracula's maintenance of law and order.*]

5. Once Dracula ordered throughout the land that whoever was old or sick or poor should come to him. And there gathered at the palace a huge multitude of poor and old people, who expected a great act of mercy. And he ordered that all these miserable people be gathered together, in a large palace which was prepared with this idea in mind. And he ordered that they be given food and drink in accordance with their wishes. So they began to eat, and they became happy. Later on Dracula personally came to see them and spoke to them in the following way: "What else do you need?" And they answered him in unison, "Our good lord, God knows how to give, and your highness surely understands the wishes of God." He then said to them, "Do you want me to make you without any further cares, so that you have no other wants in this world?" And

they all expected some great gift and they answered, "We wish it so, my lord." Then he ordered that the palace be locked and he set it on fire, and all of them perished within it. Later he told his nobles, "Know that I have done this so that these unfortunate people will have no further burdens, and so that there should be no more poor in my land but only rich people, and in the second place I freed these people so that they no longer suffer in this world either because of poverty, or because of sickness." [*Dracula's killing of the sick and poor is a favorite theme in Romanian folklore. One critic has suggested that the prince's motive was control of the plague.*]

6. Once there came from Hungary two Roman Catholic monks looking for charity. Dracula ordered them to be honored. And he first of all called one of these monks down below into the courtyard, where there were countless people on stakes and spokes of wheels. And he asked the monk, "Have I done well? How do you judge those on the stakes?" And the monk answered, "No, lord, you have done badly. You punish without mercy. It is fitting that a master be merciful, and all these unfortunate people whom you have impaled are martyrs." Dracula then called the second monk and posed the same question. The second monk answered, "You, lord, have been assigned by God as a ruler to punish those who commit crimes and to reward those who do good. Certainly they have committed some crime and have been punished in accordance with their misdeeds." Dracula then recalled the first monk and told him, "Why have you left your monastery and your cell, to walk and travel at the courts of great rulers? You know nothing. Just now you told me that these people are martyrs. I also want to make a martyr out of you so that you will be together with these other martyrs." And he ordered that he be impaled from the bottom up. But to the other monk, he ordered that he be given fifty ducats of gold and told him, "You are an understanding man." And he ordered that a carriage be prepared for him in order that he be driven with honor to the Hungarian border. [*Note different ending in Romanian Story No. 6. Note, too, that the Russian version seems designed to support one-man rule, however cruel.*]

7. Once a merchant, a foreign guest from Hungary, came to Dracula's capital city. Following his command, the merchant left his carriage on the street of the city before the palace and his wares in the carriage and he himself slept in the palace. Someone came and stole 160 golden ducats from the carriage. The merchant went to Dracula and told him about the loss of the gold. And Dracula told him, "Wait, this night your gold will be returned." And he ordered his henchmen to look for the thief throughout the city and said, "If you do not find the thief, I will destroy the city." And he ordered that the gold be placed back in the carriage during the night. But with one additional gold ducat. The merchant got up and found his gold and he counted the pieces once, twice, and found one additional golden ducat. He went immediately to Dracula and told him, "My lord, I have found the gold, but look there is one additional golden ducat which does not belong to me." And then they also brought the thief who had the original gold with him. And Dracula told the merchant, "Go in peace. If you had not told me about the additional golden ducat, I would have been ready to impale you, together with the thief." [*This tale reoccurs in Romanian folklore. Russian version is obviously meant to stress Dracula's sense of justice.*]

8. If a woman made love with a man who was not her husband Dracula ordered that her vagina be cut and he skinned her alive and tied her skin to a pole. And the skin was usually hanging on the pole in the middle of the city right there in the market place. He did the same thing with young girls who had not preserved their virginity and also widows. In some cases he cut the nipples of their breasts. In other cases he took the skins from their vagina and he placed an iron poker, reddened by fire, up their vaginas so far upwards that the iron bar emerged from their mouths. They remained naked, tied to a pole until the flesh and bones detached themselves or served as

food for the birds. [*A favorite theme in the German pamphlets is Dracula's austere standards for women.*]

9. Once Dracula was walking down a street and he saw a poor man with a shirt torn and dirty. And he asked that man, "Have you got a wife?" And he answered, "I have, Lord." Then Dracula said, "Take me to your house, so that I can see her." And he went to the house of the man, saw that he had a young and healthy wife, and he told her husband, "Did you work this spring, did you sow flax?" And the husband answered, "Lord, I have much flax." And he showed much flax to him. Then Dracula said to his wife, "Why are you lazy towards your husband? It is his duty to sow and to reap and to feed you. But it is your duty to make nice clean clothes for your husband. But you do not even wish to clean his shirt, though you are quite healthy. You are guilty, not your husband. If your husband had not sown or reaped, then your husband would be guilty." And Dracula ordered that both her hands be cut off and that her body be impaled. [*See comment for Story 8.*]

10. Once Dracula was feasting amid the corpses of many men who had been impaled around his table. And he liked to eat in their midst. There was a servant who stood right in front of him. But he could not stand the smell of the corpses any longer. So he plugged his nose. And he drew his head to one side. Dracula asked him, "Why are you doing that?" The servant answered, "My lord, I cannot endure this stench." Dracula immediately ordered that he be impaled, saying, "You must live way up there, where the stench does not reach you." [*Dracula's macabre sense of humor is highlighted in German pamphlets.*]

11. On another occasion an ambassador, a great nobleman from Matei the Hungarian king, came to Dracula's court. Dracula ordered him to stay at his royal table in the midst of the corpses. And set up in front of the table was a very high thick golden stake. And Dracula asked, "Tell me, why did I set up this stake?" The ambassador was very afraid and said, "My lord, it would seem that some nobleman has committed a crime and you want to reserve a more honorable death for him." And Dracula said, "You spoke fairly. You are indeed a royal ambassador of a great ruler, I have made this stake for you." The ambassador answered, "My lord, if I have committed some crime worthy of death, do what you wish because you are a fair ruler and you would not be guilty of my death but I myself would be." Dracula broke out laughing and said, "If you had not answered me thus, you would really be on that very stake yourself." And he honored him greatly and gave him gifts and allowed him to go, saying, "You truly can go as an envoy to the capitals of great rulers, because you are well versed in knowing how to talk with great rulers. But others let them not talk with me, but let them first learn how to speak to a great ruler." [*See comment for Story 10.*]

12. Dracula had the following custom: whenever an ambassador came to him from the sultan or the king and he was not dressed in a distinguished way and did not know how to answer the twisted questions, he impaled them, saying, "I am not guilty of your death but your own master, or you yourself. Don't say anything bad to me. If your master knows that you are slow-witted and that you are not properly versed and has sent you to my court, to me a wise ruler, then your own ruler has killed you. And if somehow you would dare to come as an ignorant boor to my court, then you yourself have committed suicide." For such an ambassador he made a high and golden stake and he impaled him in front of all and to the master of such a foolish ambassador he wrote the following words: "No longer send to a wise prince a man of such a small mind and a man so uncultured." [*See comment for Story 10.*]

13. Dracula ordered his artisans to make some iron bells. Dracula ordered these bells to be filled with gold and put in the river. And Dracula ordered that these artisans be killed, so that no one would know the crime committed by him except for the devil whose name he bore. [*The story of*

the person who kills the workmen who hid his treasure occurs the world over, thus this episode can be considered as a mythical one.]

14. On one occasion the Hungarian King Matei set out with an army against Dracula. He fought against Dracula and in the battle they captured Dracula alive, because Dracula was betrayed by his own men. And Dracula was brought to the Hungarian King, who ordered him thrown in jail. And he remained in jail at Vishegrad on the Danube up from Buda for twelve years. And in Wallachia the Hungarian King ordered another prince to rule. [*Dracula's presence in Hungary is confirmed by Hungarian sources, reports by papal representatives in Buda, and the memoirs of Pius II.*]

15. After the death of that prince the Hungarian King sent a messenger to Dracula who was in jail to ask him whether he would like to become prince in Wallachia as he had been before and if so, he should accept the Latin faith and if he does not wish it, he wishes to die in jail. Dracula, however, loved the sweetness of the earthly world much more than that of the eternal world, and abandoned Orthodoxy and forsook the truth and light and received the darkness. Unfortunately, he could not endure the temporary difficulties of the prison and he must have been prepared for the unending sufferings of hell by abandoning our Orthodox faith and accepting the deceiving Latin faith. The king did not only give him the rule in Wallachia but also gave him his sister as a wife. From her he had two sons, he lived for another ten years and in this heresy he ended his life. [*Sources given in comment above confirm Dracula's restoration in 1476, and his heresy in eyes of the Orthodox Church.*]

16. It was said about him that even when he was in jail, he could not abandon his bad habits. He caught mice and bought birds in the market. And he tortured them in this way: some he simply impaled, others he cut their heads off, and others he plucked their feathers out and let them go. And he also taught himself to sew and in this way he fed himself while in jail. [*This incident is not recorded in any other known sources.*]

17. When the king freed him from jail, and brought him to Buda where he gave him a house located in Pest, which is across from Buda, and at a time when he had not yet seen the king, it so happened that a criminal sought refuge in Dracula's courtyard in order to save himself. And those chasing the criminal came into Dracula's courtyard and began looking for him. Dracula rose up, took his sword and cut off the head of the prefect who was holding the criminal and liberated the criminal. The other guards fled and went to the municipal judge and told him what had happened. The judge and his men went to the Hungarian King to complain against Dracula. The king sent a messenger to ask him: ''Why have you done this crime?'' Dracula answered in this way: ''I did not commit a crime. He committed suicide. Anyone will perish in this way should he thievingly invade the house of a great ruler. If this prefect had come to me and had explained the situation to me, and if the criminal had been found in my own home, I myself would have delivered the criminal to him or would have pardoned him of death.'' The king was told about this, and began to laugh and wonder about his candor. [*Not found elsewhere.*]

18. The end of Dracula came in this way: while he was ruling Wallachia, the Turks invaded the country and began to loot. Dracula attacked the Turks and put them to flight. Dracula's army began to kill the Turks without mercy and chase them out of the country. Out of sheer joy Dracula ascended the hill in order to see how his men were killing the Turks. Detached from his army in this way and from his men, he disguised himself as a Turk. Those in his immediate vicinity thought that he was a Turk and hit him with a lance. Dracula, seeing that he was being attacked by his own men, immediately killed five of his would-be assassins; then he was killed by many arrows and thus he died. [*That Dracula died in 1476 is certain; whether he died in the circumstances related here is not known.*]

19. The king took his sister and the two sons of Dracula to Buda in Hungary. One of these sons still lives with the king's son, the other was with the bishop of Oradea and has died in our time. I saw the third son, the eldest, whose name was Mikhail, in Buda. He fled from the Turkish sultan to the King of Hungary. Dracula had him by a certain woman when he was unmarried. Steven of Moldavia, in accord with the wish of the king, helped establish in Wallachia a prince's son called Vlad. This same Vlad was in his youth a monk, later a priest, and subsequently the abbot of a monastery. He then took the final vows and was set up as a prince and married. He married the wife of the prince who ruled a little later after Dracula, and who was killed by Steven Valacu [*"the Wallachian"; perhaps this reference should have been to Steven the Great*]. He took the latter's wife and now rules Wallachia, the same Vlad who previously was a monk and abbot. This was first written on February 13, 1486; later, on January 28, 1490, I have transcribed [*the text*] a second time, I, the sinner Efrosin. [*The historical references here are fairly accurate, Dracula's son here called "Mikhail" was also known as Mihnea. Specific mention of Vlad "a former monk" as "the present ruler" points to Vlad the Monk and supports authenticity of the date of the manuscript.*]

APPENDIX III

ROMANIAN STORIES

Translations by Radu Florescu of folktales handed down by word of mouth. First rendering of this material into another language.

One of the central points made in this book is that the general themes in the oral Romanian folktales concur with those in the printed German and the manuscript Russian sources dating to the 15th and 16th centuries. Since the Romanian narratives are longer, often containing a moral, only a few examples are presented here.

1. *THE FOREIGN MERCHANT.* [In Romanian folklore there are three variants of this story. Variant A is closest to Russian story No. 7. Variant B is very Romanianized and probably developed later; for instance, the Romanian currency *lei* are cited instead of *ducats*. Variant C takes a new form altogether, thus it, too, is probably a more recent development. It should be noted that Variant C shows that in Romania itself the name Dracula was associated with ''The Impaler.'']

Variant A: When Dracula ruled Wallachia, an important Florentine merchant traveled throughout the land, and he had a great deal of merchandise and money.

As he reached Targoviste, the capital of the country at the time, the merchant immediately went to the princely palace and asked Dracula for servants who might watch over him, his merchandise, and his money.

Dracula ordered him to leave the merchandise and the money in the public square and to come to sleep in the palace.

The merchant, having no alternative, submitted to the princely command. However, during the night, someone passing by his carriage stole 160 golden ducats.

On the next day, early in the morning, the merchant went to his carriage, found his merchandise intact, but 160 golden ducats were missing. He immediately went to Dracula and told him about the missing money. Dracula told him not to worry and promised that both the thief and the gold would be found. He ordered his servants to replace the gold ducats from his own treasury, but to add an extra ducat.

To the citizens of Targoviste he ordered that they immediately seek out the thief and that if the thief were not found, he would destroy his capital.

In the meantime, the merchant went back to his carriage, counted the money once, counted it a second time and yet again a third time, and was amazed to find all his money there with an extra ducat.

He then returned to Dracula and told him: ''Lord, I have found all my money, only with an extra ducat.''

The thief was brought to the palace at that very moment. Dracula told the merchant: ''Go in peace. Had you not admitted to the extra ducat, I would have ordered you to be impaled together with this thief.''

This is the way that Dracula conducted himself with his subjects, both believers and heretics. [Mihail Popescu, ed. *Legende istorice ale romanilor din cronicari*, Bucuresti, 1937, pp. 16-18.]

Variant B: In times gone by when Prince Vlad the Impaler was reigning, a merchant, who was traveling throughout our land, yelled at all the crossroads that he had lost a moneybag full of one thousand leis. He promised a hundred leis to whoever would find it and bring it to him. Not long after that, a God-fearing man, as the Romanians were at the time of Prince Vlad the Impaler, came up to the merchant and said to him: ''Master merchant, I found this moneybag on my way at the turn in the crossroad at the back of the fish market. I figured that it must be yours, since I heard that you had lost a moneybag.'' The merchant replied: ''Yes, it is really mine, and I thank you for bringing it to me.''

As the merchant began to count the money, he was at wits' end to find a way of not giving the promised 100-lei reward. After he had counted the coins to the amazement of the other man, he put them back in the moneybag and said to the man who had brought it: ''I have counted the money, my dear, and I noticed that you have taken your promised reward. Instead of a thousand leis, I found only nine hundred. You did well, since it was your right. I thank you once again that you saved me from the tight spot in which I was to fall. God keep you in his grace.'' The Christian answered: ''Master merchant, you erroneously and without cause tell me that you are missing one hundred lei. I did not even untie the moneybag to look inside, and I did not even know how much money it contains. I took it to you as I found it.'' ''I told you,'' replied the merchant cuttingly and with a double meaning, ''I had lost a moneybag with one thousand leis. You brought it to me with nine hundred. That's how it is. Even if I should wish it, I cannot give you more. In the last resort, make out a petition and put me on trial.''

The merchant blushed to his ears for shame when he realized that the peasant suspected him. He did not say a word but left bidding farewell, and he went straight to the prince to complain. ''Your Highness,'' he said, ''I bring this charge, not because of the promised one hundred leis, but because of the fact that he suspects that I am not an honest man when I know that I was as honest as pure gold, and when it did not even cross my mind to deceive him.'' The prince recognized the trickery of the merchant, since the prince himself was a clever fellow, and he ordered that the merchant be brought to him. Both the plaintiff and the accused were present. The prince listened to both, and when placing both versions in the balance of justice, the prince realized on which side it weighed. Looking the merchant straight in the eye, he said, ''Master merchant, at my court people do not know what a lie is. It is strongly suppressed. You have lost a moneybag containing one thousand leis and you have found it proper to proclaim this at all the crossroads. The moneybag which this Christian brought you contained nine hundred leis. It seems quite obvious that this was not the moneybag which you lost. On the basis of what right did you accept it? Now, give the moneybag back to the man who found it and wait until the moneybag which you lost is found. While you, fellow Christian,'' added the prince, turning to the accused, ''keep the moneybag until the man who lost it shows up.'' And so it was done, since there was no way of doing otherwise.

[Petre Ispirescu, ed., *Povesti despre Vlad Voda Tepes opera postuma*, Cernauti, Story 4, 1935, pp. 83 and 160.]

Variant C: Once there reigned in Wallachia a Prince Dracula, also known as the Impaler. This prince was very severe, but also just. He would not tolerate thieves, liars and lazy people. He did all in his power to extirpate such men from his land. Had he reigned longer he would probably have succeeded in freeing his land from such parasites and perhaps even prevented that others of that kind be born. But no such luck today!

At that time a merchant from the city of Florence in Italy was returning to his native land with inestimable wares and a large sum of money. He had to pass through Targoviste for there was the seat of the prince at that time. Since he had heard the Turks relate that half had perished at Dracula's hand, he thought that the Romanians were dishonest—as bad as forest thieves. As he reached Targoviste, the merchant went straight to Dracula with a great gift and told him: ''Your Highness, fate has compelled me to pass through the land that you rule, with all my fortune which I have accumulated through the sweat of many years of Jewish work in Eastern countries. This land of yours is supposedly Christian. I don't want to have to relate in the West where I am going that a Christian was robbed by Christians, particularly when he was able to escape the sword of the pagan. On my knees I beg Your Highness to loan me a few guards to look after my goods until such time as I leave.''

Dracula who was as quick as fire frowned with his eyebrows when he heard that request and said: ''Keep your gift, you Christian. I order you to leave all your possessions in any square or any street, in any part of the city which will appear to you most isolated. Leave your fortune there unguarded until morning. If some theft should occur, I shall be responsible.''

This was no joking matter. Dracula's command had to be obeyed—otherwise he would have lost his temper. The Florentine, heart frozen with fright, submitted to the order. He did not sleep a wink because of worry and doubt.

In the morning the merchant returned only to find his possessions intact, as he had left them. He looked at them and could hardly believe his eyes. He went to Dracula, told him that all his possessions were found untouched, and praised his land. He had never seen such a thing in any of the other countries that he had visited and he had been traveling since childhood. ''What is the worth of the gift you intended to give me?'' asked Dracula. The merchant was somewhat hesitant to reveal it. Dracula insisted on finding out the amount of the gift the merchant had intended to pay. Dracula then told him: ''Tell whomever you meet what you have seen in my country.''

[Ispirescu, Story 4, 1935, pp. 83-84.]

2. *DRACULA AND THE TURKISH AMBASSADORS.* [Compare with Russian story No. 1 and German story No. 32.]

It is said that during the reign of Dracula in Wallachia, Sultan Mohammed II sent some ambassadors.

The latter having entered the reception hall of the Prince paid homage in accordance with their custom of not taking their fezzes off. Dracula then asked: ''Why do you behave in this way? You introduce yourselves to me and then do me dishonor.'' The Turkish representatives answered in unison: ''This is the custom with the rulers of our country.'' Dracula then spoke to them in this way: ''I, too, would like to strengthen your customs, so that you may adhere to them even more rigidly.''

He then immediately ordered his retainers to bring him some nails in order to secure the fezzes on the heads of the Turkish ambassadors.

Having done this, he allowed the envoys to leave and told them: ''Go and tell your master that he may be accustomed to suffer such indignity from his own people. We, however, are not so accustomed. Let him not send either to this country or elsewhere abroad, ambassadors exporting his new customs, for we shall not receive them.''

[Popescu, pp. 15-16.]

3. *THE BOYAR WITH A KEEN SENSE OF SMELL.* [Compare with Russian story No. 10 and German story No. 18.]

There were times when for whatever crime, whether judged or not judged, a man would lose his life. It is well that those times are now remote, may they never come back. It is well that we can now afford to relate these methods and not be victims anymore.

Some unruly boyars had been ordered impaled by Dracula. After some time Dracula, being reminded of the victims, invited yet other boyars to watch the spectacle with their own eyes and see how he could punish—seeing is believing. Perhaps Dracula simply wished to find out whether he could recognize some of the boyars—for within his retinue were many of the other faction [*Danesti*]. One of these boyars either because he had been involved in the intrigues of the impaled victims, or perhaps because he had been friendly to some of them, and fearing not to admit that he was overcome by pity, dared to tell Dracula: "Your Highness, you have descended to this spot from the palace. Over there the air is pure, whereas here it is impure. The bad smell might affect your health." "Do you mean to say it stinks?" asked Dracula, quickly leaning towards him and looking at him intently. "This is so, Your Highness, and you would do well to leave a place which might be detrimental to the health of a prince who has the good of his subjects at heart."

Perhaps because Dracula had finally penetrated into the depths of the mind of the boyar, or perhaps in order to shut up the remarks of other boyars he shouted: "Servants, bring me a stake three times as long as those that you see yonder. Make it up for me immediately in order that you impale the boyar, so that he may no longer be able to smell the stench from below."

The unfortunate boyar begged on his knees. He wanted to kiss Dracula's hands on both sides, all in vain. After a short time he was struggling on a stake much higher than all the others and he moaned and groaned so vehemently that you heaved a sigh.
[Ispirescu, Story 6, 1935, pp. 25-27.]

4. *THE LAZY WOMAN.* [Compare with Russian story No. 9 and German story No. 27.]

Dracula was a man with grey matter in his brains and he insisted on good order in his state. Woe to any soldier whom he saw improperly attired, he rarely escaped with his life. He liked to see his citizens cleanly attired and looking smart. Around him, he could not tolerate anyone who floundered or was slow in his work. Whenever he noticed a libertine or a rake he lost his temper.

One day he met a peasant who was wearing too short a shirt. One could also notice his homespun peasant trousers which were glued to his legs and one could make out the side of his thighs when he saw him [*dressed*] in this manner. Dracula immediately ordered him to be brought to court. "Are you married?" he inquired. "Yes, I am, Your Highness." "Your wife is assuredly of the kind who remains idle. How is it possible that your shirt does not cover the calf of your leg? She is not worthy of living in my realm. May she perish!" "Beg forgiveness, My Lord, but I am satisfied with her. She never leaves home and she is honest." "You will be more satisfied with another since you are a decent and hard-working man."

Two of Dracula's men had in the meantime brought the wretched woman to him and she was immediately impaled. Then bringing another woman, he gave her away to be married to the peasant widower. Dracula, however, was careful to show the new wife what had happened to her predecessor and explained to her the reasons why she had incurred the princely wrath.

Consequently, the new wife worked so hard she had no time to eat. She placed the bread on one shoulder, the salt on another and worked in this fashion. She tried hard to give greater satisfaction to her new husband than the first wife and not to incur the curse of Dracula. Did she succeed?

It is just as well that Dracula does not rule our country today, for he would have had to expend many stakes, which might have eliminated from our land the innumerable drones who wither the very grass on which they sit.
[Ispirescu, Story 5, 1935, pp. 21-25.]

5. *THE BURNING OF THE POOR.* [This tale has a particularly moral bent to it. Compare with Russian story No. 5 and German story No. 30.]

The tale relates that there were a great number of people out of work at the time of Prince Vlad the Impaler. In order to live they had to eat, since the unmerciful stomach demanded food. So, in order to eat they wandered aimlessly and begged for food and they subsisted by begging without working. If a man, as I say, were to ask one of these beggars why they didn't work a little too, some would answer: "Don't I wander around all day long? If I cannot find work, am I to blame?" One of that kind, an onlooker could set straight with the proverb: "I am looking for a master but God grant that I don't find one." The others also always found a pretext for not working, such as: "The furrier strains his legs day and night, but does not get anything out of it; the tailor works all his life and his reward is like the shadow of a needle; the shoemaker bends and stoops until he gets old and when he dies he is buried with an empty collection plate." And in this way they found something wrong with all the trades.

When the prince heard of this and saw with his own eyes the large number of beggars who were really fit for work, he began to reflect. The Gospel says that man shall earn his daily bread only through the sweat of his brow. Prince Vlad thought: "These men live off the sweat of others, so they are useless to humanity. It is a form of thievery. In fact, the masked robber in the forest demands your purse, but if you are quicker with your hand and more vigorous than he you can escape from him. However, these others take your belongings gradually by begging—but they still take it. They are worse than robbers. May such men be eradicated from my land!" And after due reflection, he ordered that the announcement be made throughout the land that on a certain day all beggars should assemble, since the prince was going to distribute a batch of clothes and to treat them to a copious meal.

On the appointed day, Targoviste groaned under the weight of the large number of beggars who had come. The prince's servants passed out a batch of clothes to each one, then they led the beggars to some large house where tables had been set. The beggars marveled at the prince's generosity, and they spoke among themselves: "Truly it is a prince's kind of grace—even this charity is at the expense of the people. Couldn't the prince give us something out of his own pocket for a change?" "Hey, the prince has changed: He is no longer the way you knew him." "A wolf can change his fur, but not his bad habits."

Then they started eating. And what do you think they saw before them: a meal such as one would find on the prince's own table, wines and all the best things to eat which weigh you down. The beggars had a feast which became legendary. They ate and drank greedily. Most of them got dead drunk. As they became unable to communicate with one another, as one might say, incoherent, they were suddenly faced with fire on all sides. The prince had ordered his servants to set the house on fire. They rushed to the doors to get out, but the doors were locked. The fire progressed. The blaze rose high like inflamed dragons. Shouts, shrieks and moans arose from the lips of all the poor enclosed there. But why should a fire be moved by the entreaties of men? They fell upon each other. They embraced each other. They sought help, but there was no human ear left to listen to them. They began to twist in the torments of the fire that was destroying them. The fire stifled some, the embers reduced others to ashes, the flames grilled most of them. When the fire finally abated, there was no trace of any living soul.

And do you believe that the breed of poor was wiped out? Far from it—don't believe such nonsense. Look around you and ascertain the truth. Even today times are not better than they were then. Beggars will cease to exist only with the end of the world.
[Ispirescu, Story 8, 1936, pp. 1-6.]

6. *THE TWO MONKS.* [Compare with Russian story No. 6 and with German story No. 19.]

A crafty Greek monk who like many others was beginning to travel throughout the land happened to meet a poor Romanian priest, an honest God-fearing man. Every time they met, the two clerics argued and between them there arose a fiery dispute. The Greek monk was constantly belittling the priest and criticizing Romanians. The native answered:"If you find Romanians stupid and uncouth, why don't you return to your land among your subtle and wily Greek compatriots? Who has brought you hither and who has called you like a plague on our heads?''

News about the two clerics reached Dracula's ears. He wished to see them and ordered that on a certain day they both be brought to the palace.

They came on the appointed day. He received them in separate rooms. The Greek monk was proud to have been received by the prince, but he did not know that the native cleric had also been invited. The latter was astonished and could not understand how Dracula had found out about him, but he determined that should he find him well disposed he would place a good word for his parishioners. Dracula, however, wished to probe their innermost thoughts, for His Highness was crafty in this respect. When the Greek monk entered the chamber, Dracula asked him: ''Reverend priest, you have traveled through my country in the service of the church. You had occasion to speak to good and bad people, with the rich and the poor. Tell me what do the people say about me?''

To such an obvious question the priest thought that he had the obvious retort. With a craftiness of which only a Greek is capable, he answered in a honeyed and false way: ''Your Highness, from one end of the land to the other everyone praises your name. Everyone is pleased with your reign. They say that such a just ruler has never reigned in Wallachia. To which compliment I shall add that you need to do one more thing: Be kinder to those of your subjects who come from the Holy Places [*Greeks*] and give them financial aid, so that they may bring consolation for the misfortunes suffered by their monks at these Holy Places. Then your name will be blessed of the angels with undying praise.'' ''You are lying, you unworthy priest, like the villain that you are,'' shouted Dracula, angered and frowning with his brows. It was obvious that he had been informed about the priest. Even the proverb states that even the sun cannot give heat to everyone. Opening the door he ordered his retainers who were on guard: ''Soldiers, this wicked unworthy being must be executed.''

The order was immediately obeyed and the monk was impaled. Then going to the Romanian priest who was ignorant of all that had happened, Dracula asked him the same question: ''Tell me what do people say about me?'' ''What should they say, Your Highness? People have not spoken with one voice. Recently, however, they are beginning to castigate you everywhere and say that you no longer lessen their burdens, which were small in the days of your predecessor.'' ''You dare to speak fairly,'' said Dracula in a gleeful tone of voice. ''I will think about that. Be the court confessor from this point onwards and go in peace.''

[Ispirescu, Story 7, 1935, pp. 27-32.]

7. *DRACULA'S MISTRESS.* [Compare with German story No. 21 and Russian story No. 8.]

Dracula had a mistress. Her house was located in a dark and isolated suburb of Targoviste. When Dracula went to see her he was oblivious of everything, for this woman unfortunately happened to be to his taste. For her, he had mere physical attraction, nothing else.

The unfortunate woman tried in every way to be pleasing to Dracula. And he reciprocated all the outward manifestations of love which she showed him. One might almost say that Dracula expressed a certain gaiety when he was by her side.

One day when she saw his expression somewhat gloomier, she wished in some way to cheer him up and she dared tell him a lie. ''Your Highness, you will be glad to hear my tidings.'' ''What news can you give me?'' answered Dracula. ''The little mouse,'' she answered allegorically, ''has entered the milk churn.'' ''What does this mean?'' questioned Dracula, grinning. ''It means, Your Highness, that I am with child.'' ''Don't you dare prattle such tales.'' The woman knew Dracula's method of punishing lies and wished to justify her statement. ''It is, Your Highness, as I have said.'' ''This will not be,'' said Dracula, frowning with his eyebrows. ''But if it were possible I reckon that Your Highness would be glad,'' dared she continue. ''I told you this will *not* be,'' retorted Dracula, rudely stamping his foot, ''and I will show you it will not happen.'' Unsheathing his sword, he opened her entrails in order to see for himself whether she had spoken the truth or had lied.

As the woman lay dying, Dracula told her: ''You see that it cannot be.'' He left while she agonized in great pain. She was punished because, hoping to cheer up her lover, she had told a lie.

[Ispirescu, Story 3, 1935, pp. 14-16.]

8. *VLAD THE IMPALER.* [In their characterization of the tyrant prince, the following accounts concur with the Russian and German sources.]

Variant A : And the old folks said that this village of ours, ''Vladaia,'' including its property, takes its name from a prince of the land called Vlad the Impaler. This prince had here, where the town hall now stands, a big house in which he sentenced the guilty and impaled them. Even today one may find in the soil the remains of those who had been impaled on the hill near the fountain. And perhaps if so many cruel battles had not taken place at Vladaia during the time of Vlad the Impaler as in more recent days, one would find even today the house where the judgments were made, as well as the dreadful impalement stake.

[Told by Dinu Dimitriu, age 60, of Vladaia, Mehedinti district.]

Variant B : Good God, times were bad because of the Turks at the time of Vlad the Impaler! The tax collectors came and took men either as hostages or to enroll them as their soldiers. They even took our herds—one out of every tenth one—and what was better and more plentiful than sheep at that time? The poor sheep: ''Come summer, they sweeten you, come winter, they warm you.'' Milk was so plentiful that at that time our ancestors made *mamaliga* with milk, instead of water, as the milk was cheap. And all that was the reason why Prince Vlad hated the Turks. He pursued them to the last man and when he caught them, he had them impaled.

Prince Vlad also punished the boyars who were often conniving with the Turks or did not behave honestly with people such as we. On one occasion, in order to trip them up more easily, he gave a great feast and also summoned those boyars against whom he bore a grudge. But when they came, he impaled them.

[Told by Ghita a lui Dinu Radului of Almajel, Mehedinti district.]

Variant C: Mother! It is said that Vlad the Impaler was a terribly harsh ruler. He impaled whomever he caught lying or behaving badly towards the elderly or oppressing the poor. He also impaled the Turks who came, from time to time, to rob our country. It is said that this prince had a house in some bigger villages, where he sat in judgment and where he also had stakes and gallows.

The house where justice was administered was in our village, Albutele, near Beleti. Whomever he caught red-handed was sentenced and hanged there. And after he had taken his life, he impaled them.

[Told by Marga Bodea Matusa, age 76, of Muscel district; recorded in ''Legende, traditii si amintire istorice adrurate din Oltenia si din Muscel,''*Ac. Rom. din viata poporului Roman Culigeri si Studii*, Bucuresti, 1910.]

BIBLIOGRAPHY

ANCIENT DOCUMENTS AND MODERN WORKS ABOUT DRACULA

The oldest document concerning Dracula is the manuscript in the Monastery of St. Gall, Switzerland. It was written in Low German, probably in 1462. For our translation of it, see Appendix I. Examples of the Dracula pamphlets printed from 1482 onward survive in various libraries in Western Europe. The only one in the United States is owned by the Philip H. and A.S.W. Rosenbach Foundation, Philadelphia. (See Frederick R. Goff, *Incunabula in American Libraries*, New York, 1964, p. 221.) Most of the modern studies relating to the historical Dracula are in the Romanian language.

Beheim, Michel. *Die Gedichte des Michel Beheim.* Band I Einleitung Gedichte Nr I-I47 herausgegeben von Hans Giele und Ingeborg Spriewald. Berlin, 1968. (Deutsche Texte des Mittelalters herausgegeben von der Deutschen Akademie der Wissenschaften zu Berlin, Band LX.) This is the most recent edition of the troubadour Michel Beheim's poem, which is rich in anecdotes about Dracula, was written in Wiener-Neustadt in 1463, and probably was directly inspired by stories told by refugee monks from Transylvania.

Bentley, Juliette. "Vlad Voivode Dracula," *Supernatural*, no. 2. Bournemouth, 1969. Unscholarly, superficial attempt to link the historical Dracula to Stoker's vampire.

Bogdan, Ioan. *Vlad Tepes si naratiunile germane si rusesti asupra lui.* Bucharest, 1896.

Bonfini, Antonio. *Rerum ungaricarum decades . . . ,* 4 vols. Leipzig, 1936-41. Latest edition of the chronicle by the official Hungarian historian at the court of King Mathias Corvinus (1458-90). Bonfini, who probably knew Dracula personally from 1462 onward, may or may not have gotten his Dracula anecdotes firsthand. A part of his chronicles, *Decades tres . . . ,* was published in Basel, 1543; the first complete edition, in Basel, 1568.

Cazacu, Matei. "La Valachie et la bataille de Kossovo," *Revue des Etudes Sud-Est Europeennes*, vol. 9 (1971), pp. 131-51. Useful for establishing the chronology of Dracula's first reign (1448), which the author arrived at on the basis of novel documentation.

Chalkokondyles, Leonikos. *Atheniensis historiarum, libri decem. Corpus scriptorum historiae Byzantinae.* Bonn, 1843. Earlier translations in French done in Paris, 1577; in Rouen, 1660. Of the Byzantine chroniclers, Chalkokondyles gave by far the most complete account of Dracula's campaign in 1462.

Conduratu, Grigore C. *Michael Beheim's Gedicht uber den Woiwoden Wlad II Drakul mit historischen und kritischen Erlauterungen.* Leipzig-Bucharest, 1903. A scholarly analysis of the work of the troubadour Michel Beheim; places the song in its historic context. By far the best work on this subject.

Czabai, Stephen. "The Real Dracula," *The Hungarian Quarterly,* Autumn 1941, pp. 327-32. Tendentious and without historical value.

Dlugosz, I. *Historica Polonica libri XIII ab antiquissimus temporibus.* Leipzig, 1711-12. This Polish chronicle contains interesting information on Dracul's crusades against the Turks and on Dracula's early career.

Degaudenzi, J.L. "Mythe et realite: le veritable Dracula," *Midi-Minuit*, no. 22, Paris, 1971. A highly fantasized and in part inaccurate interpretation but based on some original research.

Doukas, Michael. *Historia Byzantina recognovit et interprete . . .* Bonn, 1834. Although not so informative as Chalkokondyles, the Byzantine chronicler is probably the most impartial commentator on Dracula's 1462 campaign against Mohammed II.

Ebendorfer, Th. *Chronica regum Romanorum.* Mittheilungen des Institut's fur osterreichische Geschichtsforschung; III Ergangzungsband; Innsbruck, 1890-94, pp. 202-4. A new edition of the chronicle was published in 1968. Includes the early German Dracula manuscript written in 1462.

Engel, Johann Christian von. *Geschichte der Moldau und Walachey. Nebst der Historischen und Statistischen Literatur beidjer Lander,* vol. 1 (actually volume IV of *Geschichte des Ungarisches Reiches und Seine Nebenlander*) pp. 75-80. Halle, 1804. Contains reprints of the Dracula pamphlets, plus an analysis of them.

Giese, F., ed. *Asik-Pasa-Zade. Tevarih-i al-i Osman.* Leipzig, 1929. Although not a direct witness of Dracula's night attack on Mohammed II's camp, Asik-Pasa-Zade left an interesting account of it from the Turkish point of view.

Giurescu, Constantin C. *Transylvania in the History of Romania: An Historical Outline.* London, 1969. The best general synthesis in English; written by one of Romania's leading historians.

Halecki, Oscar. *The Crusade at Varna: A Discussion of a Controversial Problem.* New York, 1943. Of interest in accounting for the Dracul-Hunyadi feud, which led to Dracul's murder in 1447.

Heiman, Leo. "Meet the Real Count Dracula," *Fate*, March 1968, pp. 53-60. Account of "Count" Alexander Cepesi, who has operated a small blood bank in Istanbul since 1947 and who claims to be a descendant of Dracula.

Hirn, Joseph. *Erzherzog Ferdinand II von Tirol.* Innsbruck, 1885. 2 vols. Standard biography of Archduke Ferdinand II, in whose gallery at Castle Ambras Dracula's portrait is to be found.

Iorga, Nicolae. *Les aventures "sarasines" des francais de Bourgogne au XIieme siecle. Melanges d'histoire generale.* Clug, 1927. Commentary on the narration of the Burgundian De Wavrin, who participated in crusades against the Turks. De Wavrin's chronicle first published as: *Anchiennes croniques d'Engleterre par Johan de Wavrin seigneur de Forestel,* Mlle Dupont, ed., Paris, 1858-63, vol. 2, pp. 1-162. This firsthand testimony is invaluable for Dracula's early career.

————. *Histoire des roumains et de la romanite orientale. Les chevaliers*, vol. 4. Bucharest, 1937. Somewhat disorganized interpretation of Dracula's reign by Romania's leading historian.

Kirtley, B. "Dracula, the Monastic Chronicles and Slavic Folklore," *Mid-West Folklore*, vol. 6 (1956), no. 3. Superficial 3-page speculative treatment of the Slavic Dracula manuscript.

Kittenberg, Hubert. *Schloss Ambras bei Innsbruck.* Innsbruck, 1949. Useful guidebook to Castle Ambras collection.

Karadja, C.I., ed. "Die Altesten Gedruckten Quellen zur Geschichte der Rumanen," *Gutenburg Jahrbuch,* pp. 114-46, Mainz, 1934. Sketchy compilation of the few German Dracula pamphlets known at that time by Karadja, who was a pioneer hunter of Dracula memorabilia. (Most of his collection is now at the Central State Library in Bucharest.)

Kritoboulos of Imbros. *History of Mehmed the Conqueror* (translated by C.T. Riggs). Princeton, 1954. Of marginal interest to Dracula's anti-Turkish campaign of 1462. A very mediocre English translation of the Byzantine chronicler.

Lurie, I. S. *Povesti o Dracule.* Moscow, Leningrad, 1964. The most substantial and scholarly study of the origins of the Dracula narratives, but has not been entirely accepted by Romanian Slavicists and Germanists. Reproduces hitherto unknown Dracula pamphlet printed in Leipzig in 1493.

Modrussiense, Niccolo (Modrusa), in G. Mercati, ed., *Opere Minori,* vol. 4. Vatican City, 1937. The reports of this papal legate contain precious firsthand information on Dracula's cruelties and a very complete, unique literary portrait. The legate presumably met Dracula after 1462 and during his period of Hungarian imprisonment.

Munster, Sebastian. *Cosmographiae Universales*, Libri VI. Basel, 1572. Contains most of the early German anecdotes about Dracula and his cruelties; had a wide circulation. Munster may also have inspired the work of the archbishop of Prague, Ian of Puchov, first published in Czech in 1554.

Nandris, Grigore. ''A Philological Analysis of Dracula and Rumanian Placenames and Masculine Personal names in a/ea,'' *Slavonic and East European Review*, vol. 37 (1959), pp. 371-77. Very personal interpretation; has not won general acceptance by other Romanian philologists.
———. ''The Dracula Theme in the European Literature of the West and of the East,'' *Literary History and Literary Criticism*. Edited by Leon Edel. New York, 1965. (Also see ''The Historical Dracula,'' essentially the same theme, in *Comparative Literature: Matter and Method*, University of Illinois, Urbana, 1969.) A scholarly but incomplete study of the German and Slavic texts.

Pall, F. ''Notes du pelerin William Wey a propos des operations militaires des Turcs en 1462,'' *Revue Historique du Sud-Est Europeen*, vol. 22 (1945), pp. 246-66. Firsthand account of an English pilgrim returning from the Holy Land and reporting a Dracula victory over the Turks.

Pius II (Enea Silvio Piccolomino). *Memoirs of a Renaissance Pope; the Commentaries of Pius II.* An abridgment of *Commentarii rerum memorabilium . . .* , Rome, 1589, translated by F.A. Gragg, New York, 1959. See also Pius II, *De Bello Turcorum et Hungarorum*, Cologne, 1472. These commentaries include references to Dracula; although obtained secondhand, they are invaluable for an understanding of the complex diplomatic situation which preceded and followed Dracula's campaign against the Turks in 1462.

Rosetti, Dinu. ''Les Fouilles de Snagov,'' *Sapaturile arheologice de la Snagov*. Bucharest, 1935. Brief summary of the main findings of the 1931 archaeological excavations at Snagov, including reputed site of Dracula's tomb.

Sauter, Lilly V. ''Ein Schloss in Tirol,'' *Du Atlantis*, April 1966, pp. 237-69. Scholarly article in popular magazine on the collection at Ambras castle; written by the current curator.

Seton-Watson, R.W. *A History of the Rumanians.* Cambridge, 1934. Still the best general synthesis of Romanian history by an English scholar. Interprets Dracula's reign rather severely.

Striedter, J. ''Die Erzahlung vom walachischen vojevoden Drakula in der russischen und deutschen Uberlieferung,'' *Zeitschrift fur Slawische Philologie*, vol. 29 (Heidelberg, 1961-62), pp. 398-427. A comparative analysis of Russian and German Dracula narratives to be read in conjunction with that by Nandris.

Schwob, Monika Ute. *Kulturelle Beziehungen zwischen Nuremberg und die Deutschen im Sudosten im 14 bis 16 Jahrhundert*, Munich, 1969. A general monograph on German cultural contacts with Southeastern Europe containing a reference to a Nuremberg printed Dracula pamphlet. In appendix, see rare impalement frontispiece dated 1499.

Tappe, Eric. *Documents Concerning Romanian History, 1427-1601; Collected from the British Archives.* The Hague, 1964. Contains the letter of the English pilgrim William of Wey which reports a Dracula victory over the Turks in 1462.

Thuroczy, I. *Der Hungern Chronica inhallend wie sie anfengklich ins land kommen . . . von irem ersten Konig Athila*, Nurnberg, 1534. (See also *Chronica Hungarorum ab origine gentis*, Latin translation by I.G. Schwandter, Vienna, from 1746.) Oldest Hungarian chronicle referring to the early portion of Dracula's career—during the rule of John Hunyadi and Vlad Dracul. Undoubtedly subsequent chroniclers, such as Dlugosz and Bonfini, drew on this work for information about Dracul.

Wey, William [*of*]. *The Itineraries of Wey.* London, 1857.

ELIZABETH BATHORY

Baring-Gould, S. *The Book of Werewolves*, London, 1865. Contains chapter on the Blood Countess which may well have been read by Stoker.

Dezso, Rexa. *Bathory Erzsebet, Nadasdy Lerencne.* Budapest, 1908. Based on the work of Turoczi (see below).

Elsberg, R. von. *Elisabeth Bathory (Die Blutgrafin). Ein Sitten—und Charakterbild mit einem Titelbilde.* S. Schottlander, Breslau, 1904. Author apparently did not use original documents, relying instead on the data gathered by Dezso.

Leydi, Roberto. "Dracula era una dona," *L'Europeo*, no. 1 (January 1972), p. 42. Theorizes that Stoker may have been inspired in part by the crimes of Elizabeth Bathory.

Penrose, Valentin. *Erzsebet Bathory, La Comtesse sanglante.* Mercure de France, Paris, 1962. Romanticized presentation with no new historical evidence.

Ronay, Gabriel. *Exploding the Bloody Myths of Dracula and Vampires.* Gollancz, London, announced for 1972. Argues that Stoker's Dracula is based on Elizabeth Bathory.

Turoczi, Laszlo. *Erzebet Bathory.* Budapest, 1744. First published account of the Blood Countess. Contains record of trial.

MAJOR VAMPIRE STORIES IN ENGLISH LITERATURE (ARRANGED CHRONOLOGICALLY)

Polidori, John William. *The Vampire.* London, 1819. First appeared in April, 1819 under Byron's name in the *New Monthly Magazine*. In this tale Lord Ruthwen, a vampire, saps the life blood from his victims.

Prest, Thomas Preskett. *Varney the Vampire or the Feast of Blood.* The first installment of this penny novel appeared in 1847. Entire work, edited by Sir Devendra P. Varma, published by Arno Press, New York, 1970. A very popular Gothic horror story in which a well-educated, gentleman-vampire, Sir Francis Varney, plagues the Bannesworth family.

Le Fanu, Joseph Sheridan. "Carmilla," in *In a Glass Darkly*. London, 1872. In this novelette Le Fanu created the most famous female vampire in English literature; this masterpiece of Gothic horror inspired Stoker to write a vampire story of his own.

Stoker, Bram. *Dracula.* London, 1897. Numerous editions up to the present day. Contains the most famous, most fascinating, vampire in English literature. If one could read only one piece of vampire fiction, this should be it.

———. *Dracula's Guest and Other Weird Stories.* London, 1914. Stoker originally wrote "Dracula's Guest" for inclusion in his novel *Dracula*, but it was cut out of the initial editions. His widow, Florence Stoker, saw to its publication after Stoker's death.

Matheson, Richard. "Drink My Blood." A short story first published in 1951; republished in Peter Haining, ed., *The Midnight People*, Popular Library, New York, 1968. This incredibly gripping story is about a strange young boy named Jules who becomes fixated on the Dracula image in movies and literature. Jules wants to become a vampire, steals a vampire bat from the zoo, and in the end is met by Dracula himself.

Rudorff, Raymond. *The Dracula Archives.* Arbor House. New York, 1971. A novel recreating Bram Stoker's style and mixing up Elizabeth Bathory and Stoker's Dracula image.

MODERN ANTHOLOGIES CONTAINING VAMPIRE STORIES

Carter, Margaret. *Curse of the Undead.* Greenwich, Conn., 1970. Literary tales about vampires.

Haining, Peter, ed. *The Midnight People.* Popular Library, New York, 1968. Short stories related to the vampire theme.

———. *The Ghouls.* Pocketbooks. New York, 1972. A selection of short stories which illustrates how they inspired specific horror films; includes Bram Stoker's ''Dracula's Guest,'' which inspired the film *Dracula's Daughter.*

Tolstoy, Alexis. *Vampires: Stories of the Supernatural.* 1969. Includes story of a family of vampires from Serbia.

Vadim, Roger; Volta, Ornella; and Riva, Valeria. *The Vampire: An Anthology.* London, 1963. Includes short selections from major vampire stories, by authors such as Merimee, Le Fanu, and Tolstoy.

STUDIES OF THE VAMPIRE IN LITERATURE, HISTORY, AND MYTH

Epaulard, Alexis. *Vampyrisme, necrophilie, necrosadisme, necrophagie.* Lyon, 1901. The psycho-pathology associated with ''living vampires.''

Faivre, Tony. *Les vampires.* Paris, 1962. One of the best of the current serious books on vampire beliefs. The author traces the historical records about vampires from ancient times to the present in a semi-scholarly manner. There are some mistakes, such as claim that in Moldavia the word ''Dracul'' refers to a vampire. The historical data is not well related to the narrative, but the illustrations of the vampire in art are most interesting.

Frazer, James G. *The Fear of the Dead in Primitive Religions*; especially vol. 2, London, 1934. The famous author of *The Golden Bough* delivered these lectures at Trinity College. He dealt with the walking dead in a somewhat out-dated rationalistic manner.

Gerard, Emily de Laszowska. *The Land Beyond the Forest.* London, 1888. The author includes a good deal of Transylvanian folklore, including some on who becomes a vampire and how to kill one. Her article ''Transylvanian Superstitions'' was published in *The Nineteenth Century*, vol. 18, London, 1885, pp. 130-50.

Glut, Donald F. *True Vampires of History.* H.C. Publishers, New York, 1971. A presentation of records about vampire cases; no critical analysis.

Hill, Douglas, and Williams, Pat. *The Supernatural.* Aldous Books. London, 1965.

Hock, Stefan. *Die Vampyrsagen und ihre Verwertung in der Deutschen Literatur.* Berlin, 1900. Vampire themes in German literature.

Hurwood, Bernhart J. *Monsters and Nightmares.* Belmont Productions. New York, 1967.

———. *Monsters Galore.* Fawcett Publications. New York, 1965.

———. *Terror By Night.* Lancer Books. New York, 1963. Republished as *The Monstrous Undead*, Lancer, 1969. One of the finest studies of the belief in vampires, including probings into the reality behind reality.

Jellinek, A. L. ''Zur Vampyrsage,'' *Zeitschrift des Vereins fur Volkskunde*, vol. 14, 1904, especially pp. 234 ff. A scholarly treatment of the vampire theme in folk literature.

Murgoci, A. ''The Vampire in Rumania,'' *Folklore*, vol. 37, 1926. A brief but excellent study of the vampire theme in Romanian folklore.

Murgoci, A., and Murgoci, H. "The Devil in Rumanian Folklore," *Folklore*, vol. 40, 1929.

Rogo, Scott. "Reviewing the Vampire of Croglin Grange," *Fate*, vol. 21, no. 6 (June, 1968), pp. 44-48.

———. "In-Depth Analysis of the Vampire Legend," *Fate*, vol. 21, no. 9 (Sept., 1968), pp. 70-77.

Seabrook, William. *Witchcraft: Its Power in the World Today.* Harcourt, Brace. New York, 1940. Paperback: Lancer Books, New York, 1968. Part Two contains a fine analysis of the vampire and the werewolf.

Smith, Warren. *Strange Monsters and Madmen.* Popular Library. New York, 1969.

Sturm, Dieter, and Volker, Klaus. *Von den Vampiren oder Menschensaugern.* Munich, 1968. An excellent, scholarly, work, including texts about vampires from literary and official documents dating back to ancient times and up to the present. The book concludes with two fine essays: one on the literary traditions of the vampire, another on the historical traditions.

Summers, Montague. *The Vampire: His Kith and Kin.* Routledge and Kegan Paul. London, 1928. Republished by New Hyde Park, New York, 1960. Summers was one of the pioneers in the field of the occult. This work, though serious, fails to distinguish between significant and insignificant details.

———. *The Vampire in Europe.* Routledge and Kegan Paul. London, 1929. Republished by New Hyde Park, New York, 1966. A general treatment; has same defects as in work cited above.

Varma, Devendra P. *The Gothic Flame.* 1957. Excellent study of the Gothic Romance, with some references to the vampire literary strain.

Villeneuve, Roland. *Loups-garoux et vampires.* Paris-Geneva, 1963.

Volta, Ornella. *Le vampire, la mort, le sang, la peur.* Editions Jean-Jacques Pauvert. Paris, 1962. Translation by Raymond Rudorff: *The Vampire*, Tandem Books, London, 1965. A look at the vampire from an erotic viewpoint; many bizarre illustrations.

Wright, Dudley. *Vampires and Vampirism.* William Rider and Son. London, 1914. A superficial treatment.

STUDIES OF THE VAMPIRE IN FILM

Borst, Ron. "The Vampire in the Cinema" *Photon*, no. 19. Mark Frank, ed. & pub. Brooklyn, N.Y., 1970. This is the best, most comprehensive listing of its kind.

Butler, Ivan. *Horror in the Cinema.* International Film Guide Series. New York, 1971. First published in 1967 as *The Horror Film*; second revised edition, 1970. Contains brief references to vampire films. Filmography at the end is weak.

Clarens, Carlos. *An Illustrated History of the Horror Film.* Longmans, Canada, 1967; New York, 1968. References to vampire films appear throughout the text. The filmography omits several vampire films, but the general text is adequate.

Douglas, Drake. *Horror!* Collier Books, 1969. First published by The Macmillan Company, 1966.

Eisner, Lotte H. *The Haunted Screen: Expressionism in the German Cinema and the Influence of Max Reinhardt.* University of California Press, 1969. First published under the title *L'Ecran Demoniaque*, in France, 1952; revised and reissued, 1965, by Le Terrain Vague. A classic. Contains a superb analysis of the pre-Nazi German films of the 1920's by one who understood German expressionism and film. Book includes an admirable chapter on Murnau's *Nosferatu*.

Gifford, Denis. *Movie Monsters*. London, 1969. Chapter entitled "The Vampire" quickly traces historical development of the vampire image in film.

Michel, Jean-Claude. "Les vampires a l'ecran," *L'Ecran Fantastique,* 2 serie, no. 2, Paris, 1971. One of the most comprehensive filmographies on the vampire, plus perceptive comments on the films.

Reed, Donald A. *The Vampire on the Screen.* Inglewood, California, 1964. A small but pioneering work by the President of the Count Dracula Society.

————. *Midi-Minuit Fantastique*, nos. 4-5, January 1963, Paris. An excellent summary of cast and credits of all the Dracula films until the early 1960's. Many photos from the films.

FILMOGRAPHY

DRACULA-VAMPIRE FILMS, 1896-1971

Most of the early, and by now obscure, silent films about vampires are actually about "vamps"—female flirts who entice or captivate men. The first real vampire movie is F. W. Murnau's classic *Nosferatu* (1922), which was based on Stoker's novel *Dracula* (1897).

SILENT FILMS 1896-1928

1896. *Le Manoir du Diable*. Robert-Houdin film, France; director Georges Melies. American title: *The Haunted Castle*. English title: *The Devil's Castle*. In one scene a huge bat in a medieval castle becomes transformed into Mephistopheles. A cavalier arrives with a crucifix; confronted with it, the devil "throws up his hands and disappears in a cloud of smoke." Despite the film's imagery, the devil-figure does not drink blood, thus is not a real vampire.

1909-22. This period included among others the following films, which are listed here out of historical interest. *Vampire of the Coast*, 1909 USA. *The Vampire's Trail*, 1910 USA. *Vampyrn*, 1912 Swedish short. *Vampe di Gelosia* (The Vamp's Jealousy), 1912 Italian short. *The Vampire*, 1912 Messter short. *Danse Vampiresque*, 1912 Danish short. *The Vampire*, 1913 USA Kalem film; *director*, Robert Vignola. *In the Grip of the Vampire*, 1913 USA. *Vampires of the Night*, 1914 Greene's Feature Photo Plays. *The Vampire's Trail*, 1914 USA; *director*, Robert Vignola. *Vampires of Warsaw*, 1914 USA. *The Vampire's Tower*, 1914 USA, Ambrosia film. *Saved from the Vampire*, 1914 USA. *Les Vampires*, 1915 French serial; *director*, Louis Feuillade. *The Vampire's Clutch*, 1915, Knight film. *Was She a Vampire?*, 1915 Universal film. *Kiss of the Vampire*, 1915 USA. *Mr. Vampire*, 1916 USA. *A Night of Horror*, 1916 German film; *director*, Arthur Robison. *A Vampire Out of Work*, 1916 Vitagraph film. *Ceneri e Vampe*, 1916 Italian film. *A Village Vampire*, 1916 USA. *The Beloved Vampire*, 1917 USA. *The Vampire*, 1920 Metro film. *The Blond Vampire*, 1922 USA.

1922. *Nosferatu oder eine Symphonie des Grauens*. Prana Films, Germany; director, Friedrich Wilhelm Murnau; screenplay by Henrick Galeen. Released on March 5, 1922 in Germany; in the U.S. as *Nosferatu, the Vampire* in 1929. Count Orlock, played by Max Schreck, is the vampire Nosferatu (Dracula). The script was an adaptation of Stoker's novel. Since Murnau had not secured the proper copyright, he changed the setting from the Balkans to the Baltic area, and he also changed the names of the main characters. This is the first Dracula vampire film. Visually it ranks as one of the greatest horror films of all time. Murnau filmed it in an outdoor, realistic setting. Despite some technical gimmicks which cause modern audiences to laugh, such as the speed-up of the sequences of Dracula's carriage and his loading of coffins, this film is a masterpiece.

1927. *London After Midnight*. Metro-Goldwyn Mayer, USA. Producer and director, Tod Browning; screenplay, by Tod Browning and Waldemar Young, from a novel by Tod Browning entitled *The Hypnotist*. Film released in England as *The Hypnotist*. Lon Chaney appears as Inspector Edmund Burke, alias Mooney (the vampire). In this film Lon Chaney, "the man with a thousand faces," plays a vampire in human form.

1928. *The Vampire*. United Pictures, USA. Released in France, 1928, as *Vampire a du Mode*. A seductive image is portrayed here, not a real vampire.

TALKIES 1931-71

1931. *Dracula*. Universal Studios, USA. A Tod Browning Production; producer, Carl Laemmle Jr.; director. Tod Browning; screenplay, by Garret Fort, from the play by Hamilton Deane and John F. Balderston, based on the novel *Dracula* by Bram Stoker; additional dialogue by Dudley Murphy. Dracula is played by Bela Lugosi, who had the stage role on Broadway. This is the first real vampire talkie. It remains one of the most popular films of all time, though most film critics do not hold it in high regard. The photography is unimaginative; the music contains snatches from Tschaikovsky's "Swan Lake"; but Bela Lugosi's authentic Hungarian accent and presence reach out to make *his* Dracula image a part of contemporary American "folklore."

1931. *Dracula*. Mexican-Universal; co-producer, Carl Laemmle, Jr.; director, George Melford. Mexican version of the Browning-Lugosi film cited above, filmed at the same time.

1932. *Vampyr*. Les Films Carl Dreyer, France; producer, Carl Dreyer; screenplay, by Carl Dreyer and Christian Jul, freely adapted from the story "Carmilla" by Sheridan Le Fanu. Released in America as both *The Vampire* and the *Castle of Doom*; in England as *The Strange Adventures of David Gray*. This film is an example of what a real horror film should be. The dreadful is sensed rather than seen. Blood-drinking is suggested rather than portrayed. The entire film has a distant, grainy quality which is reminiscent of a Seurat painting. This quality actually was an "accident" in filming, and Dreyer turned it into an asset. Unfortunately, the mood it creates remains unique; no successors have ever duplicated, much less equaled, it.

1933. *The Vampire Bat*. Majestic, USA; producer, Phil Goldstone; director, Frank Trayer; screenplay by Edward Lowe. Lionel Atwill plays a mad doctor who tries to cover up his weird experiments by fomenting a vampire scare among the inhabitants of a far-off Balkan village.

1935. *The Mark of the Vampire*. Metro-Goldwyn Mayer, USA; producer, E.J. Mannix; director, Tod Browning; screenplay, by Guy Endore and Bernard Schubert, from the story by Tod Browning. Bela Lugosi plays Count Mora (Dracula) in the film. His female vampire is played by Carol Borland. This is an elaborate remake of *London After Midnight* (see above). In the film Lionel Barrymore, an occultist, insists that a vampire is behind the murders in a gloomy castle, but in the end the supposed vampires turn out to be local actors. The real killer was a human who had drained the blood of his victim. This film was re-released in 1972.

1935. *Condemned to Live*. Chesterfield-Invincible, USA; producer, Maurey M. Cohen; director, Frank Strayer; screenplay by Karen de Wolfe. In Africa, a woman bitten by a vampire bat gives birth to a baby who becomes a vampire-like werewolf.

1936. *Dracula's Daughter*. Universal, USA; producer, Carl Laemmle, Jr.; director, Lambert Hillyer; screenplay, by Garret Fort, adapted from Bram Stoker's story "Dracula's Guest" and a story by Oliver Jeffries. Gloria Holden played Dracula's daughter, Countess Marya Zaleska. The daughter tries to conquer her inherited blood lust without success.

NOTE: During the 1940's Dracula-vampire films fell on hard times. Such films as *Frankenstein Meets the Wolfman*, *The House of Dracula*, *Abbott and Costello Meet Frankenstein*, toy in a frivolous, titillating way with the main elements of fiction and folklore. One cannot escape the feeling that these films were made to satisfy the public's desire for a ridiculous encounter of monsters and comedians. This encounter reached its nadir in 1952 with *Old Mother Riley Meets the Vampire*.

1940. *The Devil Bat*. Producer Releasing Corp., USA; producer, Jack Gallagher; director, Jean Yarbrough; screenplay, by John Thomas Neville, from George Bricker's story "The Flying

Serpent.'' Bela Lugosi played Dr. Paul Carruthers, a mad scientist who raises huge vampire bats to become his agents of revenge.

1941. *Spooks Run Wild*. Banner Production-Monogram, USA; producer, Sam Katzman; director, Phil Rosen; screenplay by Carl Foreman and Charles R. Marian. Bela Lugosi played Nardo, a stage magician suspected of being a vampire-like monster.

1943. *Le Vampire*. France; director, Jean Painleve. Documentary filmed on location in the Gran Chaco, South America. Includes scenes of the actual vampire bat stalking its victim and drinking blood.

1943. *Son of Dracula*. Universal, USA; producer, Ford Beebe; director, Robert Siodmak; screenplay, by Curt Siodmak, suggested by Bram Stoker's novel *Dracula*. Lon Chaney, Jr. played Count Alucard (Dracula spelled backward). The count emigrates from Europe to the United States in search of fresh blood.

1943. *Dead Men Walk*. (Other titles: *The Vampire* and *Creatures of the Devil*.) Producers Releasing Corp., USA; producer, Sigmund Neufield; director, Sam Newfield; screenplay by Frank Myton. George Zucco played the vampire Dr. Lloyd Clayton.

1943. *Return of the Vampire*. Columbia, USA; producer, Sam White; director, Lew Landers; screenplay, by Griffin Jay, based on an idea of Kurt Neumann; additional dialogue by Randall Faye. Bela Lugosi played the role of Armand Tesla (Dracula) who appears in England during World War II. Here, he seeks revenge against those who first tried to kill him.

1943. *Frankenstein Meets the Wolfman*. Universal, USA; director, Roy William Neill; screenplay by Curt Siodmak. Lon Chaney, Jr. played the role of Dracula. The titillating variation on the traditional theme of horror is now a clearly marked tendency, which crests in the 1940's.

1944. *House of Frankenstein*. Universal, USA; producer, Paul Malvern; director, Eric C. Kenton; screenplay, by Edward T. Lowe, based on an original story by Curt Siodmak. John Carradine appeared in his first role as Count Dracula, alias Baron Latoes.

1945. *The House of Dracula*. Universal, USA; producer, Paul Malvern; director, Erle C. Kenton; screenplay by Edward T. Lowe. John Carradine again appeared as Baron Latoes, the alias for Count Dracula in *The House of Frankenstein*.

1945. *Isle of the Dead*. RKO Radio Pictures, USA; producer, Val Lewton; director, Mark Robson; screenplay by Ardel Wray and Joseph Mischel. Boris Karloff played a Greek general who has come back to the island where his wife has been entombed. He accuses a young girl of being a vampire (*vrykolaka*).

1945. *The Vampire's Ghost*. Republic Pictures, USA; associate producer, Rudy Abel; director, Lesley Selander; screenplay, by Leigh Brackett and John K. Butler, after a story by Leigh Brackett. John Abbott is cast as a vampire in a small African village.

1946. *Devil Bat's Daughter*. Producers Releasing Corp., USA; producer, Franck Wisbar; director, Franck Wisbar; screenplay by Griffin Jay, based on an idea of Leo T. McCarthy, Franck Wisbar, and Ernst Jaeger. A murdering doctor tries to blame his crimes on the daughter of the ''Devil Bat'' doctor.

194?. *Dr. Terror's House of Horrors*. U.S. Independent. Reissue of parts of four earlier horror films, including sections from Dreyer's *Vampyr*.

1946. *Valley of the Zombies*. Republic, USA; associate producers, Dorrell McGowan and Stuart McGowan; director, Philip Ford; screenplay, by Dorrell McGowan and Stuart McGowan, based on a story by Royal K. Cole and Sherman T. Lowe. Ian Keith portrays a resurrected body dependent upon constant blood transfusions in order to stay alive.

1948. *Abbott and Costello Meet Frankenstein*. Universal, USA; producer, Robert Arthur; director, Charles Barton; screenplay by Robert Lees, Frederic Rinaldo, and John Grant.

Released in England as *Abbott and Costello Meet the Ghosts*. Bela Lugosi played Dracula. A light-hearted satire—typical of vampire films, especially since 1943—on Dracula, Frankenstein and the Wolf Man; Dracula ends up as a bat in the claws of the Wolf Man.

1951. *The Thing from Another World*. RKO Radio Pictures, USA; producer, Howard Hawks; director, Christian Nyby (and Orson Welles, according to rumor); screenplay, by Charles Lederer, based on the novel *Who Goes There?* by John W. Campbell, Jr. First film to link the classical vampire with science fiction. A figure from outer space crash-lands on Earth and survives on blood.

1952. *Old Mother Riley Meets the Vampire*. Renown, Great Britain; director, J. Gilling; screenplay by Val Valentine. Released in America as both *Vampire over London* and *My Son the Vampire*. Bela Lugosi played Van Housen the vampire in this British comedy.

1953. *Drakula Istanbulda*. Demirag, Turkey; producer, Turgut Demirag; director, Mehmet Muktar; screenplay, by Unit Deniz, after the novels *Dracula* by Bram Stoker and *The Impaling Voivode* by Riza Seyfi. First and only film to fuse Stoker's Dracula with Vlad the Impaler, although the references are slight. A balding Alif Kaptan plays Dracula, and the story is set in Istanbul.

NOTE: The popularity of the horror film declined during the late 1940's and early 1950's; but the late 1950's brought renewed interest and once again Dracula and vampire films were being made.

1956. *Planet Nine from Outer Space*. Distribution Corporation of America, USA; producer and director, Edward D. Wood, Jr.; screenplay by Edward D. Wood, Jr. Second title: *Grave-Robbers from Outer Space*. Lugosi played Specter. This was Lugosi's last film.

1957. *The Vampire*. Gramercy Pictures Prod., United Artists, Great Britain and USA; producers, Arthur Gardner and Jules V. Levy; director, Paul Landres; screenplay by Pat Fiedler. American title: *Mark of the Vampire*. John Beal accidentally takes pills which turn him into a vampire at night.

1957. *Blood of Dracula*. Carmel Production, American International Release, USA; producer, Herman Cohen; director, Herbert L. Strock; screenplay by Ralph Thornton. Released in England as *Blood Is My Heritage*; in Canada as *Blood of the Demon*.

1957. *Not of This Earth*. Allied Artists, USA; producer, Roger Corman; director, Roger Corman; screenplay by Charles Griffith and Mark Hanna. Science fiction and vampirism.

1957. *I Vampiri*. Titanus-Athena, Italy; director, Riccardo Freda; screenplay, Piero Regnoli, Rik Sjostrom, and Riccardo Freda. Released in America under the titles *The Vampire of Notre Dame, The Devil's Commandment,* and *Lust of the Vampires*. Not a real vampire film at all.

1958. *The Return of Dracula*. Gramercy United Artists Release, USA; producers, Arthur Gardner and Jules V. Levy; director, Paul Landres; screenplay by Pat Fiedler. Released in England as *The Fantastic Disappearing Man*, and on American TV as *The Curse of Dracula*. Francis Lederer plays Bellac (Dracula), the vampire come to California to spread the cult.

1958. *The Horror of Dracula*. Hammer Films, Great Britain; producer, Anthony Hinds; executive producer, Michael Carreras; director, Terence Fisher; screenplay, by Jimmy Sangster, adapted from the novel *Dracula* by Bram Stoker. Dracula is played by Christopher Lee. This is a fine work which ranks with the earlier horror films such as *Nosferatu* and *Vampyr*, which surpass the merely terrifying. The final scene is superb: Van Helsing (played by Peter Cushing) traps Dracula as he is rushing to get back to his coffin at break of day. Van Helsing in a desperate leap rips the drapes to let in the light, fashions a cross from two huge gold candelabras, and forces Dracula into the sunlight, where the vampire disintegrates into dust.

1958. *Blood of the Vampire*. Tampean Productions, Great Britain; producers, Robert S. Baker and

Monty Berman; director, Henry Cass; screenplay by Jimmy Sangster. Sir Donald Wolfit played Dr. Callistratus, a medical doctor with a blood deficiency who carries on research among the helpless victims in his prison hospital.

1959. *Curse of the Undead*. Universal, USA; producer, Joseph Gershenzon; director, Edward Dein; screenplay by Michael Pate and Mildred Dein. First film to mix the vampire legend with the traditional American folklore of the western.

1959. *El Vampiro*. Cinemagrafica ABSA-Mexico; producer, Abel Salazar; director, Fernando Mendez; screenplay by Heinrich Rodriguez and Ramon Obon.

NOTE: Beginning in the late 1950's and continuing on into the early 60's a series of Italian potboilers emerged. It appears that Italian film-makers tried to give new life to the vampire theme by introducing playgirls or musclemen into the films.

1959. *Tempi Duri Per I Vampiri*. Maxima, Italy; presented by Joseph E. Levine; producer, Mario Cecchi Gori; director, Pio Angeletti; screenplay by Mario Cecchi Gori and others. Released in America as *Uncle Was a Vampire*. Christopher Lee as Uncle Rinaldo, the vampire, in an Italian comedy.

1960. *The Brides of Dracula*. Hammer Films, Great Britain; producer, Anthony Hinds; executive producer, Michael Carreras; director, Terence Fisher; screenplay by Jimmy Sangster, Peter Bryan, and Edward Percy. David Peel performs as the vampire-baron, Baron Meinster.

1960. *L'Ultima Preda del Vampiro*. Nord Film, Italy; producer, Tiziana Longo; director, Piero Regnoli. Released in America as *The Playgirls and the Vampire*. A sexploitation film.

1960. *Et Mourir de plaisir*. EGE Films-France-Italy; producer, Raymond Eger; director, Roger Vadim; screenplay, by Roger Vadim, Claude Brule and Claude Martin, based on a story by Roger Vadim and also Sheridan Le Fanu's "Carmilla." Released in America as *Blood and Roses*. Vampire enters the body of a young girl, and through her carries out his vampire practices.

1961. *Maschera del Demonio*. Jolly-Galatea, Italy; director, Mario Bava; screenplay, by Ennio de Concini and Mario Serandrei, based on the story "Viy" by Gogol. Released in America as *Black Sunday*; in England as *Revenge of the Vampire*. Barbara Steele played Princess Ada Vajda, the vampire-witch. An excellent film.

1961. *Il Vampiro dell'Opera*. N.I.F. Rome, Italy; director, Renato Polselli. A vampire haunts an old opera house.

1961. *L'Amante del Vampiri*. C.E.F. Consorzio-Italo-Films, Italy; producer, Bruno Bolognesi; director, Renato Polselli; screenplay by Renato Polselli, Giuseppi Pellegrini, and Ernesto Castaldi. Released in America as *The Vampire and the Ballerina*. An imitation of the 1960 film *L'Ultima Preda del Vampiro*. A vampire and his servant prey on showgirls.

1961. *Ercole al Centro della Terra*. Omnia SPA Cinematografica, Italy; producer, Achille Piazzi; director, Mario Bava; screenplay by Alessandro Continenza, M. Bava, Duccio Tessari, and Franco Prosperi. Released in America as *Hercules in the Haunted World*. Christopher Lee played Lyco. A muscleman epic.

1961. *El Vampiro Sangriento*. Azteca-Mexico; producer, Rafael Perez Grovas; director, Miguel Morayta; screenplay by Miguel Morayta. Released in America as *The Bloody Vampire*. Count Frankenstein is a vampire, and in the end he remains uncaught.

1961. *Ataud del Vampiro*. Cinemagrafica ABSA-Mexico; producer, Abel Salazar; director, Fernando Mendez; screenplay, by Ramon Obon, after a story by Raul Zentino. Released in America as *The Vampire's Coffin*. A mad doctor resuscitates a vampire in this sequel to *El Vampiro Sangriento* of the same year.

1961.*El Mundo de la Vampiro.* Cinemagrafica ABSA-Mexico; producer, Abel Salazar; director,

Fernando Mendez; screenplay, by Ramon Obon, based on an idea of Raul Zentino. Released in America as *World of the Vampire*. Vampire on the trail of revenge ends up on a stake.

1962. *Maciste contre il Vampiro*. Ambrosiana Cinematografica, Italy; producer, Paolo Moffa; directors, Giacomo Gentilomo and Sergio Corbucci; screenplay by Sergio Corbucci and Duccio Tessari. Released in America as *Goliath and the Vampire*. Muscleman-vampire versus superhero.

1962. *La Strage dei Vampiri*. Italy; producer, Dino Sant'Ambrosio; director, Robert Mauri; screenplay by Robert Mauri. Released in America as *Curse of the Blood Ghouls*. Italian Gothic.

1962. *La Invasion de los Vampiros*. Mexico; producer, Rafael Perez Grovas; director, Miguel Morayta; screenplay by Miguel Morayta. Released in America as *The Invasion of the Vampires*. A vampire called Count Frankenhausen acts in this further sequel to *El Vampiro Sangriento* (1961).

1962. *House on Bare Mountain*. Olympic International, USA; producers, David Andrew and Wes Don; director, R.L. Frost; screenplay by Denver Scott. Sexploitation with all three classic horrors—Dracula, the Frankenstein monster, and the Wolf Man. Comparable to *Abbott and Costello Meet Frankenstein* (1948).

1962. *La Maldicion de los Karnsteins*. Hispaner Films, NEC Cinematografica, Spain-Italy; director, Thomas Miller (alias Camillo Mastrocinque); screenplay, by Julian Berry, after "Carmilla" by Le Fanu. Christopher Lee played Count Ludwig Karnstein. Released in England as *Crypt of Horror*; in America as *Terror in the Crypt*. The third film version of Le Fanu's tale, to which it adheres rather closely.

1963. *Tre Volti della Paura*. Emmerpi-Galatea-Lyre, Italy; director, Mario Bava; screenplay by Marcello Fondato, Alberto Bevilacqua, and M. Bava. Released in America as *Black Sabbath*. Three stories in one film, one of which is based on Alexis Tolstoy's "The Wurdalak" about the Urfe family of vampires. Boris Karloff, the narrator, also played Gorca, the head of the vampire household.

1963. *Kiss of the Vampire*. Hammer Films, Great Britain; producer, Anthony Hinds; director, Don Sharp; screenplay by John Elder (alias Anthony Hinds). American TV title: *Kiss of Evil*. A well-made film about a couple honeymooning in Bavaria, where they become involved in the vampire cult.

1964. *The Last Man on Earth*. Co-production: Produzioni La Regine and American International, Italy-USA; producer, Robert L. Lippert; director, Sidney Salkovo; screenplay, by William Leicester, after the novel *I Am Legend* by Richard Matheson. Vincent Price portrayed Robert Morgan, the last human in a land of vampire-like creatures following atomic holocaust.

1964. *Dr. Terror's House of Horrors*. Amicus, England; producers, Milton Subotsky and Max J. Rosenberg; director, Freddie Francis; screenplay by Milton Subotsky. Death in the guise of Dr. Schreck, played by Peter Cushing, predicts the death of five passengers on a train. One sequence contains a vampire.

1965. *Dracula—Prince of Darkness* or *Blood for Dracula*. Hammer Films, Great Britain; producer, Anthony Nelson Keys; director, Terence Fisher; screenplay, by John Sansom (alias Jimmy Sangster), from an idea of John Elder (alias Anthony Hinds) based on the characters in Bram Stoker's *Dracula*. In this sequel to *Horror of Dracula* (1958), Christopher Lee played Dracula, who is revived by blood flowing into his ashes.

1965. *Terrore nella Spazio*. Castilla, Italy; producer, Fulvio Lucisano; director, Mario Bava; screenplay by Ib Melchior and Louis M. Heywood. Released in America as *Planet of Blood*; for TV as *Planet of Terror*. Beings from another planet try to take over human bodies.

1965. *Devils of Darkness*. Planet Films, Great Britain; producer, Tom Blakeley; director, Lance

Comfort; screenplay by Lyn Fairhurst. Count Sinistre, a vampire, tries to ravish modern-day victims from Brittany.

1965. *La Sorella di Satana*. Italian-Yugoslavian; directors, Michael Reeyes and Charles Griffiths. Released in America as *The She-Beast*. A vampiress in modern-day Communist Transylvania.

1966. *Billy the Kid Vs. Dracula*. Circle Productions, Inc.-Embassy, USA; producer, Carroll Case; director, William Beaudine; screenplay by Karl Hittleman. Dracula, played by John Carradine, preys on a western town until he is killed by the outlaw Billy the Kid, played by Chuck Courtney.

1966. *Blood Bath*. American International, USA; producer, Jack Hill; directors, Jack Hill and Stephanie Rothman; screenplay by J. Hill and S. Rothman. American TV title: *Track of the Vampire*.

1967. *Le Bal des Vampires*. Cadre-MGM, France, Great Britain; producer, Gene Gutowski; director, Roman Polanski; screenplay by Gerard Brack and Roman Polanski. Released in America as *The Fearless Vampire Killers or Pardon Me, But Your Teeth Are in My Neck*. A well-filmed satirical approach to vampires. Polanski correctly uses the occult symbols; ironically this was the last film played in by Sharon Tate—Polanski's wife and one of the victims in the Manson murder case.

1967. *A Taste of Blood*. Creative Film Enterprises, Inc., USA; producer, Herschell Gordon Lewis; director, H.G. Lewis; screenplay by Donald Standford, with characters based on those in Stoker's novel *Dracula*. An American, John Stone, unknowingly drinks the blood of his ancestor Count Dracula and becomes a vampire, killing the descendants of those who executed the original Dracula.

1968. *Dracula Has Risen from the Grave*. Hammer Films, Great Britain; producer, Aida Young; director, Freddie Francis; screenplay by John Elder. Christopher Lee's third appearance as Dracula, in a dull film with a garbled story line. Knocked from the battlements, Dracula is impaled on a huge stake with gore galore.

1968. *Le Viol du Vampire*. An ABC "television movie" presented by SNA; producer, Sam Selsky; director, Jean Rollin; screenplay by J. Rollin.

1969. *The Blood of Dracula's Castle*. Paragon International Film, Crown International, USA; producers, Al Adamson and Rex Carlton; director, Al Adamson; screenplay by Rex Carlton. A poor film.

1969. *Malenka la Vampire*. Victory Films SA (Madrid) and Cobra Film (Rome) Spain, Italy; director, Armando de Osorio.

1969. *The Blood Beast Terror*. Great Britain; producer, Arnold Miller; director, Vernon Sewell; screenplay by Peter Bryan.

1970. *Jonathan, Vampire Sterben Nicht*. Beta Films, Germany; director, Hans W. Geissendorfer; screenplay by H.W. Geissendorfer. An erotic film, freely adapted from Bram Stoker's novel.

1970. *Taste the Blood of Dracula*. Hammer-Warner Pathe, Great Britain; producer, Aida Young; director, Peter Sandy; screenplay, by John Elder (alias Anthony Hinds), based on characters in Stoker's novel *Dracula*. Christopher Lee played Dracula.

1970. *Count Dracula*. England-Spain; producer, Harry Alan Towers; director, Jesus Franco. Based on Stoker's novel. Dracula, played by Christopher Lee, sports a mustache as does Stoker's vampire.

1970. *Count Yorga, the Vampire*. Erica Films-American International Pictures, USA; producer, Michael MacReady; director, Bob Kelljan; screenplay by Bob Kelljan. Released in America as *Loves of Count Yorga*. Robert Quarry played the count, a vampire from Eastern Europe, who appears in a California setting in search of fresh blood. A success among the college youth.

1970. *Blood of Frankenstein.* USA; Zandor Vorkov played Count Dracula.

1970. *Lust for a Vampire.* Hammer Films, Great Britain; producers, Harry Fine and Michael Style; director, Jimmy Sangster; screenplay by Tudor Gates. Yutte Stensgaard played a character reminiscent of Le Fanu's Carmilla.

1970. *The Vampire Lovers.* Hammer Films, Great Britain; producers, Harry Fine and Michael Style; director, Roy Ward Baker; screenplay by Tudor Gates. This is the fourth film version of Le Fanu's ''Carmilla.'' Ingrid Pitt as Carmilla played the role of a vampire who lives through three generations and raises havoc among the village inhabitants. Some of the faint lesbian suggestions in Le Fanu's novelette come through in this film.

1970. *Countess Dracula.* Hammer Films, Great Britain; producer, Alexander Paal; director, Peter Sandy; screenplay by Jeremy Paul. Ingrid Pitt had the lead as a female sadist who bathes in the blood of her victims.

1970. *Scars of Dracula.* Hammer Films, Great Britain; producer, Aida Young; director, Roy Ward Baker; screenplay by John Elder. Christopher Lee played Dracula. This film is particularly good in showing the ways in which the vampire stalks his victim and compels the victim to drink his blood.

1970. *Guess What Happened to Count Dracula?* A Merrick International Picture, USA; producer, Leo Rivers; executive producer, Laurence Merrick. The nadir of horror films. Blatant sex-ploitation. Made three times on the same set: once with actors wearing clothes, under the original title; secondly with actors in the buff in *Does Dracula Suck?*, and thirdly, as a degenerate romp under the title *Does Dracula Really . . . ?* No taste, no talent, bad filming techniques, and poor acting.

1971. *The Return of Count Yorga.* Director: Bob Kelljan. Superior sequel to the first *Count Yorga, the Vampire* film (1970). At the end of the film the count is destroyed, but one of his pursuers has become a vampire, so the cult lives on.

NOTE: See Chapter 8 for 1972 and current films.

Designed by Ray Ripper
Graphic Production by Frank De Luca
Composed in 12/15 Garamond with Palatino display
    by JD Computer Type Inc.
Printed and bound by Halliday Lithograph Corp.